Copyright © 2025 by Mary-Pat Ross

All rights reserved.

No part of this book may be reproduced in any form or by any electronic or mechanical means, including information storage and retrieval systems, without written permission from the author, except for the use of brief quotations in a book review.

Scripture quotations are from the **World English Bible (WEB)**, which is in the public domain.

Scripture quotations taken from the **Holy Bible, New International Version®, NIV®**. Copyright © 2011 by Biblica, Inc.® Used by permission. All rights reserved worldwide.

Disclaimer: This is a memoir based on the author's personal experiences. Some names, locations, and identifying details have been changed to protect the privacy of individuals.

ISBN: 978-0-473-74515-8

Front cover photo credit: Chris Low

Back cover photo credit: Sue Fosse

Map credit: Althea Barr and author

Cover design by Susanna Schollum and Nina Ruth

Editing and layout by Susanna Schollum (www.linebyline.co.nz)

Proofread by Althea Barr

Called to a Sun-Scorched Land

Missions to Mozambique

Mary-Pat Ross

Dedication

I dedicate this memoir to the courageous Mozambicans who taught me so much. As Christ loves us, we believers unite in love for each other. I treasure the friendships made during those years and continue to uphold the missionaries still there—and even beyond those borders—in prayer.

"Even when I am old and grey, do not forsake me, O God, till I declare your power to the next generation, your might to all who are to come" (Psalm 71:18, NIV).

Contents

Introduction	15

Part 1: Old Life, New Life, and the Call to Missions

EARLY DREAMS OF AFRICA	19
Forest Lookout Towers	23
A Hospital Job	28
EAST AFRICA AND BEYOND!	31
Sailing on a Small Yacht in the Indian Ocean	33
South Africa, an Immigrant Ship to New Zealand, and Beyond	34
A Permanent Return to New Zealand	37
NEW LIFE AT FIFTY-TWO	40
The Call to 'Go'	42
My Career or God's Direction?	46
Released from Preschool Job	48
A Long-Term Mission Training Course	50
EXPLORATORY TRIP	56
Decisions and Preparations	57
Learning More about Mozambique Missions	60
Sharing My Desire to Serve in Africa	61
FOUR WEEKS IN MOZAMBIQUE	64
Whitewater Farm and Preschool	68
Prayer and Preschool	72
Baobabs and a Glimpse of Bush-Bush Villages	74
The Good Samaritan Programme	76
A Women's Seminar	78

TANZANIA	81
The E.G. Foundation and Preschool	83
An Orphanage Visit	85
NAIROBI, KENYA	87
Kibera Slums	88
A Safe Place for Young Children to Learn	89
Mama Mercy and Moses	90
Women Refugees	91
Yellow Roses and an Ethiopian Restaurant	93
An International Church and a Game Park	94
Another Orphanage, Then Time to Go	95
God Answers and I Hear Him!	97
PHOTOS	100

Part 2: Portugal and World Outreach Internship 2014

THE PROPOSAL: PORTUGAL FIRST	111
So Much to Prepare!	113
Time to Go, and An Angel Escorts Me	117
Language Lessons in Portugal	118
SOUTH AFRICA, VISA GRANTED, AND MOZAMBIQUE—FINALLY!	126
Internship at Whitewater Farm	131
Drumbeats at Night	135
A Diverse Community	137
SERVING WITH WHITEWATER MINISTRIES	140
Our Unique Routines at the Farm	141
What a Subsistence Lifestyle Looks Like	146
PRESCHOOL HERE IS DIFFERENT	149
My First Visit to the New Model Preschool	151
Learning and Laughing Through Language	154

Part 3: First Year as a Missionary

SERVING AT WHITEWATER FARM	159
The Whitewater *Escolinha*/Preschool Model	162
Teaching Volunteers to Make Resources	164
A Bush-Bush Seminar	168
Latrine Building	170
MY NEW HOME COMPLETED	172
Wildlife Outside and Inside	174
BAPTISMS	176
RELATIONSHIPS HELP GROW LANGUAGE	181
Growing in Confidence	185
Encouraged by a New Zealand Missions Pastor	189
Marion's Good Samaritan Health Clinic Opens	190
Taking the Jesus Film to the Bush-Bush	192
October/November: FIRE Season and Mangoes!	196
PREPARATIONS FOR LEAVING	199
Packing Up for the Rainy Season	204
Home for Christmas and a Surprise Visit	206
Back to New Zealand to Prepare	208
PHOTOS	210

Part 4: The Return and In Town 2015

BACK TO MOZAMBIQUE	219
Temporary Housing	222
Floods	224
Prayer Walks for Exercise	225
Language Lessons Begin in Town	226
Preschool Plans	228
Exploring the Town	229
Finding Bread Buns and Beef Meat	232

FINALLY MOVING TO ANYA'S	234
Anya's Brother and His Family	241
The Giant Lizard and Fat Snake Battle	242
Motorbikes and My Big Red Honda Hero	243
Two Ramps, an Iron Gate, and the Kitchen Padlock	246
A Change of Motorbike and on the Highway	247
Bible Studies	249
Three Different Churches	249
PLANS AND IDEAS FOR THE YEAR AHEAD	252
Preschool Volunteers Training Together	253
Finding Beauty in the Brokenness	258
Watching our Faith Grow	263
The Good Samaritan Orphan Programmes	268
Storytelling Props: Dolls and Lions	270
Rabies and Rosso	274
Puppies Finally Appear, Only to Escape	276
Superstitions and Witchcraft Practices	278
WO'S GLOBAL CONFERENCE IN THAILAND	283
WO Leadership Seminar at Whitewater Farm	286
PRACTICAL MISSIONS	288
Motorbikes to a Bush-Bush Village!	292
Practical Help and Prayers for Healing	295
An Old Wheelbarrow and a Freshly Painted Wall	297
Eye Clinics and Drilling for Water	298
END OF YEAR ACTIVITIES	303
A Small Island	305
Looking Back and Looking Forward	308
Packing and Preparing for a Return to New Zealand	311
YWAM Base on My Way Home, and Delayed!	313
Home for a New Zealand Christmas	316

Part 5: The Return 2016

CHANGE OF PLANS!	321
RETURN TO MOZAMBIQUE	327
Motorbike Licence Renewed by Myself!	330
Discipleship Programme	332
A Surprising Development	333
EXCITING OCCASIONS	336
Another Orphans' Programme	338
My Honda Hero Takes Me to Cedru's Family	341
A Surprise Visitor Who Helps!	344
My Solar Panel Finds a Home!	345
Anya's Baptism	349
MEETING NEEDS	352
A Surprising and Timely Seminar	356
UNFORESEEN CHANGES	359
A Door, Donations, and a New Owner for the Hero!	363
Plans to Leave, but for How Long?	367
Surprising Detour to Zimbabwe	368
Finally, Home in New Zealand!	372
PHOTOS	376
Epilogue	383
Postscript, or Where to From Here, Lord?	385
Afterword	387
Acknowledgments	389
About the Author	391

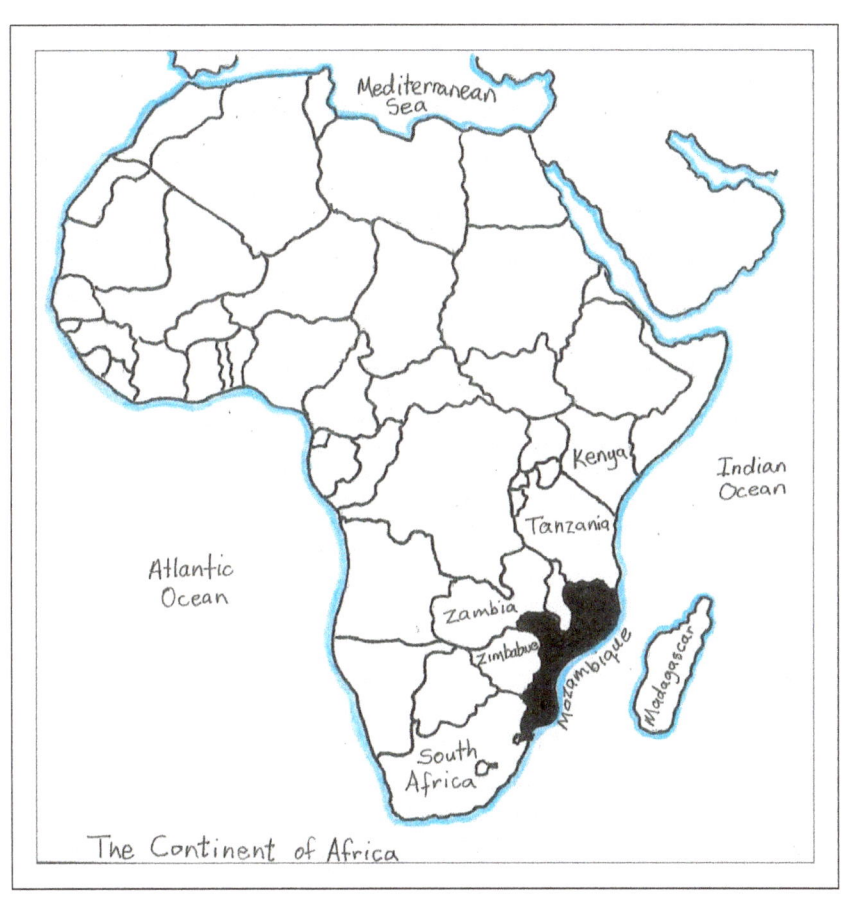

The Continent of Africa

Introduction

The dry afternoon heat of northern Mozambique beat down on me as I donned my red motorbike helmet and short leather boots, then fitted wide sun goggles over my glasses.

"*Muito calor, Anya! Eu vou agora na minha moto. Até logo,*" I said. "Very hot, Anya! I'm going on my motorcycle now. See you later."

I was living with Anya and her extended family to learn better Portuguese while serving a second year with a mission team in a rural area. I exited their courtyard and headed to the highway, pleased to be able to use the language I was learning.

How did I arrive at this later stage of my life, riding a red Honda Hero on sandy, dusty roads and a challenging highway? The call to Africa began at a young age. Four significant influences contributed to my first adventures in Africa as a child and teenager: *National Geographic* magazines, Peace Corps volunteers, a roommate's return from Africa, and summers spent alone in forestry lookout towers. After two years of university that lacked focus, I had a change of heart towards formal education.

Introduction

One day I decided that only travel and worldwide experiences would help me find meaning and purpose to my life. The dream was born. My destination? Kenya! Although I had grown up with a social conscience, my desire to help disadvantaged people quickly evaporated in the port of Mombasa when I met an international group of 'hippies afloat' sailing around the world for adventure. Goodbye, college days and social work. Hello, high seas!

However, it would be nearly forty years later, after adventures and family life, that I finally returned to Africa—but not on my own. This time, I was a follower of Jesus, and I heard God call me to missions in Africa.

The answered prayers, both big and small, the God-coincidences, and the angelic interventions I experienced before, during, and since my time as a missionary testify to God's goodness, protection, and provision with remarkable answers to challenging situations.

Part 1: Old Life, New Life, and the Call to Missions

Early Dreams of Africa

I dashed inside the house with one thing on my mind. "Please don't slam the door!" Mom shouted over the noise of the cake mixer.

"Sorry." I threw my school bag onto the sofa and checked the top of the cabinet to see if anything had arrived in the mail addressed to me.

"Hasn't the magazine arrived?" I called, feeling the anticipation of exploring the world by reading about faraway places fade away.

"It's in your bedroom. Before you get lost in the pages, how was your day at school? And come into the kitchen and say hello. Whatever's wrong with you these last few months?"

I replaced the family's unopened mail and turned from the cabinet, my sense of excitement rising again. I could wait five minutes to do the decent thing and say hello. The day had been long, the bus ride home noisy and distracting. Now that school was over for the summer break, I had a couple of months to become lost in my dreams. The rising urge to explore the world had become an obsession.

"Sorry, Mom. What kind of cake are you making?" I asked.

"A German chocolate cake, everyone's favourite."

My story began as an impressionable ten-year-old girl. Although I was raised as a Catholic, I was unaware of God's faithfulness. I also didn't know that a dream was forming in my heart to go to Africa, nor the many astounding twists and turns I would travel before it became a reality.

In the fifties and sixties, our family lived in a small town in southern Oregon. I was the oldest of four children. It was a settled and happy childhood; in those days of innocence, we knew no fear. Our neighbourhood of children had simple pleasures, like playing ball games; riding bikes or skateboards made by nailing steel roller-skates onto a board; making kites, stilts, and go-carts; and resting on the grass looking for four-leaf clovers. We had a wide area to roam and play in with our parents' expectation of being home in time for dinner.

Unbeknown to me, in my adult years, I would mix with children in another country who had not known these luxuries.

During the holidays, we travelled to my grandparents' little farm in northern California. Grandpa and I studied the *National Geographic* magazine, especially the map of Africa, lost in wonder at the size of the continent.

"Is America bigger or smaller than Africa, Grandpa?" I asked.

"Let's work that out for ourselves," he replied.

He reached for a ruler out of the bib pocket in his pin-striped overalls. We placed it on the map from west to east and counted the segments marked on the wooden ruler. "How many are there?"

"Four inches, I think. I'll check again. One, two, three … well, four-and-a-half inches. What does that measure on the scale?"

With our fingers, we stretched the ruler across and discovered Africa measured seven inches, so it was larger from west to east than the United States' land mass.

Early Dreams of Africa

"See if you can find the continent of Africa on my new globe," said Grandpa.

He helped me search, spinning the globe and finding not only Africa but also the United States, learning it was on a continent too, called North America.

"See those blue lines running north and south from the poles and across the globe east to west? Those lines are another way to measure distances on the globe. They are called longitude and latitude."

Years later, I would sail from East Africa into the Indian Ocean and learn that these imaginary global lines were essential for navigating by sextant, chronometer, and charts.

"Wow, Grandpa, it's so amazing to see these countries on the globe. Can I have your old globe to take home, please?"

"Of course. It would be a pleasure to see it being used by someone who is so interested."

My heart leapt. Now I could read our own *National Geographic* magazines at home and find these places on Grandpa's globe.

On another holiday, Grandpa brought out his special *National Geographic* hardcover books showing people in different countries. This was the first time I saw African children with no clothes on, skinny but with big tummies, living in mud huts with no toys in sight. The women carried babies in a sling on their backs and walked barefoot on red, dusty paths with water containers balanced on their heads.

A light ignited like an unquenchable fire within. Grandpa fuelled it by paying for an annual *National Geographic* subscription for my family.

I wonder how he would feel knowing those hours spent together during our weekend holidays shaped me to take a step of faith, travelling along sandy, dusty paths in Mozambique alongside people I was to love.

As a child, my interest in Africa—its diversity of nations and its extraordinary birds and animals—carried over into a school project. One of our home assignments was to make a topographical map of a country of our choice on a plywood base. I chose the entire continent of Africa and, using flour, salt, and water paste, moulded and painted yellow, brown, and green landscapes, surrounding the continent with three oceans of blue. From memory, Dad took it to school in his work truck, as it was such a big project. I loved creating that big African map.

I also developed a desire in my teenage years to go to Africa as a volunteer and help people there. Learning to serve people in our community through my Catholic education nurtured this desire. I listened to stories of helping people in underdeveloped countries by a couple who were friends of my parents and served in the Peace Corps in Central America.

High school focused on academics with an emphasis on English and Religious Studies. I learned typing skills and a love of the written word.

"You should keep writing," my grandmother encouraged me. "You show a natural ability."

Latin studies, though, I found pointless. However, they contributed to my understanding of language and sentence structures. Study skills were greatly encouraged so I would be capable of going on to university.

When I graduated from high school, I was shy about making new friends, even at the nearest college. I made a shocking revelation: *I've never had to make new friends!* I was unsure of my direction at university and terrified of making mistakes. Yet my curiosity about many subjects drew me to enrol each year in vastly different subjects, trying to find my way to a purpose in life.

When the Peace Corps came to recruit volunteers, I was instantly attracted to joining this international venture. The recruitment officer asked me, "Do you have a degree in teaching or nursing? Or do you have a skill to offer?"

"No," I replied. "I've only completed two years of different subjects." I wondered whether to share that I had an overwhelming desire to go to Africa and help in some way. *Looks like that's not enough to be accepted by the Peace Corps.*

"See you in a couple of years when you have a degree."

I discovered other worldviews and belief systems through my sociology, anthropology, and philosophy classes and threw out my Catholic religious upbringing. A growing revelation formed: *I've been brainwashed! Maybe I will be an atheist and search the world for experiences.* That was the start of my quest to find 'truth'. Decades later, I came to appreciate the Christian foundation laid in my early years.

Forest Lookout Towers

"How about a summer job on a forest lookout tower?" my mother asked me one day. "My good friend's husband works for the forest service and can put in a good word for you."

The three summer months between studies in the early 1970s saw me employed with the Oregon State Forestry Department as a Fire Lookout Tower Attendant. Southwest Oregon's primary industry was timber. I accepted a position for the three to four hottest summer months to protect the nation's woodlands. I was fortunate to be one of the last solo women to 'man' two different towers over consecutive summers: Round Top and White Point.

My dad had been hunting deer in the area and knew both locations. "Hey, you can drive your car right up to the Round Top lookout tower."

My little white 1965 VW bug climbed up the last rocky track with supplies for a three-week period, returning for five days in town. I looked up at the top of a few flights of wooden stairs. A small glass cubicle sat atop a wooden tower. Climbing up, I discovered a single bed, a table, and a fire finder pillar as well as a gas cooker and tiny fridge in the middle of the tiny room. A wooden deck encircled the glass windows, and at night I could secure a trap door so no unwanted two or four-legged creatures disturbed me.

Forest rangers collected water at the nearest springs and brought it up the steep stairs for me. Two large stainless steel milk cans held this precious water. Bathing was at a minimum, but I was alone, so it didn't matter too much.

Before I left at the start of the hot summer months, Dad offered me his .22 rifle. Shooting empty tin cans off stumps below gave me something to do during the day. It was a simple life, and my only contact with people for over three weeks was by shortwave radio during the twelve-hour periods I was on duty.

I assured the base that all was well at regular intervals. "10–4 good buddy, over and out."

All too often, when looking through the binoculars, I grabbed the radio receiver. "I have a 10–33 [fire] up a canyon ..."

Thankfully, not many fires got out of control.

At night, sudden lightning storms frequently swept through the area, prompting me to crouch on a small stool with glass insulators on the legs, hoping my tower did not get struck by lightning. I was in awe of the power and beauty in these midnight thunder and lightning displays.

Lightning started fires on dead trees called snags. Early the following morning, I'd get busy with binoculars, locating any fires and pinpointing their exact locations using the fire finder and a map with coordinates.

I'd spend the entire summer following the sun, moon, stars, and clouds, while daydreams formed like clouds on my personal horizon. *I wonder if there is any purpose in life. What should I pursue at college? What is the meaning of life? Is it true there is only one God, or are there many gods? What is truth?*

By the second season of having so much time on my hands while looking for and reporting fires from White Point lookout tower, I was bored. My longing to follow my dream of travelling to Africa prompted questions. *What would I do to help people? Which country would I go to first? Should I train to be a teacher or a nurse?*

I took up carving wooden objects and completed three acrylic paintings. Looking back, I see they were signposts of what was to come. I carved a big sun and a sailboat, and painted a beach with sunshine, a wide sea and clouds with no land in sight, and an enormous white dove with outstretched wings and rays behind it.

Down at the forestry depot, while I had a day or two to shop for the next three weeks' supplies, I shared my dream of going to Africa with an older employee who was about to retire.

"Why do you want to go there?" he asked. "You could have a career in the Oregon State Forestry in the most beautiful state in the Pacific Northwest. Why would you want to go all the way over to Africa with all its problems?" He just shook his head when he saw I was determined to go.

They were good questions but didn't deter me at all. I can only think it was because God had planted a dream in my heart long before, although I was still not ready to know Him yet.

During my second year at university, living in a communal house with other students, I bought a whole pineapple at the supermarket.

"Did you know you can grow a pineapple plant from cutting the top?" my flatmate asked.

That will be amazing! I looked out my window at pine trees and large oaks. "A subtropical plant here?" Sure enough, the green tip from the pineapple grew roots, and I planted it in a red clay pot. It continued to whet my appetite to travel to exotic countries, especially Africa.

One flatmate, Kathy, had just returned from Kenya. Her stories captivated me. "When you go there," she said, "you've got to visit the island of Lamu on the Indian Ocean coast of Kenya."

"Why's that?"

"It's like stepping back in time, with only donkeys for transport, or walking, as there are no vehicles allowed on the island. But the most interesting part is the handmade boats called dhows."

"Dhows?"

"Yes, they're built on the coast with hand tools to trade between coastal countries as far away as the Red Sea. They have billowing sails hoisted up like a huge triangular cloth on a lateen rig, nothing like our sailboats. There's something old-world about them as they silently sail by without engines. And, of course, you must visit a game park with lions, elephants, and giraffes. I saw them all at Tsavo East and West Game Parks."

To see those big African animals in real life will be thrilling! I had never even been to a zoo.

By the end of that year, I was determined to work and save for travelling to Kenya. But first I had to convince my parents, who wanted me to get a degree. Before enrolling in my third year, I spoke to them about my plans. "I'm thinking of taking time out of school to work and save to go to Africa."

"Why?"

"I think going to Africa will give me some insight or clue into what sort of career to pursue. And I won't be gone for more than six weeks at the most."

"Where would you go? Which country?" asked Dad.

"My friend just visited Kenya in East Africa during a semester break. She said it's a settled, fairly peaceful, safe country, with

Jomo Kenyatta as president. They speak English too," I reassured him.

In the early 1970s, I had no access to *Lonely Planet* guides or Google to assist with travel preparations. As a budding atheist, I also had no church connections. I just went by myself.

Why this was so surprising was that I grew up in a very small community. Most of my peers went to Europe during the summer months and relaxed with their families. But here I was, planning to go halfway around the world to an underdeveloped country. I had no thought of the risks of being on my own, nor did I know where I would stay or what I would do. My heart still had a nagging desire to help the people there.

My parents, especially my mother, were very supportive of my new direction.

To fund this adventurous idea, I shared a car ride with a friend of a friend of a friend. In other words, I didn't know him! He was going through Colorado. *Hey, this would be a good place to work and earn money. I could ski on my days off!*

"I can drop you off in Boulder on my way east," he said.

"How long will it take to drive there?"

"About two days and a night. It's around 1,200 miles from Oregon."

Travelling in a car rather than a bus meant I could carry my precious pineapple plant as well as a backpack and my downhill skis.

Waving goodbye, he dropped me off in Boulder at a friend's place.

"I think I will continue to Denver, as I will find more work there. Can you take me to the bus station?" I asked my Boulder friend after staying a couple of nights.

After arriving at the Denver bus station, I found a newspaper with many jobs advertised. The one that I noticed was for someone to sand wooden shutters in a small factory. Poking some coins into the payphone, I rang the number. "I'm interested. Where are you located? Can I come and talk with you?"

The job was just around the corner. The boss hired me on the spot. He suggested I ask the spray painter where he lived and maybe find a place to rent near him so we could share a ride to work together.

"I live on the other side of Denver, and there are rooms in houses for rent over there," the painter told me.

Coming from a small town, I had no idea how to ride a city bus, so I set off to walk there. I was young, fit, and loved walking. However, the journey of walking thirty-six city blocks became unbearable with all my belongings.

I plucked up my courage and asked a bus driver how to get to that suburb. He was very kind, helping me ride and transfer onto other buses.

I found a double-storied brick house with a room for rent and a shared bathroom. My pineapple plant enjoyed a sunny spot in the window upstairs, and I carpooled to work the following week.

A Hospital Job

Months later, I decided sanding all day long was not for me anymore. Having found my way around the city somewhat, I applied to a local hospital for a job as an admissions clerk in the emergency room and front counter. This paid much higher wages, boosting my funds to Kenya. I'd never worked in a hospital before, especially getting details from trauma patients in the emergency room. The doctors and nurses seemed too cheerful, but this was where I learned the term "compassion fatigue." This would serve me well overseas in a developing country years later.

The job had a surprising health benefit to prepare me for going to an underdeveloped country.

"What are you saving up for?" I was asked one day.

"Africa!"

When they heard about my plans to go to Africa, they informed me this hospital offered training opportunities for dentists and doctors.

"Maybe you should get your wisdom teeth out before you go," they suggested.

"Why is that?"

"Wisdom teeth can cause dental problems later, and it won't cost you much here."

"How much?"

"The oral surgeon only asks for a bottle of Chivas Regal whiskey!"

Deciding I could save a lot of future health issues and money, I considered the extractions along with yellow fever and typhoid vaccinations to be part of my health preparations for heading off to what I thought could be a third-world country with limited health resources.

As a hospital employee, I got an examination.

"Why do you want all these wisdom teeth out?" the surgeon asked. "I can't see any problem with them. They appear to be well settled in your mouth."

"I'm saving up to go to Africa in a few months for an unknown period."

"Well, we can extract all four at once as long as you're happy with having a student dental surgeon in training on one side of your mouth."

This sounded cost-saving and efficient, so I booked the procedure. Fortunately, I'd moved into a communal house where people could transport me and look after me following the ordeal. I was under so much pain medication that I didn't know if I was coming or going for the next ten days!

After nearly one year of working, I shared a ride with a friend going back to Oregon, still holding my pineapple plant and with my skis on the roof rack.

I left everything with my parents, only carrying what would fit in my backpack. I wore sturdy leather boots for climbing mountains and a red parka with many pockets for holding essential items.

"Well, Mom and Dad, this is it. The time has finally come for the big adventure to Africa!"

"We'll take you to the bus station with your brothers and sister to see you off."

With a lump in my throat, my heart pounding, and a few doubts trying to derail my adventurous plan, I fought to hold back tears as I hopped on the bus. I felt relieved yet faint at the prospect of the unknown journey ahead.

I secured a flight on a cheap charter from Toronto, Canada, flying over Iceland to Paris and then London.

In Paris, I suddenly felt a lack of courage and rang my mother, crying. "I want to come home!"

"You have been wanting to go to Africa for a long time. Keep going! You can do this."

Reassured by my mother's encouraging comments, I set off to find cheap flights to Nairobi, Kenya from London. I wasn't sure where to find them. When I found the agency that handled those things, I discovered these flights weren't regular.

Now what should I do? Sitting on a bench in Earl's Court, I considered my options.

East Africa and Beyond!

I bought a round-trip ticket and finally made it to Nairobi in January 1975 for my twenty-second birthday. No books, guides, or internet were available to help me plan this trip halfway around the world—just dreams, *National Geographic* maps, and a few travel stories from a friend who had been here.

After the formalities of entering Kenya, I staggered out into bright sunlight with my not-so-light backpack.

I thought I would try out my newly learned Swahili greeting and find a place to stay. "*Jambo.* Can you tell me please where the nearest youth hostel is to stay for a night or two?"

Unfortunately, I learned the hostel close by had been transformed into a school dormitory for young women.

Walking further, I spotted a small museum and escaped the sunshine and heat into its cool, dusty-smelling interior. One other person was inside, also sheltering from the heat.

Nervous, I spoke my one Swahili greeting, "*Jambo.*"

A friendly young Kenyan man dressed in office clothes and

speaking delightful English asked me, "Where have you come from today?"

We struck up a conversation, and when Omari found out I had nowhere to stay and no one to meet, he invited me to stay with him and his brother in the local suburb where the East African Railways employees were housed. I simply trusted him with good intentions, which he honoured. I lived with him and his brother for a few months and even took a train with him to his home village, Kisii, near Lake Victoria. *What would it be like to marry, settle here in Kenya, and have African children?* It was a rather naive thought. Finally, we realised our futures would never be compatible, so I headed to the coast where I would find other travellers.

Any thought of returning to university simply evaporated in this hot African sun. Adventure was on my radar and was to be my focus for quite a while. I fell in love with travelling and being on this continent, discovering a new passion through these adventures of living with local Kenyans, meeting world travellers on yachts in Mombasa, climbing Mt Kenya, and hearing stories from Peace Corps volunteers heading back to the States. A love of the ocean and beach found me drifting to Twiga Lodge, a backpacker and overland traveller beach campground.

Listening to outrageous adventures by sailors and overlanders convinced me this type of lifestyle was my newfound direction. I abandoned my earlier half-baked idea of volunteering to help the less fortunate. My decision a few years earlier that there was no God in my life anymore facilitated this self-focused pursuit of adventure and truth-seeking. I was drifting rapidly away from a religious concept of God, searching for truth through experiences. Needless to say, some character traits were underdeveloped, and my maturity was lacking.

Sailing on a Small Yacht in the Indian Ocean

After six months of travelling in Kenya and hanging out with adventurous people from four countries on an old wooden schooner, I found myself rowing over to a smaller yacht to apply for a crewing position. I had no sailing experience, and some of the lads thought it would be funny to send me over with an umbrella for the owner. Unbeknown to me, an umbrella was considered bad luck on a boat!

"Have you any sailing experience? And how much baggage do you have, as this is a small 36-foot yacht with very little storage left?"

My heart sank, thinking I would be put ashore. With only $50 left, I would have to return home. "I've never sailed before and only kayaked in some lakes. But I only have a small bag of belongings, as I sold my backpack and climbing boots."

"That's great news! You are just who we want, as you will follow the skipper's instructions for steering the boat. And with only that small bag, no problems."

After interviewing six other lads as well, they informed me I would be their fourth crew member. The owner wore a red headband. The skipper, known as PJ, sported a bushy black beard and a gold earring.

PJ hailed from New Zealand. I later found out he voted for me to join the crew rather than any of the other guys. This was the start of our relationship and a lifestyle of travelling and sailing for nearly two decades.

Heading into a rough Indian Ocean voyage, my courage evaporated. I was extremely seasick, convinced we were going to tip over and drown. I cried out to God one night as I was hanging on to the tiller for dear life. When we successfully anchored at a deserted island after fourteen turbulent days, I decided I was not an atheist.

Maybe I'm an agnostic, believing in a higher power. At any rate, after that experience, I forgot about God for a while.

When we sailed into the most beautiful place that I'd ever seen, with white sandy beaches, papaya and coconut trees, and clear, warm, turquoise Indian ocean waters with a myriad of colourful fish, I was hooked. *What a fantastic way to see the world! Yet a week ago, seasick with seven more days of sailing before we anchored, I would have flown out if there was an airport!* After a week of drying out and washing our salty bedding in an abandoned water reservoir, I looked forward to another leg of the journey.

We continued to Madagascar, then over to Mozambique, finally arriving in South Africa three months after leaving Kenya.

South Africa, an Immigrant Ship to New Zealand, and Beyond

By now, I'd been in and around Africa on land and by sea for a year. From South Africa, we looked west towards sailing to Brazil or east towards New Zealand. PJ and his brother had built a house bus before sailing took them overseas. When he suggested we could live in the bus and work around New Zealand, I was sold on that idea!

A telegram to his father for a loan of money helped us secure passage on a ship in Cape Town with 1,650 immigrants heading towards Australia and New Zealand. After three weeks, we arrived in Auckland and travelled by train to Central Otago to spend Christmas with his family. Train travel gave us time to adjust from sailing. Views from the windows created a strong heartfelt sense of loving this country. I felt in my soul that this was to be my home. *Why does this feel like home to me? I have a lovely family back in the Pacific Northwest of America.*

It was love at first sight of the 1948 Bedford bus, which was painted bright yellow and red with the name 'Paradise' down the sides. It had been a tourist bus up the Paradise Valley in Lake Wakatipu years earlier. We parked the bus in an apricot orchard near a factory processing my favourite stone fruit, apricots. Once we had paid back PJ's father for our passage from South Africa, we travelled north and parked in a campground in the middle of Christchurch. Delivering campervans between the North and South Islands while cleaning rental vehicles for a small firm helped us save money for future travels.

One morning we awoke to find snow on the roof of our bus! Our days sailing in the tropics seemed distant memories.

"Where should we go next?" PJ asked.

"I don't know, but I think my visa is running out soon. Maybe we should get married first!"

"Good idea! I could get a green card to work in America."

It was settled. Our sense of adventure and spontaneity led us the next week to taking a longer morning break from our job. When we came back to work, we told the boss. He ordered a box of cream buns for afternoon tea to celebrate! Sadly, we were not very considerate of our parents or family with our decision to get married at a Registry Office. In the South Island in 1976, this was quite an unusual ceremony! We didn't give it a thought.

Leaving Addington campground, we drove further north to some warmer weather, crossing the Cook Strait on one of the big rail ferries. It was an exciting three-hour passage, turbulent but scenic. We parked in another campground on the north shore of Auckland. With only car licences and a five-week training course, we both donned green bus uniforms and drove the public buses. I loved driving the electric trolley buses and pre-select Daimler and Leyland buses. PJ was more experienced with the double declutch buses, so he drove the North Shore buses.

After one year in New Zealand, with enough funds saved to fly to England, we sold the bus. We both felt the call to go overseas again. But where?

"What about buying a double-decker bus in England and taking people to India?" suggested PJ, while looking at our National Geographic atlas one night.

"Sure, why not?"

We enjoyed living in a house bus and driving buses. Filled with enthusiasm but not much wisdom, we got busy making bamboo-framed backpacks and old sail bags. We even took our big atlas and hand-built skateboard! Waving goodbye to the new owners of Paradise bus, we headed to the airport.

We visited my parents and family on the way to England. *How am I going to tell them we got married a few months ago?* My initial plan of being away for six weeks had become more than two years before I saw them all again. University wasn't even discussed. I was well and truly a world adventurer now. I was thankful my parents shared my enthusiasm for this new lifestyle. They seemed very supportive, despite our spontaneous marriage. My younger siblings still at school kept them occupied.

When we arrived in the south of England during the cold, wet UK winter, PJ's brother gave us a contact to inquire about buying a double-decker bus. However, this was not a well-thought-out plan, not to mention the fact that the bus company did not want one of their beloved buses travelling to India!

"Oh well, what about visiting our friend in the Canary Islands?" suggested PJ. "She offered a place for us to stay on Lanzarote, remember?"

"Sure, why not? Sounds interesting. Let's go!"

One place led to another, which led to another, and on and on.

Our "wanderlust gene" took us travelling together around the world overland and on yachts for years, experiencing wild adventures between our times of employment. Adventurous and a bit rebellious, we lived a hedonistic lifestyle, though at the time we just thought it was fun.

However, living for the moment became boring and unsatisfying after years of one-way destinations. After a critical time when we almost ended up in a foreign jail with friends, my search for spiritual truth became more important. While waiting for PJ to return from sailing, I joined a Hindu ashram in Denver. Three months later, I gave up on that and rejoined PJ for Mardi Gras in New Orleans.

A Permanent Return to New Zealand

As I turned thirty, I realised to my amazement that I wanted to get off the merry-go-round of constantly changing locations. I yearned to settle in one place and start a family in New Zealand. This was not an easy change of direction. After seven years of numerous residences and jobs, first in the South Island, then in the North, we finally settled for a time.

Soon, another big change came.

"Guess what? We're pregnant!"

Welcoming our son, Ross, into our lives was incredible and an answered prayer from my wavering faith walk. I now believe finally starting a family was a miracle and blessing from God. However, back then, I simply returned to a mixture of beliefs and new-age practices. I was an older mother with a young-at-heart attitude.

This addition to our family filled me with delight and satisfaction. I loved being a mum and having a settled family life off the high seas of crazy adventures. We qualified for a Housing Corporation loan and bought a little cottage in West Auckland. PJ set about teaching himself how to weld and started building a yacht in our backyard.

Plans to sail the Pacific with our son evaporated. Changes came about too quickly for me, although not for PJ. First the boat sold, then our house, and we were heading off again overseas, this time with a two-year-old. *I guess it will take PJ a while to settle down. Sigh. Oh well, maybe our son will have some time with his grandparents.* I had to look on the bright side. *At least, we will be living on an island in the Pacific Northwest.*

After our eight-month trip to Puget Sound, we flew back to New Zealand with little money, no job, and no house. A long-time friend and yachtie offered us his 50-foot yacht, built of recycled materials, to live on at the marina while we found our feet again. PJ got serious about building houses with another friend, and we paid off the loan for his tools and van. Meanwhile, I was busy with playgroup and friends with three-year-olds again.

When our son started school, we thought the Kerikeri area would be the best place for him to grow up. By some miracle, we bought a small one-acre property in the Bay of Islands and built our own little cottage. This was a dream come true. *Now maybe we can settle long term!* We both loved it and couldn't imagine any place better.

The school bus stopped by the road, picking up Ross and other boys from neighbouring houses. PJ was employed with house building, while I worked part-time as a teacher aide. Planting trees and having a garden, watching the seasonal changes, and living in an area with real kiwi was so satisfying after our many travels. Seeing our son grow up building tree huts, fishing and swimming at the wharf, and having so many friends to play with was a real joy.

I realised another dream when I was trained to be a teacher through online distance learning at Massey University in New Zealand. As an older student in my late forties, I had to learn how to use a computer and navigate the seas of higher education. I clearly recall being totally daunted by just the application process!

Step by step, I gained a BEd (Bachelor of Education) degree in primary teaching.

I worked as a beginning teacher for a year and a half before my life fell apart. Neither PJ nor I knew how to sail these high seas of the stress of a mortgage, health issues, self-employment, me developing a career in teaching, and a son entering his teenage years. Our marriage was floundering, and we didn't know how to adjust our sails.

New Life at Fifty-Two

I had an ever-growing sense of my spiritual void growing bigger and bigger. This brought me to a place of surrender and ultimately led to me accepting Jesus Christ as my Saviour, after many years of trying to find peace through Hindu and new-age practices.

This dramatic change, which I found to be a lifesaver, was met with resistance on the home front and set into motion a series of events that I had no idea would follow. Tragically, my marriage fell apart. Although our relationship was already struggling, I didn't know how to fix it. My biggest concern was the effects of our split on our teenage son. As the storms raged like nothing I had ever experienced at sea, my anchor lay in my new faith. It became a lifeline and comfort for me.

My understanding of this faith grew through being discipled and studying how to apply biblical truths to my daily life. I found freedom from past emotional hurts and peace in accepting who I was now in the eyes of a God who loved me with a tangible and deep love.*

The next step for me in my faith walk was being water baptised as an adult as a public demonstration of my confession of faith in Jesus Christ. The Bible tells us Jesus got baptised as an adult and instructed his disciples before He returned to heaven. I learned that baptism is an outward testimony of an inward transformation. As a disciple of Jesus, it is an act of obedience. Three months after my first step of choosing a faith walk with Jesus, I knew I needed to be baptised. When I heard a baptism event was coming up and that it was at the beach, I knew this was the right time and place for me.

On Easter Monday at Matauri Bay beach and campground, with believers from a local church as well as a little Pentecostal church up north, three youths and I were water baptised in the sea under sunny skies. Someone played the guitar while we sang worship songs. My son and some of his friends were playing not far down the beach, waiting for the baptisms to be over so they could enjoy some lunch from the many plates of food shared by everyone.

As I stood waiting my turn in the small waves at Matauri Bay, looking back at over a hundred people watching and curious bystanders in the campground coming to watch us as well, it was easy to imagine this as a scene out of The Book of the Acts of the Apostles two thousand years earlier.

Standing in waist-high water off the beach, with my friend Joy holding me on one side and the pastor on the other, the pastor asked me a question before putting me under the waves. "Do you realise you will be born again, never to be the same, and a new person in Christ?"

"Yes, I understand." I'd spent the past two weeks studying Bible

---

* *Do not be afraid or terrified because of them, for the Lord your God goes with you; He will never leave you nor forsake you.* (Hebrews 13:5, NIV)

passages with a friend to understand more about what this bornagain experience and what being baptised as an adult signifies.

I felt like a new person coming up out of the water, that the old me was washed away. That significant event sparked a transformation within me, giving me courage and comfort in navigating through an unsettling time. Raising a teenage boy within a broken marriage was not at all what I envisioned, nor was being a solo parent. I felt comforted by the new Scriptures I was learning, assuring me that God would never leave me and that he was healing my broken heart.*

Walking out my faith daily got me through with some joyful moments as well as mistakes and disappointing outcomes. My emotional and mental battles with fear and anxiety were met with a stronger belief and a growing level of faith that came from renewing my mind with Bible verses.

Another season of my life was dawning. This time I would be on my own and a solo parent. Though it was a daunting thought, I looked forward to this new chapter with a growing measure of hope.

The Call to 'Go'

I spent six years healing through prayer with supportive friends, navigating the changes of a broken marriage, retraining in care for the elderly, and solo parenting. Then an opportunity arose for me to fly to Oregon to see my mother. Dad had passed away the year before. These three weeks away from New Zealand visiting family and friends gave me the opportunity to seek God for a new direction for my life. I returned to distance learning as a postgraduate student in early childhood education, unaware that this would be

---

* *He heals the broken in heart, and binds up their wounds.* (Psalm 147:3, WEB)

an important step leading to my heart's desire to serve in Africa as a missionary.

Secretly, I questioned, *How will this be possible for me, a latecomer to this living faith?*

As a new believer, I was yet to read more of the Bible and what Jesus taught about sharing the 'Good News'. In the gospel of Matthew, Jesus' words about going into all nations struck me. *This seems to be speaking to me!*

Those early years as a believer saw me interested in the worship music and Bible teachings broadcast from a church in California. Checking out their website for upcoming events, I discovered there was to be a women's conference at the time I was in Oregon. My heart soared. I sensed this would be pivotal in finding out God's direction for my life as a single, 'empty-nester' older woman.

However, the distance from southern Oregon to northern California was considerable—over 800 miles or 1,287 kilometres. *How will I travel without a car on a shoestring budget, and where will I stay?*

Homestay options were provided for people visiting the conference, for the cost of sharing food. The bus fares and timetable looked as though they could work. As the travel and accommodation fell into place, my excitement grew. My naturally adventurous spirit reawakened after years of parenting, reigniting a sense of going offshore to serve God wholeheartedly.

After a great time in Oregon with family and friends, I hopped on a bus for the ten-hour trip. I found the bus service hadn't changed from years ago when I first rode Greyhound buses, stopping at random places and waiting with others for the toilet stops, hoping there was enough toilet paper.

The homestay woman had informed me that the other person attending the women's conference would have a rental car and could pick me up from the bus station. She could also take me to and from the conference, as her house was out of town. When Becky came to the bus station, we immediately connected.

"I'll need the toilet before we go to our homestay. And then you can tell me where you've arrived from!" I ran to get my bag off the bus, and after a pit stop at the loo, I jumped into her rental car.

"I've been a long-term missionary in China, teaching English to students and holding a home church for new believers."

Wow, a real missionary in China! Through meeting someone equally passionate about serving the Lord and inspired by this church, God started to show me my next direction.

I listened with excitement as she shared her stories from China. Part of her mission involved travelling by bus up a steep mountain range to another region, where she'd been invited, along with others, to share a discipling course for a group of *lamas* (monks) curious about Jesus. It was a journey of danger and yet rewards in evangelising a remote part of the world. I was in awe of hearing the stories firsthand.

The conference gave me space to fervently seek the Lord for direction. One afternoon session provided personal space to pray. I noticed prophetic paintings placed around the room. When I stood in front of a painting titled Mozambique, a lightbulb moment flashed an internal message to my heart.

At the end of the conference, I shared with Becky about my growing excitement in sensing a calling from God to be a missionary, probably to Africa. Jumping on the bus, I prayed for her. "Blessings and favour on your return to China. May God protect you, especially in your adventurous bus rides up into the mountains."

On the long bus ride back to Oregon, I thought of my inner excitement at hearing stories of life in China with my roommate during the week-long conference, and the stirring in my heart from seeing the painting of a missionary in Mozambique. I had over ten hours on that bus trip back to my parents to think about my experiences, since the bus broke down in an isolated area of northern California and the rescue bus took five hours to reach us. Still, I was excited to be on this adventure, even while stranded on a highway of dry, rolling hills.

After a short time of recovering from the travel and conference, I walked to a local grocery store. On the notice board, I spotted an advertisement for a Christian TV channel. It looked out of place amongst ads for meditation classes, crystal healings, and Hindu teachers at local ashrams. Something in me was drawn to viewing whatever programme was on this channel.

Arriving back at my parents' house, I asked for help in finding the channel on a tiny black-and-white TV in a back room. As soon as I turned it on, the programme began with a volunteer teacher in a school in Mozambique, of all places!

I had asked God to make His plan and purpose for my life clear and unmistakable. The mission-based teaching programme in Mozambique was captivating; more so was my growing confidence that God was pointing me towards being a missionary in Africa, and possibly Mozambique. I stored this revelation in my heart along with some scriptures that seemed to point towards 'going!' to the continent of my heart's desires again, but this time with God.

At the airport, boarding the plane back to New Zealand, I waved goodbye to my mother and brother with a lump in my throat and tears forming. Over the thirteen-hour flight, I became aware of a growing excitement, of sensing a call of God to go to Africa as a missionary and single woman.* A glimpse of a hope-filled future

---

* *I took you from the ends of the earth, from its farthest corners I called you. I said, "You are my servant"; I have chosen you and have not rejected you. So do not fear, for I am with you; do not be dismayed for I am your God. I will strengthen you and help you; I will uphold you with my righteous right hand.* (Isaiah 41:9–10, NIV)

filled my vision and, with it, the unveiling of another new chapter. *Where in Africa will I go? What will I do there? Will I be with other missionaries?*

For some years, my church had been supporting Kevin and Ginnie, a missionary family from New Zealand, in northern Mozambique. Once a year, the family returned with photos and stories about new churches planted in remote villages, their Bible Training School, supporting the locals in cashew and goat-raising ventures, providing a feeding programme for children and babies during the hunger season, and more recently, their plans to create a Bible-based preschool programme in rural villages.

At this time in my early walk with the Lord, I believed that as a follower of Jesus, I could be involved in going to foreign nations. Again, a well-known verse came to mind: "Therefore GO and make disciples of all nations" (Matthew 28:19, WEB). Missions can be in our own backyard, but some of us are called to go to the other side of the world for God's plan and purpose.

I had a growing awareness that I could be one of these people!

My Career or God's Direction?

I had much to think about as I returned to the early childhood centre with a team of dedicated teachers. Kelly, my manager, encouraged me to develop my passion for preschool education. She would also prove to be a strong and essential supporter of my mission-sending team. It was so satisfying to find a job that was meaningful, interesting, and allowed me to develop parts of myself I'd buried or never explored. I can only say God opened this up. He is faithful in creating pathways to realise long-buried dreams.

Pondering this new Africa-focused direction in my life, I recalled prophetic visions shared with me a few years earlier in my Connect group from church. Checking my journals, I discovered someone in 2008 had seen me sitting under a big tree with African children.* Another prophecy, before I went to visit family in Oregon, was similar, with African children grouped around me. *But, Lord, I have only just realised my passion for early childhood education! Are you asking me to give it up?*

I received my first prophetic vision at a distressing time. During a heated moment of our separation, my husband blurted out, "You're going to be a missionary in Africa!" He'd perceived, after my born-again experience, something I did not yet anticipate. Still, it seemed impossible at the time.

Though my marriage crumbled, and I crumbled too (until God restored me with His everlasting love), I was to discover a silver lining years after the divorce: God was indeed calling me to missions in Africa. Following my visit to Oregon and California—years after my husband foretold it—I shared this realisation with my prayer partners.

God's methods of providing what I needed were unbelievable.† After completing my post-grad in ECE, I owed a debt of around $3,500 to an Auckland-owned daycare franchise. My ECE qualification was to be paid off over years of continuing employment, working four days a week, as agreed when I embarked on the study.

When I had to go to other ECE centres for practicum training sessions, the employers kept my job open and hired a reliever. I didn't get paid for time spent training and had to take a student loan to make ends meet. While grateful for how the franchise

---

* *Jesus came to them and spoke to them, saying … "GO and make disciples of all nations, baptising them in the name of the Father and of the Son and of the Holy Spirit, teaching them to observe all things that I commanded you."* (Matthew 28:18–20, WEB)

† *Do not be conformed to this world, but be transformed by the renewing of your mind, so that you may prove what is the good, well-pleasing and perfect will of God.* (Romans 12:2, WEB)

enabled me to study and work as a solo parent, I emerged with a sizable debt.

Though challenging, childcare had its rewards. It never bored me and provided ongoing professional development training. I finally felt as though I was working in a worthwhile profession to help train up and love the next generation of children.

Released from Preschool Job

I had a growing awareness that God was calling me to Africa to serve less advantaged people. When and where I did not know. It seemed such a complex situation. Thankfully, my son was now independently working and living in a city four hours away. I missed him yet was pleased he'd found employment immediately. I knew he needed to find his own way in life. My former husband had moved permanently to Australia to be near some of his family.

One thing was certain: Africa! But I was looking at impossible obstacles. *How will I get there? How will it be financed? Whereabouts will I be?* Plus, with this debt of $3,500, I had a commitment to the childcare centre for a few more years, at least. And I was nearly sixty!

But for God, I was realising, none of this was complicated. He was to show me how He can do extraordinary things outside the scope of my imagination.

The franchise from Auckland was implementing changes that seemed to compromise too much of the well-being of the children. Understandably, there were pressures on them as a business. However, having just trained as an ECE teacher, the wellbeing of the children was paramount in my mind.

Our poor manager was stuck in the middle between the owners and the teachers. As pressures mounted, the three of us who were

Christians (myself, the manager, and one other teacher) felt led to pray at the end of each week on a Friday when all the children had gone home. With crucial changes being implemented for how we cared for and managed young children, we prayed for guidance, peace, and strength to maintain a positive environment for everyone.

Things shifted, but not as we expected. God was working things out for me to go to Africa much sooner than I anticipated. The head teacher, very experienced as well as outspoken, was mysteriously dismissed without any communication with us. This was strange and unsettling. The manager, my friend and sister in Christ, also resigned due to mounting health issues. I drafted a letter to the owners about how the environment did not create a beneficial work/play space and asked the new manager to read it before I sent it off.

Soon after, I was summoned into the office. *This is not good*, I thought. My diary records the date as Friday, 11/11/11.

"The owners would like to talk with you on a Skype call about your situation here," the temporary manager told me. "They understand you are finding the drive to the daycare very long and difficult and want to offer you a solution."

This is strange! I'd never once complained about my commute to work. I wondered what was going to be proposed and why.

The franchise owners started by saying how they understood I was finding the work difficult with a long commute from home, and they were also aware of the $3,500 loan I was to repay over time from my ECE training.

To my shock, they offered me a deal to resign immediately. They would wipe the debt from my studies and pay me for one month from today's date. (My eyes were getting wider.) Then they offered holiday pay as well, which was a couple of thousand dollars. On top of that, they offered to write me a positive recommendation for future employers and promised to speak highly of me if contacted for a verbal reference.

The conditions were that I drop any complaints, resign immediately, not breathe a word of the details negotiated with any other teachers or talk to anyone about it, and leave that afternoon. I was speechless, having never had such an experience in my life. I was quietly excited about this change of direction yet nervous about what lay ahead.

My new manager was listening. Her mouth dropped in amazement. Adding up all they'd offered, she worked out it was a payout of thousands. She had never witnessed anyone else receiving such an amount. I was beginning to find out that with God, all things are possible!

Could this be my release to go to Africa? Not only was I free from debt, but I now had the exact funds to enrol in a seven-week intensive cross-cultural mission course in Sydney, Australia starting in a couple of weeks. *Hopefully, this course will guide me to where in Africa God is leading me!*

A Long-Term Mission Training Course

God was answering my prayers sooner and more effectively than I could ever have imagined. I immediately contacted Calvin and Glenda, the couple teaching the upcoming course, who had been missionaries in Papua New Guinea for over twenty years.

"I can come!" I said excitedly. "But where will I stay for those seven weeks?"

We had to organise our own accommodation. I'd never been to Australia and had no contacts. I didn't even know where Parramatta was, let alone the new location of the Christian college.

With only ten days to go until the start of the course, time was running short. Glenda emailed me to say that a friend she'd known previously, Sarina, sat down next to her at a church service. Sarina leaned over and whispered, "Do you know if any students need a room with meals for the upcoming course? I have a bedroom available."

Glenda shared the news with me immediately, asking if I still needed room and board.

"Yes! Book me in."

Less than one month after being made redundant, I left Kerikeri by bus to catch the flight to Sydney.

Originally from Indonesia, Sarina had lived in Sydney for many years. Staying with someone from another country who shared a passionate faith in God while embarking on this cross-cultural training course felt extra meaningful. Having a car, she drove us from her home in Parramatta to a Pentecostal-style church in Baulkham Hills. I was thrilled to go there every Sunday, as I knew many of their worship songs.

I found it amazing how God orchestrated the provision for this course and accommodation. This was the first time I had witnessed such a move of God and His dramatic, speedy provision. It further confirmed I was on the right path with His plan for me.*

God graciously only revealed bit by bit what He planned for me regarding the timing and location. I was grateful, aware that I might faint at the prospect of it all or, worse still, race ahead out of step with His perfect timing.

Sarina's lovely apartment turned out to be close to campus, so I could walk to my mission course. My board payments even included delicious, home-cooked Indonesian dinners! I love Indonesian food, so it was such a blessing to have that provided. I

---

* *Forget the former things; do not dwell on the past. See, I am doing a new thing! Now it springs up; do you not perceive it? I am making a way in the wilderness and streams in the wasteland.* (Isaiah 43:18–19, NIV)

supplied my own breakfast, then purchased lunch from cafés near the campus. Her Bible study group included friends from Indonesia, Malaysia, and the Philippines.

"I'm living in a cross-cultural situation 24/7. How cool is that?!" I texted friends back home.

Sarina took me to the Vietnamese area of town to shop for vegetables and fruit. There I discovered strange new fruits like dragon fruit as well as a passion for mangoes! A $10 box of ten big mangoes lasted me a week. She showed me how to halve and cut them into cubes, then invert them so they looked like armadillo shells. "The cubes of mango are easier to eat that way," she explained.

I rediscovered my heart for people from other countries, along with my love of adventure and exploring new places. Only this time, it was to be on my own—except God was with me. My faith was growing. Saturdays were a time to relax and explore Sydney once my homework was done. The ferry across the harbour to the zoo was refreshing after being in the classroom all week. This zoo was one of the best animal habitats I've seen.

More than seeing tourist attractions, it was special to be with a group of passionate, mission-minded believers, both at the college and at Sarina's home. We all wanted to share the Gospel wherever God led us, introducing a positive change in people's lives and giving them hope.

I enjoyed meeting and listening to other folks preparing for their long-term mission experience. I particularly learned a lot from Calvin and Glenda, who shared their knowledge and experience from years living in Papua New Guinea. All the adults in the course were looking to become long-term missionaries. The topics of church planting and training locals to be effective pastors and teachers were appropriate for them. *What is going to be important for me to learn?*

I was in awe of those goals and loved learning everything about going to another country to share the Gospel. This course claimed to shorten the outcome of making an impact with the Gospel from seven to three-and-a-half years. *I know I'm to be here too, but I wonder what God's plans are for me, and where am I going?*

One of the valuable aspects I learned was how to share the good news of Jesus and the Bible in a culturally acceptable way. The extensive curriculum covered many topics for long-term mission outreach. The topic of animism intrigued me. This was also where I first heard the term syncretism, when Christianity is mixed with other beliefs. Gathering financial support, learning time-management strategies, a short study of other religions (including a visit to a Hindu temple), IT, and practical administration skills were other topics covered.

The most frequent phrase was 'Not wrong, just different!' We were encouraged to be open to viewing the world through fresh eyes, not with our own cultural bias.

One practical skill drilled into us was to back up any writing on a USB stick. This proved very useful in managing information shared in newsletters and the documentation of events. As Wi-Fi connections or electricity supplies in remote areas were frail and inconsistent, one could unexpectedly lose all work in one moment as it vanished from the screen. In remote and rural areas, we could not depend on a nearby IT specialist to help retrieve it!

Will I need to learn a tribal language? I had many questions and wondered at these possibilities, particularly as I was not gifted in languages.

The innovative and fast method of learning a local 'heart' language (or mother tongue) by recording speech intrigued me, and I was excited to learn methods for cross-cultural living. When bringing the Gospel to an unreached people group, communicating in their 'heart' language makes a more positive impact. It enables them to identify with the Bible's message of 'Good News' within their own culture, not a Westernised version. *Will this learning technique be necessary for me to learn?*

They strongly recommended we join a mission organisation when serving overseas. Not only would we gain their expertise, a mentoring process, a network of connections, and a prayer team, but also protection in an evacuation process if needed.

Although I still did not know some essential details, this course contributed to a valuable knowledge base for missions. At any rate, I felt better prepared for where God was leading me.

I met a lovely couple from just over the Blue Mountains who were passionate about making a difference in a South-East Asian country. Before they left, they invited me for a weekend away to meet with their church family and see some Australian countryside. This couple had a very supportive, mission-focused church to partner with them. I was humbled and touched to receive some encouraging words about going to Africa from members there.

One woman gave me a little wallet-sized card, which I carried with me for years. Reading the verse on it rescued me many times from sinking feelings of insecurity. We never know how a small gesture of kindness or a word of advice can help someone, even years after.

Learning about cross-cultural mission outreach and getting to know these long-term missionaries was such a privilege. Most of them had been disciples of Jesus in their own countries much longer than me; they also knew which country they were preparing to go to serve. Although I was not at this point, I was certain God had clearly orchestrated the steps to me attending this course.

Those seven weeks we spent together encouraged me in my new direction. I had a lot to think and pray about. Not knowing where I was going to serve or for how long was unsettling. But importantly, I was learning to trust God with this unknown destination. *Where God, where?* I tried not to sound too impatient!

Exploratory Trip

Africa is a big continent. I had fond memories of East Africa from my time in Kenya as a twenty-two-year-old. Kevin and Ginnie, the missionaries our church supported in Mozambique, served with an organisation called World Outreach (WO). Their global vision was to evangelise and disciple unreached people groups, equipping them to disciple their own and other peoples.

Serving in Mozambique through World Outreach was high on my list of preferred places, but I also had a heart for East Africa. I was fortunate that Ron and Lyndie, at that stage the African WO field directors, were visiting New Zealand. I organised an interview with them, and we met at a café in Whangarei Basin.

Over coffee, I expressed some doubts. "I'm not sure where God is calling me to go, as I have enjoyed East Africa and I've been involved in supporting Whitewater Ministries. My only skill to offer is being recently trained and having experience in preschool education. Where do you think I could be useful?"

"World Outreach is just beginning a one-year internship for

people considering long-term missions but who are not sure how long a commitment they can make. You might like to apply for that position," they suggested. They also recommended undertaking an exploratory trip to wherever God was leading me, months before actually moving long-term to the 'new' country.

After meeting Ron and Lyndie to discuss the prospects of visiting various mission projects over seven weeks, they secured contacts in four different countries. The timing and connections were amazing.

Only God could have brought it together in such a rapid way. He knew who I needed to know and where I needed to go. It was like I was on a fast track. I was continually in awe of how many things were falling into place in such a short time.

Decisions and Preparations

Preparing to visit various mission centres in four countries required me to first return to work and save money; finish my New Zealand ECE teacher registration; complete the World Outreach application process; update my passport and vaccination documents; learn IT skills on my smartphone for communication, photos, and information; and invite others to join me on this journey, financially and/or prayerfully.

All this was a huge undertaking in addition to full-time work. I was thankful for my church family, who supported and prayed with me and assisted me in practical ways, and for the WO process that helped me achieve these requirements.

As I returned to work, I wondered exactly when or where I was going to end up in Africa. God was soon to answer in a unique way that reassured my questions.

On my return from Sydney, I accepted a three-month temporary position in a local early childhood centre, with the option for a permanent position. My confidence in God's call on my life strengthened on my first morning when a CD of African music was playing in the four-year-olds room. Not only that, but a new book had arrived, and I was asked to read it to the children at mat time. It was called *Teddies Visit Africa* and had pictures of safari animals. I felt as though God was reminding me of His calling me to Africa. I hadn't spoken to anyone there yet about my vague plans.

Even though this centre was a delightful one to work in, I considered carefully whether to accept a permanent position. I was now qualified and in my late fifties. I had to choose my path. I shared with them my heart and my expectation of moving to Africa in the near future. Although I didn't know many details about how this journey was going to work out, I felt it was imperative for me to trust God in His direction for my life.*

I declined an offer of security in employment and applied for another temporary position in nearby Kaikohe. 'Trust in the Lord' sprang to mind, confirming this decision.

Part of my Africa preparation was to have my New Zealand passport updated and current, along with evidence in a yellow health passport that I'd had the necessary vaccinations to enter these countries. Tanzania, in particular, required proof of a yellow fever vaccination in the health passport before entry. Over the next few months, I took trips to a travel clinic to get vaccinated against typhoid, yellow fever, rabies, and Hepatitis A. Meanwhile, I completed my New Zealand teacher registration and worked in preschools, which helped fund the hundreds of dollars for these vaccinations.

Whenever I heard of anything to do with overseas missions, my ears pricked up. One organisation held a weekend seminar for

---

* *In their hearts humans plan their course, but the Lord establishes their steps* (Proverbs 16:9, NIV)

Exploratory Trip

returning missionaries, which I thought could be a good place to hear actual experiences of being on the field.

During that seminar, someone asked me, "Do you know another language? Did you know it's quite difficult for an older person to learn a new language? Have you thought about choosing an English-speaking country such as Kenya for your mission experience?"

Maybe I should consider that? Doubts crept into my mind. It was a valid point. But after some prayer, I felt that if God was going to call me to a country where I needed to learn another language, He would also equip me to learn that language. I was reminded of Moses in the Old Testament and how he told God he was slow in speech. But God still called him to lead the Israelites out of Egypt to the Promised Land, despite Moses being nearly eighty years old and slow in speech. There was still hope for me!

One day, as I glanced at my list of preparations, I wondered how I was to learn the phone skills I needed. Almost immediately, I bumped into an acquaintance from another church. A friend was just coming out of the local library with his phone in hand, excited to have downloaded some apps for his upcoming mission trip. He had just finished his teacher training with a Christian college and was off to a refugee camp with the Karen people group for six months.

He shared with me the most helpful apps to put on my phone—time zones, money conversions, weather, and even Portuguese language learning. *Am I going to need that?* He also suggested starting a blog to inform other people of my plans to go to Africa. *A blog? Not sure about that!* It was one of the many ways God put other people in my path to help me on this journey.

Learning More about Mozambique Missions

During the Christmas holidays, Kevin and Ginnie visited our church to update us on the progress and needs of Whitewater Ministries. Their current brochure described the outreach as a 'community of believers bringing a holistic presentation of the Gospel to the rural people through community development, medical missions, and church planting/leadership training'.

In the mid 1990s, there was a large group in northern Mozambique that World Outreach considered unreached. This group had no access to the Gospel of Jesus Christ and no churches or training centres, and had geographical, literacy, and cultural restrictions in hearing or reading about the Good News. There wasn't even a Bible translated into their own language.

After homeschooling their four children, Kevin and Ginnie had a vision of training local Mozambicans to teach preschool with a simple Christian or biblical perspective in their local villages. Young children would have an opportunity to learn Portuguese through practical and fun activities relevant to them starting school.

Whitewater Ministries was to build a model preschool and provide volunteers with training through intensive preschool seminars they could implement back in their own villages. The focus was to give the locals ownership of the preschool training programme, which would ultimately equip them to be independent volunteer teachers. The baby-feeding programme was thriving, and a few local churches had been established in the area, though still as mud and thatched-roofed huts.

Ginnie approached me about helping in this endeavour when she learned I had a heart for missions and was trained in early childhood education. I didn't think I had enough experience to develop a program, but I was definitely interested in assisting a team set it up in whatever ways I could.

Exploratory Trip

Ginnie later connected with two women from Europe, Tina and Rita, who had developed a training programme called *Preschool in a Box* for poor rural communities worldwide. With Ginnie, who had served for over a decade, they adapted the programme to meet the needs of Mozambicans in this isolated rural area. Most importantly, it needed a biblically based training programme for children up to eight years old.

The focus in training the adults was for them to understand themselves as volunteers, having a heart for the children and making a difference by helping them apply God's truth in a sensorial, child-friendly environment.* The training needed to be in Portuguese and with bilingual residents who could translate into the local language.

Help! Speaking is not my strength, Lord, even in English.

Sharing My Desire to Serve in Africa

I shared with Kevin and Ginnie my belief that God was leading me into missions in Africa. They recommended I contact World Outreach and start the application process for becoming one of their interns so that I could see if long term was for me.

They suggested I go to Portugal for a short intensive language school with a teacher they had trained with many years earlier. Portuguese is the principal business and educational language in Mozambique. While I was waiting for the application process, I found a Brazilian high school student to help me start learning basic Portuguese at the local library. Something inside me sensed this was necessary for where I was destined to go.

Applying what I'd learned from the cross-cultural course, I

---

* *Therefore, if anyone is in Christ, he is a new creation. The old things have passed away. Behold, all things have become new.* (2 Corinthians 5:17, WEB) designed a small notice outlining my intentions to explore which of four possible countries God was leading me to. I shared this with local churches, including the one in the far north where I gave my heart to the Lord in 2005. Assistance came from many directions. I also prayed for the courage to go ahead.

Some timely help came in making notices to be emailed and posted for distribution amongst churches and friends who wanted to support me financially. It was good practice for when I went as a longer-term missionary. I needed to secure financial partnerships and prayer partners before I left.

By now, I knew I was going to Mozambique for three weeks to experience life and ministries at Whitewater Farm. Having only recently qualified, I asked myself, *Could I help in the early stages of pioneering an early childhood training programme?*

I also wondered about East Africa. Ron and Lyndie helped me organise another three weeks in Kenya and Tanzania through their connections. One contact was Gabriella, a long-term WO missionary in Nairobi who could show me some of the life and ministry in nearby slums. The second week's visit was organised with The Foundation in Arusha, Tanzania, which had an established preschool, primary, and high school.

Many people partnered with me. Some local friends from Zimbabwe offered use of a barbeque during their upcoming garage sale to help finance my exploratory trip with a sausage sizzle.

I went back to work with the preschool, now under new ownership, and shared my African plans to help train volunteers in early childhood for village children. The staff and owners were excited about this adventure, as were a newly arrived family from South Africa.

"Let's bring out the boxes of resources in storage from upstairs and see what we can donate to the African children," I suggested, keen for others to be involved. The children quickly found wooden

Exploratory Trip

puzzles with African big game animals and durable hardback books with photos of fruits, vegetables, and farm animals, all topics familiar to African children.

My exploratory trip was taking shape faster than I imagined. Within six months, I had enough money saved, additional generous donations, and my essential health vaccinations sorted. It was time to GO! For everything to come together so quickly was a miracle. I was learning that when God is involved and people are praying, we can expect incredibly more than we expect or hope for.[*]

My excitement built as the reality of going to Africa as a servant of God fast approached.

---

[*] *So that with good courage we say, "The Lord is my helper. I will not fear. What can man do to me?"* (Hebrews 13:6, WEB)

Four Weeks in Mozambique

Landing in The Big City and walking off the plane into the hot, humid temperature, I observed amazing huge smooth lumps of rocks that emerged from the ground. I briefly wondered how they had been formed. However, my attention immediately focused on navigating myself with my scarcely understood Portuguese. I hoped smiling at the customs and immigration officials would smooth my entry.

"*Bom dia*" (good day) seemed such a lame phrase that I also sent a quick prayer to God asking for His grace and favour in this situation.

Finally, I emerged with approval and with my luggage. What a joy to have Ginnie's familiar face greet me from Whitewater Farm. Tina accompanied her too, as they were working together on the preschool project. Tina and her husband Andy had come from the Youth With A Mission (YWAM) team to Whitewater Farm for three years. We loaded my luggage quickly. The smells of diesel and smoke were overwhelming, as was the harassment by men and boys fighting over my luggage. Both were unforgettable memories of this new cultural experience.

Though I wanted to help these baggage handlers, it would take some time to learn wisdom from others about when and how to assist people financially. I remembered the well-known phrase 'a hand up, not a handout'. This helped me say, "*Não hoje*" (not today) to the hands held out begging. The needs in Africa can be so overwhelming.

Many times, I caught myself wondering, *How can I make a positive difference in a land with such great needs?* In time, I discovered I could trust God to multiply what little I brought in ways far more than I could imagine.*

After the airport, we went to the supermarkets where South African goods were imported so we could supplement our supplies. Whitewater Farm was a few hours away from the main city, with the closest market selling only essentials. As soon as we got out of the truck, Ginnie and Tina advised me to hold on to my bags tightly and not pay anyone. Boys and men hassled us until we got near the armed guards at the entrance of the grocery store.

The store was an oasis from the crowds outside wanting something from us. When we exited, the same thing happened. We jumped into the truck and locked the doors since any opportunity to steal was possible. It was a stressful experience, and heartbreaking to see so many desperate-looking people.

"Is this always like this?" I asked.

"Yes, all the time!"

I don't think I ever got used to it.

On our way home, we stopped along the road where sellers sat

---

* *Then your light will break forth like the dawn and your healing will quickly appear, then your righteousness will go before you and the glory of the Lord will be your rear guard. Then you will call and the Lord will answer, you will cry for help and he will say "Here I am"*. (Isaiah 58:8–9, NIV) on mats in front of small piles of red onions, tomatoes, capsicums, and little lady-finger bananas. I watched as Ginnie bargained for in-season fruits and vegetables.

Finally, we left the dusty, busy, and chaotic roads of The Big City after a few hours of shopping.

"How long is our drive up to The Farm?" I asked.

"Depending on the road conditions and traffic, about two hours," replied Ginnie.

I'm sure glad I had a couple of days rest in South Africa after the long flight from New Zealand.

I got comfortable and looked out of the window as the hot wind blew in my face. Sitting in the back of the Toyota twin cab ute, time passed quickly for me as multiple new sights appeared. Traffic in these parts was a bizarre combination of vehicles. Anyone who has visited Africa will remember the incredible variety of goods carried on scooters, minivans, bicycles, and taxis, and by people walking along highways. Small Chinese motorbikes were loaded with family members plus chickens and baskets of cabbages. One bike had six trays of eggs balanced on the fuel tank, while another had a live goat strapped on the back.

Few people wore a helmet or shoes, despite flying along at top speeds. Women in colourful fabrics and headscarves walked along the busy road with buckets of water balanced on their heads, and children strolled along with school bags. Buses roared past, spewing diesel smoke, with goats, woven baskets of vegetables, and sacks of rice all on the roof. Crammed with so many people, some had to hang on outside the bus doors.

Northern Mozambique was a very poor part of the country, with health issues of malaria, cholera, diarrhoea, pneumonia, and HIV/AIDS. According to internet statistics, the average income was less than $1.50 US, and literacy was under 40 percent. As of 2018, Mozambique was the seventh poorest country in the world.

Brown mud huts with thatched roofs clustered beside the road with huge cashew trees filling in the open spaces. I marvelled at the places that seemed desolate; there was always someone walking or biking along the road.

"What are those one-litre plastic bottles filled with a yellow liquid in those little huts?"

"Gasoline!"

I learned that these were strategic stops for small motorbikes to fill up, as petrol stations were few and far between. Sometimes we saw big petrol-filled 44-gallon drums on the back of small trucks, a necessary yet dangerous solution to a scarcity of service stations.

Slowing down for police roadblocks checking documents was another first impression of being in a different country. At times, the highway passed through a small town or village where bright, colourful lengths of fabric hung on bamboo poles with odd assortments of household items dangling in the sun.

Close to the highway, people displayed bed frames strung with thick rope for woven grass mats to lie on, dressers, tables, and even chairs with upright backs and rounded spokes. They crafted these from local hardwood timber, often using only hand tools.

I was curious. "What's in those huge white sacks piled along the highway?"

"Chunks of locally made charcoal. It's their main cooking fuel, made from burning logs underground," said someone in the ute.

Sadly, this necessity destroyed dwindling forests, creating empty land with sandy soil and making it even more difficult to grow food crops. During this drive to Whitewater Farm, I was grateful for answers to my many questions. I was soaking up everything and listening to what the others had learned while living here for more than a decade.

Suddenly, we turned off the main road and followed a narrow dusty track lined with mud and straw huts. Scantily clad children, skinny goats, and curious people peered at us as we drove amongst their houses. I was shocked at how close to them we were driving, but the villagers were not. Many were smiling and waving, as the Whitewater Farm truck was well known here, involved in transporting goods and people to remote inland regions when possible.

We picked up a young woman, Hope, from her parents' home to continue working at Whitewater Farm, including with ministry projects. The Farm offered local villagers some employment picking cashew fruits and processing the nuts. A small business of raising goats was another endeavour to assist Whitewater Farm and locals with raising their own meat supply or selling for cash to buy other goods.

As we drove up, seven dogs of different breeds and sizes met us along with local Mozambican families; Ginnie's husband, Kevin; and Tina's husband, Andy. After dropping my luggage in a delightful airy room with a big mosquito net hanging over the bed, I quickly washed under a cold shower before dinner.

I knocked on the screen door of a separate cottage across from the main house. "Something smells delicious!" I called out.

Andy had been busy preparing a spicy goat stew with mashed potatoes and a creative coleslaw with roasted peanuts. Greens were in short supply, so anything went into a coleslaw, and it was present at every meal, it seemed. I grew fond of the small, sweet dark peanuts grown and harvested on the farm. This was a memorable meal after an adventurous day!

Whitewater Farm and Preschool

Northern Mozambique is in the lower latitudes, and being closer to the equator, the setting sun quickly creates instant darkness. No long twilight evenings here, so lights were prepared and torches readied before pitch blackness came crashing down. I was ready for bed soon after the meal.

"*Boa noite. Dormir ben,*" I said, practising my Portuguese, wishing all a good night and good sleep.

I slept soundly, never hearing the rats and bats in the ceiling over my bedroom.

Well rested, I was up at 5am the next morning. Checking my Portuguese phrase book, I found it was "*sexta-feira*" (Friday). Though the sun was up, the morning air was still cool. Silently, I followed the others to the community garden, where all the workers and residents spent time before breakfast. Not a word of English was spoken. Worship songs and prayers were all in Portuguese.

After that weekly prayer gathering, we all sat at the big farmhouse table.

"*Mata-bicho* this morning will be a special treat."

"*Mata-bicho?*"

Hope explained that it was the Makua word for breakfast, meaning 'to kill the little bugs (*bicho*) that eat inside and make hunger.' *What an interesting way to explain the word breakfast!*

"Oh, yum. French toast, my favourite!"

Yesterday's bread buns were sliced, soaked in egg and milk, fried, and laced with butter and syrup. Fresh papaya from trees outside, strong South African tea, and thinking about the little bugs in my tummy making me hungry created a lasting image of a memorable breakfast! I was reminded to take my daily antimalarial meds with breakfast, as others were doing, so I wouldn't forget since the days were so busy.

"Make sure to cover your bed with a sheet and put away your clothes," advised Ginnie.

"Why is that?" I grabbed my toothbrush on the way to the sink.

"Because the ceiling planks have gaps where fine black dust

from years of bat dung falls through the boards. It causes rashes and itching when it gets on our skin."

The 'delightfulness' of my room quickly vanished! I was careful from then on to cover my bedding and clothes.

After breakfast, we jumped into the Isuzu twin cab ute. There was always a lively banter between the owners regarding which was the better make, Isuzu or Toyota. It took us fifteen minutes to drive up the road to a nearby village where the preschool was being built. Ginnie gave away pumpkins from Whitewater Farm to hungry families and also met with a couple of men and women who were going to volunteer and train in this first preschool venture.

"Why are so many children and teenagers at home during the day? Shouldn't they be at school?" I asked.

"These children are orphans or from poor families who cannot afford to pay for schooling."

Instead, the children were collecting manioc roots, taking turns at pounding it into a fine powder with an enormous wooden pestle and mortar. This made a staple thin porridge that expanded in bellies to ward off hunger. This dry, sandy region suited growing manioc, a vegetable with little nutritional value. Some poorer children just sucked on the dried root and had a ring of powder around their mouth and, very often, a distended belly. Seeing these struggles in real life, not from a TV programme, was an eye-opener. Little did I know these experiences would shape my decision about where to go long term.

Buildings at The Farm were decades old and deteriorated rapidly in this harsh environment. With only screens and no glass in the windows, the houses always needed dusting and sweeping, so house workers were employed. Laundry was washed by hand in concrete troughs, and food products required labour to prepare for eating. Every employed person supported families in the nearby village, freeing the missionaries and healthcare volunteers to devote their skills to health and education.

Outside, around the occupied buildings, someone would sweep away leaves to discourage snakes or scorpions from hiding. Farm workers were employed to care for and maintain the cashew trees and goats. If there was a fire on the property, every single person helped to contain and control it.

This was a vibrant community, and my first job, feeding and exercising the seven dogs, was a means to get to know the activities and routines.

"Watch out for scorpions hiding under the pots by their bowls."

I could tell this would not be a boring task!

Any suspicious, unwell dog behaviour could be from a snake bite. Natural causes could reduce the number of dogs quickly in this region, as no veterinarians were available. Along with exercise, part of the reason for walking with the dogs around the farm was to keep an eye out for illegal fallen trees and charcoal pits nearby where locals could be creating charcoal as an income. Whitewater Farm was one of very few remaining areas of bush and vegetation, so it was necessary to protect it.

Exercising the dogs helped keep us safe on our walks, as the dogs usually located any snakes and scared them away. Having so many dogs on this expansive and remote farm added to security. Sadly, in such a poor area, people were driven to take desperate measures. Theft was common, and the dogs became the night-time alarm.

As we walked the wide track of roads around the farm, especially in the dry season, we looked for any fires that might be starting. Within the first week of arriving in the dry season, I was out there with everyone flapping out small grass fires and even driving the water truck to bigger flames. But first, we all emailed prayer partners back home to pray that the wind would die down and rain would come to drench it. It certainly was an interesting place to live, with so much to learn!

My afternoon walks with the dogs, observing the frequent deep red sunsets that were impossible to capture by camera, were often times of reflection. *What a challenging yet interesting place to serve.*

"I wonder if this is to be where God is leading me. What do you think?" I asked Taz, one of the more intelligent-looking dogs. Who knew dogs would be an essential part of this mission field and its many ministries?

On Saturday night, after a busy week out in the villages, we relaxed with some of the residents in a friendly game of dominos called Mexican Train. A simple treat of popcorn and glasses of cold Coca-Cola completed our weekly community fun time. As it was dark by 7pm, the evening usually finished by 8.30pm.

"Be ready to go to church by 8am, and bring your bilingual Bible and water bottle," I was told.

Morning came quickly. We all crammed into the twin cab ute after our chores and headed for the small village where Hope's parents lived. Hope was leading the children's church group that morning. Usually, it was a bilingual service with the local language spoken and translated into Portuguese. But as I was new, a young man offered to translate Portuguese into English for me, pleased to practise his English. After the service, everyone went outside, shaking hands and speaking blessings to each other. It was my first experience of a Pentecostal-style service in a mud hut.

Prayer and Preschool

I wonder why people pray so often here, even over the littlest things? Over time, my observations led me to believe we had unique reasons for more prayer needs, not only with this challenging environment but also with the spiritual opposition to sharing the

Gospel of Jesus Christ. One unforgettable experience of active witchcraft in the area were nights waking up to the sound of village drumbeats. Kevin and Ginnie had learned the essential need to pray during their years of living in a unique and strange environment.*

Ginnie and Tina were developing a culturally appropriate programme in remote impoverished areas, with a focus on upskilling volunteers as well as providing a stimulating experience for preschool children. I noticed they always preceded their planning by prayer, inviting the Holy Spirit into their programme planning. *I think I need to pray more often! Could God be interested in my smallest issues?*

Trialling their preschool ideas with the local farm children involved six to seven children ranging in age from four to ten, the older children including the younger ones. This curriculum provided opportunities to learn about a God who loves them and how special each child is to God. We started with a short welcome song, *Olá, como esta,* translated to mean 'Hello, how are you, and welcome!' Then we sang the days of the week in Portuguese using a simple calendar. Implementing ideas from Hope, we made up three to four different activity stations and rotated the children through each one. A drink and simple snack ended the session.

These families and volunteers were busy growing their food, fetching water daily, and undertaking other family responsibilities. It was decided that two afternoon sessions per week, each two hours long, were all that could be expected. This became a template for the other village preschools we were to visit.

It was amazing to bring out wooden puzzles, beads, and books donated by my home preschool and practise how we were going to

---

* *Rejoice always, pray continually, give thanks in all circumstances; for this is God's will for you in Christ Jesus.* (1 Thessalonians 5:16–18, NIV)

use them. Hope was helpful with teaching simple songs, but more importantly, she provided a bridge in language learning between Portuguese and the local dialect. I could see how valuable she was in encouraging locals to this new idea of a preschool in their village.

As I learned new preschool and worship songs from Hope, I thought music could be a good way to learn a language. But I found her laughter and sense of humour were the primary bridge to learning language, as it put me at ease and encouraged me to try. We had many laughs at my initial attempts.

Baobabs and a Glimpse of Bush-Bush Villages

During my three-week visit, I was fortunate to join the team going to a very remote village. It was their first visit to train local believers in how to start their own preschool. Wherever the truck went, a local person came along to show us where to go through tracks without signposts and to interpret if needed.

I loved the adventure of travelling across remote Africa through red, dusty tracks and passing enormous baobab trees under the clear expanse of a blue sky. Baobab trees were known as the upside-down trees, as they looked like they had been yanked up from the ground and replanted with their roots in the air. These flowering trees are amazing survivors in an arid environment and can grow to be over one thousand years old.

The twin cab truck carried an assortment of goods and people. Hanging on through these bumpy roads was challenging, not to mention the added challenge of 'holding on' until our destination to relieve our bladders. There were no scrubs to squat behind in this open countryside.

Most memorable for me were the curious stares of the children as we transferred building materials or sacks of dried food to the church huts for distribution. I was able to pass on some secondhand reading glasses from New Zealand to people who could no longer read their Bibles due to poor eyesight. It was such a thrill to see the big smiles on their faces when they could now read the pages. On the way, we picked up a mother carrying her very young, sick baby on her back in a piece of cloth called a *capulana*. We would take them to the hospital on our way home, as the baby seemed very weak and frail.

Finally, we reached a cluster of mud huts, and the jolting ride was over. Someone was ready to welcome us, showing us where to park and giving clear directions to a small, fenced area with a hole in the ground.

"Here, take this with you to wipe your hands," Tina suggested on one of our village visits. One of the best tips for travelling in these remote areas was to take a small supply of toilet paper and handy wipes.

The local pastor and his wife welcomed us to their small village church with broad smiles. The preschool was going to be held in the church building, as it was the only community building.

Tina and Ginnie had prepared a programme for the day, and I assisted at times, always observing and wondering if I could see myself here for the longer term. While they were setting up inside, I tried some Makua phrases I had learned at Whitewater Farm with Hope and the children.

Saying "Hello, how are you?" and "I am fine" in Makua was a real relationship builder. "*Thali*," I would call out, and immediately people came over with "*Salaama*," then "*Kihavo*," and I would reply, "*Miano kihavo*." Unfortunately, they then assumed I was fluent in Makua and would carry on until I made signs of not understanding and we would all laugh.

I connected better with the children out in the bush who knew no Portuguese if I had a smattering of Makua and did some simple action-type songs. The farm children with Hope taught me 'Jesus loves me' in Makua (*Jesu naki penta*). I sometimes got the name for God, *Muluku*, mixed up with a similar sounding word meaning 'crazy' or with the number ten in Makua, *moloko*. Sharing my little knowledge of counting and singing to Jesus in their mother tongue brought laughter to lighten the atmosphere of feeling like an alien from outer space!

The hardships of rural Mozambique created in me a fondness and respect for the people. The remoteness was interesting and challenging. However, I still needed to explore other volunteering opportunities in Kenya and Tanzania during the weeks ahead.

Coming home to Whitewater Farm after this long, challenging day was restorative, with showers and a meal fixed by Kevin after his day of teaching in the Bible School. *I have much to think about. Oh yes, God, and to pray about!*

A second connection was organised for me, visiting a health-related ministry by Marion, a woman who began her journey at Whitewater Farm many years ago with Kevin and Ginnie.

The Good Samaritan Programme

The Good Samaritan provided a unique ministry in small rural villages where access to doctors or hospitals was nearly impossible. Marion's vision was to teach locals how to make and administer natural medicines in clinics, along with an orphans' programme, including a message of God's love. She was well-known since she transported locals and materials to the nearby bush clinic in her little old Datsun pickup.

One evening, to my alarm, as we were driving out of The Farm's driveway to go to Marion's place, she shouted, "I have no steering!" Swerving abruptly, she parked the truck on the grass. However, moments later, she was laughing at this sudden change of plans.

Walking back in the dark to spend another night with Kevin and Ginnie, we were thankful this had not happened out on the main highway. In the morning, it was discovered that the steering rod had broken in the driveway. Andy offered to drive us north to try and find another one.

I quickly grabbed stuff for a day out and hopped in the back of his pickup. *I'm getting good at this!* Other people came too, making use of this opportunity to go to the next city on the coast. Meanwhile, back at Whitewater Farm, a tractor towed the Datsun over a pit, ready for some volunteers to replace the broken rod. Early morning prayers were answered by finding the necessary steering rod and making the journey home safely in one day.

The next morning, we set off again, this time with a 5am start. Marion drove, and I sat in the passenger seat. Marion's young student from Europe had arrived and sat in the back with the helpful Mozambican companion. Travelling with a local person usually ensured a successful outcome for the journey. I was looking forward to visiting a coastal town and one of the outpost natural healing clinics.

Stopping at a one-way bridge, I asked Marion, "How much longer?" I felt like I was in a washing machine!

"It's around a five-hour journey, so we have another three hours," she shouted over the noise of the truck.

Finally, we arrived at the coastal outpost clinic. I felt wobbly and slightly carsick. *Whew, I'm glad it wasn't longer!* We delivered bags of herbs from Marion's main clinic, so they could continue making herbal remedies in this remote area of the country. We all enjoyed stretching our legs on the hour-long walk to the gardens beside the local river. The vegetables and herbs grown near the water's edge provided ingredients for making natural healing ointments and syrups for simple ailments.

The dusty, narrow walking track was a busy highway of foot

traffic. Women carried huge pots of water or big bunches of firewood sticks on their heads, with babies strapped on their backs. The garden grew many plants I recognised, including some enormous beetroot. In the distance, I spied people washing their clothes in the nearby river, which also was a source of water for the plants.

Marion trained Mozambicans in a two-year programme that included the Word of God. They were not only helping physically with ailments but also spiritually able to pray for healing. Many capable, trained men and women were involved in the programme and were training others, too.

I was very impressed with Marion's courage and dream of fulfilling this passion of hers. She was a trained nurse and could see the benefits of teaching knowledge of basic cures in remote areas of Mozambique with so few hospitals and doctors. She was an inspiration to me and, I'm sure, many others.

I was realising that a better grasp of Portuguese was a determining factor in how I could best serve people here. If I came as an intern, I would need a short intensive language course in Portugal, for sure. *Can I see myself here long term? English is commonly spoken in Kenya and Tanzania. But is this where God is leading me?*

A Women's Seminar

I spent my fourth week in Mozambique at a resort with other missionaries, attending a five-day World Outreach seminar in a remote northern port city. I was thrilled to be part of this gathering of married and single women who were serving in Mozambique and Zambia. It was reassuring to find I was not the only single woman here, and I particularly looked forward to hearing how single women were effective missionaries.

The nationalities were a mixture of New Zealanders, South Africans, Europeans, and Zambians. Three women from South

Africa and Zambia had just returned from ministering in Ethiopia. It was a time of refreshing and encouraging words, listening to people's stories, and building up our understanding of God and ourselves. Stories of loss and grief were especially touching. *This is a harsh land.*

Most of the women lived with their families in isolated places, homeschooling their children. They had to deal with loneliness, spiritual battles, and keeping in touch with homelands. It was a privilege to meet these courageous women and hear real stories of living in this land and sharing the Gospel.

I had much to consider after the eventful and rich experiences of these past four weeks. I now needed to look ahead and prepare for the next part of this exploratory mission-finding trip. A dream hidden for so long looked like it was coming true.

Travelling in the back of a small pickup, or *buckie* (a South African term), from the retreat to Whitewater Farm at 7am was refreshing in this hot climate, but I was rather sore when we arrived. I quickly gathered my suitcase, ukulele, and documents to travel with Tina and Andy on the long drive to The Big City in preparation for flying out on Kenya Airways.

We arrived in time to buy some delicious periperi-BBQ chicken, chips, and ice-cold Coca-Cola with fresh lemon. Andy dropped me off at an enclosed compound for Bible translators with a settlement of houses, dormitories, and a Christian preschool. There were many bunk rooms for visitors and transiting missionaries, and a place to store their vehicles when they went home for a few weeks or months during the wet season.

I stayed overnight, waiting for my flight in the early morning. By this time, I had a slight tummy bug, so having a flush toilet across the courtyard was much appreciated, as was the cold shower. Opening my Bible for a word from the Lord, this verse was just what I needed to hear: "Then your light will break forth like the dawn and **your healing shall spring up speedily**; your righteousness shall go before you; the glory of the Lord shall be your rear guard. Then you shall call and the Lord will answer; you shall cry and he will say 'Here I am'." (Isaiah 58:8–9).

I prayed earnestly for speedy healing. I did not want to be taking a tummy bug with me to begin the next three weeks in East Africa! Exhausted by the day's travel in two vehicles, a tummy bug, and the eventful past four weeks, I was thankful to be the only visitor here.

I fell into bed and slept soundly, waking around 5am with the roosters crowing, and more importantly, without the tummy bug. I was ever grateful for that rapid answer to my prayer. I was learning to trust God in all my needs and that He could, at times, surprise me with a quick response.

A taxi took me to the airport. With renewed energy, I looked forward to the next part of my journey.

On to East Africa!

Tanzania

"*Karibu!*" (Welcome!) I smiled as I recalled these greetings after many years away. "*Jambo. Habari ako? Mzuri sana! Asante sana.*" I was so excited to be speaking and hearing Swahili again, just simple phrases I had remembered: "Hello. How are you? Very good. Thank you very much."

The three-hour flight was just enough to rest and get ready for the next three weeks' adventures. I was flying with Kenya Airways but transiting through Nairobi to land at Kilimanjaro Airport in Tanzania, near Arusha. In The Big City Airport, I tried to explain in Portuguese and English that my bags were to go on to Tanzania. I had a feeling I was not being understood. I was also anxious about the upcoming health official I was to see after the passport official in Tanzania.

God's favour, prayers, and grace blessed me again as my undetected duplicate yellow health document was met with approval in Tanzania. However, my bags did not arrive. They had been lost in transit!

I had to fill out a form about my missing luggage and, in the process, missed the last shuttle bus (unbeknown to me) into Arusha. The desk people kindly let me use the phone, as I wasn't sure how to use my cell phone without a SIM card.

"Hello, is that Belinda? I missed the last bus to your place. How do I get there now at 9.30pm?"

The small airport was beginning to empty. I was in a predicament; I had no spare clothes in my carry-on luggage, the one time I'd neglected to do that! Being at least an hour from town, with darkness all around and no transport available, I quickly sent one of those prayer darts to God that simply said, *Help!*

Faithfully, He answered me with the appearance of a lovely friendly French couple who thankfully spoke some English and offered me a ride to town. As they dropped me off, the thought came, *Were those angels in disguise?*

I was so grateful that, despite my backpack being empty of spare clothes or toiletries, I had my documents! The Foundation sent a taxi to collect me, even though it was after 10pm. Arriving around midnight, I was shown to a rondavel-style hut and literally fell into bed under the mosquito net, exhausted.

After a sound sleep, the generous women missionaries clothed me with spare clothes and even supplied me with a new toothbrush. Though I had no spare underpants, I had my ukulele, which was a comfort, and a New Zealand storybook to give to the children. I discovered that all my bags were detained in Nairobi. They caught up with me three days later.

From now on, I will pack spare clothes and toiletries in my carry-on bag! I promised myself.

Tanzania

The E.G. Foundation and Preschool

New Zealanders Belinda and her husband had been missionaries and teacher trainers here for nearly thirty years. The E.G. Foundation was now entering a new level of training, as many locals trained as teachers needed further professional development. Being only a recently trained teacher, I felt inexperienced in that realm.

However, I would investigate the preschool sector in this teacher training college. A common pattern in discerning what door was to open for me was to 'wonder, pray, and try'. If the peace of God filled me in a decision, I knew I was in His plan and that He would guide and provide for me as I needed.

An early morning start saw me wearing my newly borrowed clothes. I felt strange in the longish, somewhat formal skirts but surprisingly cool in these temperatures. The preschool and primary school started with an assembly on Monday morning at 7.45am. All students and teachers shared in singing, prayers, and thanksgiving for the coming week's learning.

Children as young as three were neatly dressed in red, blue, and white uniforms. All their shoes were lined up at the entrance to each classroom. The heat of the day could be overpowering, so an early start for Year 1 (three- to four-year-olds) and Year 2 (five- to six-year-olds) meant they finished at 12.30pm.

Their formal curriculum for three-year-olds involved writing at desks. This shocked me, as it was a different approach to learning for this age group than how I had been trained in New Zealand. I found out this was a preferred method of learning in Africa and seemed to bring good results in learning. The phrase 'not wrong, just different' sprang to mind. The children were quiet and obedient. Education was a privilege, as only some could attend while others stayed home and did chores. No behavioural issues were evident. *Wow, that's amazing!*

Morning tea for the preschoolers was possibly their only food since getting up early to walk to school. The children sat quietly in a circle on the floor, waiting to be served a thin maize porridge sweetened with sugar in blue plastic cups. *Is this type of preschool in Africa where God is calling me?*

"Would you like to share a song or read a story from New Zealand tomorrow?" one of the teachers asked me. I had brought my ukulele for this reason. Although I hadn't prepared anything, I prayed and asked God for guidance and courage.

The children played outside on some old tyres and a makeshift slide while the teachers had morning tea. I was grateful for strong, sweet tea with milk and a triple-layered white bread sandwich with peanut butter, as I hadn't had breakfast.

For lunch, the children sat in a dining room and ate a substantial meal, possibly their only one for the day. Every meal included beans and *ugali*, a thick maize porridge, with some sort of cooked greens. Locally grown moringa leaf, the nutritious new superfood, was sprinkled on the food. Everyone was satisfied, and even the cooks were beaming.

The next day, I took my ukulele to the preschool and borrowed their globe. "I come from a little country called New Zealand. Does anyone know where it is?" The children sat attentively in a circle, looking blankly at me. The two local teachers were very helpful and encouraging. I hadn't been playing the ukulele very long and knew only three chords and a few songs from the New Zealand preschool. I had brought along a children's book the day before that had *Kia ora* in it, so I taught them *Kia ora e hoa* ('Hello my friend' in Te Reo Māori). *Well, they appeared to enjoy that. But what more can I offer? They seem quite well organised here.*

Tanzania

An Orphanage Visit

"Would you like to see a local orphanage?" the girls asked when I got home from school.

When the van let us out at the two-storied orphanage, I was shocked at the level of security surrounding it. There was barbed wire on top of the walls and broken glass was cemented on top, with wires on top of more wires. It was a fortress that I was to see often in larger cities in East Africa. I felt sad for the children, but they were being cared for with food, shelter, and some education. Without this, they would be begging on the streets. We were treated to some delicious hot *chapatis* they were making for dinner later. It was sobering to see this shelter for homeless children.

We decided to forgo the bumpy van ride and walk back and had very dirty dusty feet on arrival. I was thankful for a cold shower before dinner, which was served in a private courtyard lined with bright bougainvillaea, the chairs filled with people from other countries. Everyone had interesting reasons for being there. A lovely outdoor fireplace provided a fire for light. The gentle ambience made for a welcome, relaxing evening.

My newly made friends from New Zealand took me to the markets, which were rich and varied with lush fresh fruits and vegetables since the fertile ground at the base of Mt Meru had plenty of water. The local churches had an international community and sang worship songs similar to my church back home. The ease of communicating in English everywhere was something to be considered. *Could this be the place for me?*

Back at the E.G. Foundation, we discussed the vision, including the need to write a preschool curriculum with a biblical worldview. As the training school had graduated many teachers, there was a need for leadership training opportunities. This would require someone to help in coaching, training, and mentoring the existing preschool teachers.

Not for me, I thought. *But the nearby preschools need some encouragement; could I serve there?*

It was an interesting experience that clarified my preferences. I valued this opportunity to view something quite different, and it helped me to find my calling. I was grateful to Ron and Lyndie for making the connections for me to experience different preschools in a variety of environments. However, I did not have peace from God about returning here as a missionary/teacher. I had learned by now that this peace was essential when making decisions.

Coming up next was an action-packed week-long visit to Nairobi, Kenya. I wondered what that would be like—and how it would be, after so many years, to return to my first African country, Kenya. The Holy Spirit reminded me that God is a God of restoration and is faithful to his promises. I'd been a rebellious yet soul-searching twenty-one-year-old on my first visit. This time, decades later, I knew I had God with me, which I found comforting and yet exhilarating. It was a moment to remember.

I also had my luggage, which arrived the day before I was to return to Nairobi. Small miracles do happen.

Nairobi, Kenya

What a relief to see my bags and ukulele arrive at Nairobi Airport following the short flight from Arusha, Tanzania. The airport was in a state of transition and repair. A fire on 7 August had swept through the international arrivals area and shut the airport down. An investigation into the cause was still underway. Soon after my arrival, it was determined that an electrical fault had caused the fire. The response was slow, adding to the considerable damage. Not only that, but on 21 September, twelve days before my arrival in Kenya, a terrorist attack at the Westgate Shopping Mall resulted in seventy-one people shot dead. Everyone was on edge and security was tight.

"What a relief to see you!" I exclaimed when Gabriella, a long-term missionary from Australia, met me at the airport. The traffic in Nairobi was incredibly jam-packed and chaotic. Gabriella, who had lived here for nine years, had become an aggressive driver, as one needed to be. After dumping my luggage at her flat, we proceeded to a nearby supermarket mall to get lunch and biscuits for a World Outreach prayer meeting with other missionaries (local and foreign). Security was tight at the entrance of the mall, with all bags being searched.

We battled through the traffic again to arrive at the prayer meeting, where I heard about a huge slum and some ministries going on in it. After dropping me home, Gabriella left to deliver some jewellery produced by previously trafficked women from other nations. Grateful for a break from the frantic traffic, I cooked dinner for us, using local salad produce and lasagne ingredients from the supermarket. When Gabriella returned, we enjoyed coffee and biscuits after dinner, talking late into the night about the slum and the many projects and major security issues there.

Kibera Slums

Strangely, I woke up initially excited to be visiting a slum. But my enthusiasm waned when Gabriella gave me something to sign before entering the slum area.

"What's this?"

"It's a waiver of responsibility in case you are mugged, suffer injury, have anything stolen, or are killed."

This was a sobering moment. Needless to say, we prayed before entering.

A few weeks earlier, the South African women's prayer group had prayed for my journey to East Africa. One woman said she saw a bright light and the letter 'N'. She believed it referred to Nairobi and that the bright light indicated divine protection, so I need not be afraid.*

Gabriella had contacted a local security man to escort us inside

---

* *But the Lord is faithful, who will establish you and guard you from the evil one.* (2 Thessalonians 3:3, WEB)

the slum city. We were to dress simply, taking in no food or water bottles, phones, cameras, sunglasses, or jewellery, including watches. He was dressed as an ordinary person and followed us at a distance.

According to internet statistics, in 2013, one million people were crammed into a two-mile radius. There was one toilet for 1,300 people, and due to disease and violence, life expectancy was thirty years.

I don't know what hit me first—the visual pollution or the stench. It was a comfort to know our security friend had our backs. We had to watch where we were walking as there could be 'flying toilets' on the narrow path.

"What's a flying toilet?" I asked Gabrielle quietly.

"Since the toilets are so few, and one might get raped or killed on the way, residents use plastic bags during the nights to relieve themselves and then hurl them out into the night, hoping they don't hit anyone on the way!"

We saw a few of these plastic bags on our walk.

My heart was moved, seeing children playing near these incredibly deep rivers of waste and pollution. It was heartbreaking and overwhelming, especially when they were looking for anything to eat or sell.

A Safe Place for Young Children to Learn

The first place we visited was inside a walled compound. It catered for preschool children and for older children who had left school and become street kids, then later decided to return to school. Tutoring classes were offered for primary-aged children who left school and succumbed to street life in the slum. Volunteers helped these older children so they could get caught up to the government school level and re-enter. The preschoolers (aged five to six) were mainly from families who had jobs outside the slum and needed a safe place for their children to stay during the day.

A few precious herbs, vegetables, and flowers grew in a play area for young children, creating a small sanctuary of beauty. Outside, the walled compound looked ugly and harsh.

Games and resources were set up in a creativity centre for the children to enjoy with supervision. They were short of volunteers to oversee this activity, so Gabriella and I stayed to supervise games and painting for two thirty-minute sessions with each group. The older children were not allowed to participate, which was sad, as literacy and numeracy can be learned through art. The curriculum was Bible-based, so the children could learn that God loves and cares for them along with reading, writing, and maths skills.

Before we left, I inquired about the application process for joining this organisation. *It ticks a lot of boxes.*

Mama Mercy and Moses

Back in the car, we made our way around the edge of the slum to another area.

"Where are we going now, Gabriella?" I asked.

"To visit Mama Mercy. We don't need the security guy this time, though."

However, we still took nothing in with us that could be desirable for very poor and desperate people. Gabriella had arranged for Mama Mercy, as she was known, to prepare us lunch in her little hut that clung to the side of a hill. To enter, we had to descend a rickety vertical ladder that dropped many metres, passing some vicious-looking dogs. The ladder and difficult location were deterrents for robbers.

As we entered this dwelling, we were met with the warm hospitality of Mama Mercy. I wished I had my camera to record how ingeniously the space and every scrap of anything was utilised. Mama Mercy raised her children herself, and all of them managed to attend school. Her youngest son, fifteen-year-old Moses, joined us for lunch. The family, believers in Jesus Christ and the Bible, began the meal with a simple prayer of thanksgiving. Without running water or refrigeration, Mama Mercy had prepared a meat stew with potatoes, *chapatis* (roasted flatbread-like tortillas), and cabbage. Afterwards, we sipped sweetened ginger chai or tea.

"Moses needs exam money next Monday," Mama Mercy confided.

"How much?" I asked.

As Gabriella had been friends with her for years, I was confident our donation would go towards his exam fees and not be wasted. I was shown his previous achievements in education and could tell how studious he was. *I'm sure my supporters would like to contribute towards his education.* Education was a privilege here and was regarded as a way to have a better future than living in a slum.

We had a short time of prayer for the family's needs, then climbed back up the rickety ladder to find our car.

Women Refugees

Returning to the first entrance, we met other local Kenyan missionaries with World Outreach. We checked that we weren't carrying anything that would attract attention and met our security guard again. I tried to imagine myself coming here regularly. This time we walked further than before and arrived at a community project and healthcare centre.

Gabriella filled me in on the situation. "These women are mainly refugees from South Sudan (Nubians) and Ethiopia. They come to learn how to read and write, and are also taught how to make beaded necklaces and bracelets to earn some income."

The volunteers were passionate about being involved with women refugees and committed to giving them practical education, human trafficking advice, and an insight into the God of the Bible who loves them. Most were from a sheltered background. On arriving in the slum city, they were often enticed by people who promised them jobs as housemaids or nannies overseas. Evidence showed that instead of an honest job in Middle Eastern countries, these women were sold and often subjected to sexual and violent abuse. By giving them practical skills and education in health issues and human rights, the project was helping this vulnerable part of the community.

We met three young women who had just been rescued from being sold to dubious employment in nearby countries. They gave their testimonies the following Saturday to women attending a forum hosted by a Kenyan woman doctor and her son. The place was packed with women who spoke little Swahili, shrouded in brightly coloured robes and headscarves. At first, the listeners were quiet and shy, but on hearing the girls' testimonies of how easy it was to get tricked into believing people who offer employment that sounds too good to be true, they loosened up and started asking some questions. *It's heartbreaking to hear how poverty can drive people to these situations.*

Gaining information about health issues for them and their children and babies and learning about their human rights gave these women knowledge to avoid becoming victims. Counselling was offered after the forum, along with a lunch of chai, bananas, hard-boiled eggs, bread, and *samosas* (delicious triangle-shaped savouries containing meat, potato, and peas).

As we retraced our steps through this crowded, impoverished sea of shacks, picking our way over paths of rubbish and smells of sewage, I was in awe of anyone who ventured into full-time ministry in this area. It seemed rewarding to work with the desperately poor, yet there were so many dangers and heartbreaking moments in everyday life. *Admirable, but I don't think this is for me.* Again, I turned to God. I wanted His peace in any decision I made.

Yellow Roses and an Ethiopian Restaurant

Hanging on for dear life, we battled the Nairobi traffic again. *I'm not so sure I could survive the traffic!* When we returned to the apartment, I read again in my Bible about God's protection, especially in Psalms 16–18. I was grateful for my growing faith in God's direction over every step I took and His protection in all areas. *If God is for me, who can be against me?*

The next day, we tried to go to the elephant orphanage park and the giraffe hand-feeding place, but the traffic was a nightmare because of an international trade show that school children were going to. School buses blocked the roads. Gabriella said this twenty-minute ride could easily turn into a four-hour traffic nightmare. I believed her, so we crept back to her home.

On the way, I spied a roadside stall selling gorgeous roses. The price was $3 for eighteen. "That's enough yellow roses for your flat as well as for your jewellery-maker employee."

This employee was a Christian woman who had grown up in a slum city and somehow got out. She walked and bused for ninety minutes each way to Gabriella's flat, where she created beautiful, beaded necklaces. Married with four children, she lived in a tin shed with divisions making areas of privacy for all six family members. After witnessing the living conditions in that slum, I could see that her situation was a big improvement. Her face lit up with a big smile when I presented her with a bunch of long-stemmed yellow roses to take home for her family.

A local market and international online market provided areas of support for women in crisis, mainly refugees from other African countries. I purchased a couple of necklaces and a bracelet for Christmas presents back home to inform others of this valuable ministry.

We both agreed to have a rest day. I caught up on my journaling, while Gabriella completed some ministry work.

"Have you ever been to an authentic Ethiopian restaurant and eaten *injera?*" she asked me.

"No, what's that?"

Thankfully, with Gabriella driving, we arrived safely at the courtyard restaurant. A huge brass platter arrived bearing the *injera*: large, grey-coloured, fermented flatbreads served cold, topped with tasty savoury foods. They reminded me of material like ACE bandages. We finished with small and seriously black coffees. Dessert was popcorn presented in a woven hat! The outside fire was in a huge metal dish that had been burning continuously for eight years since the restaurant's opening. It was truly a novel food experience and proved to be a popular eating spot in Nairobi.

An International Church and a Game Park

My final Sunday in Kenya arrived, and we attended a church in Karen. We drove past amazing homes and parks. Africa is a continent of contrasts! Memories of people living in shacks amidst rubbish and sewage contrasted with these big properties that provided locals with employment. At church, I met other expats from around the world, a melting pot of people.

I overheard someone commenting, "Nairobi is crawling with

missionaries and shopping malls, and with English spoken, it's a preferred destination." This comment stuck in my mind—food for thought later.

The worship music was similar to that in my home church, and the message was inspiring. I went up for prayer as I had a cold developing with sinus blockages, which doesn't do well in aeroplanes.

I certainly had seen a mixture of opportunities, both with World Outreach and other ministries. But before I made any decision, I had one more couple to stay with; Colin and Natalie were long-term WO missionaries with teaching, discipling, and evangelising ministries, and supported an orphanage. Natalie had a preschool teaching background as well, so we talked a lot about that.

Before we visited the orphanage, they organised for me to go to a game park outside Nairobi. It was another 5am start. Their lovely guide and driver took me to see the most amazing wildlife so close to Nairobi. He had a family to support, so I was pleased to help by hiring him for the day's excursion. He kindly stopped for me to take photos of big game animals, and on the way home, bought us each a long, fresh sugar cane. This proved to be tough chewing. I admire the locals' strong white teeth that can deal with sugar cane!

By nightfall, I was exhausted. It had been a full day of driving, taking photos, observing how elephants orphaned by poaching are cared for, and feeding giraffes at another animal refuge.

Another Orphanage, Then Time to Go

After a restful sleep, I was ready for the last ministry experience of this whole seven-week exploratory trip. Natalie drove me to an orphanage managed by a Kenyan woman with a husband and four children and a big heart! She provided a home for abused and neglected orphans from babies to seventeen years of age. As a local Kenyan, she was able to ascertain they were genuine orphans and not from poor families wanting a better life for their children.

She provided for them as best she could with a sewing business, but she needed extra financial assistance to care for and educate thirty-two children, as funding for the orphanage was scarce. She was looking and praying for a reliable partner with a heart full of love and patience to help with the children. This would enable her to work at her tailoring business. They had two cows to supply milk, one goat, chickens for eggs, and a garden for veggies. Her needs were huge, and we all prayed God would bring people and resources to help this very worthy enterprise. My heartstrings were pulled by this situation. I could visualise myself there, caring for the children and helping with their education.

When we got home, Colin and Natalie talked with me about my experiences and offered to pray for God's guidance and for me to gain peace in this decision. We looked at my photos of all the opportunities I'd been fortunate to visit in Mozambique, Tanzania, and Kenya. Colin suggested I keep my journals and photos and write a book about my missionary experiences. *I wonder if I will do that! It seems too big to even contemplate.*

I was very grateful to Ron and Lyndie for organising contacts and for the missionaries who made time for me and provided places to visit. Scripture readings and insights stirred my heart, and I had a passion for returning to Africa, but I needed patience and time before announcing a decision. I had long flights booked from Nairobi to Johannesburg and then onto New Zealand, with only airport transit times and no stopovers, so I would have a lot of time to process before landing in Auckland.

The international area of Nairobi Airport was still crowded due to last month's fire, but I found the shrink-wrapping place and checked my bags all the way to Auckland.

Nairobi, Kenya

In Johannesburg, I had time to look in souvenir shops. The Mozambique AA road map jumped out at me. I also found a fridge magnet of Fort Jesus near Mombasa, Kenya, which I had gone to years earlier. *Are these clues?* I also kept remembering the comment about Nairobi crawling with missionaries.

Will I hear God's voice in my inner heart? Will I understand His direction for me? It would be imperative if I was to have His peace and confidence in this very daunting adventure!

God Answers and I Hear Him!

As I relaxed into the economy seat of the aircraft, I pondered all that I'd experienced in such a short, intense time in four African countries. In one moment of that twelve-hour flight, I sensed the quiet voice of the Holy Spirit say, "Who will go to the remote areas of Mozambique with heat, dust, poverty, snakes, bandits, scorpions, and no shopping malls?"

I quietly replied, "Here I am, I will go there."

What!? Did I hear correctly?

It was a revelation moment—shockingly soon, I thought. However, I kept it quiet in my heart until I had more confirmation that this was God's direction for me.* The verse 'If God is for us, who can be against us?' (Romans 8:31, NIV) came to mind, reassuring me in my growing faith walk.

From Sydney to Auckland, new thoughts occupied my mind. I sensed there would be opposition to God's plan for me to return to Africa. *Maybe I'm too old, being in my early sixties?* There were practical logistics to consider, too. *If I return to Whitewater Farm as a one-year intern by March or April 2014, can I get the funds*

---

* *I heard the Lord's voice saying, "Whom shall I send, and who will go for us?" Then I said, "Here am I. Send me!"* (Isaiah 6:8, WEB) *together in time? I will only have a few months. Will I have enough people to back me for an undetermined amount of time? And can I learn a language at my age?*

Other people had already sown seeds of doubt, so I really had to listen for God's thoughts on the matter. I read some Bible passages that encouraged my faith to grow in knowing that God is bigger than anything else, that He will provide, and that His ways are not my ways.

I sensed God speaking directly to me while reading the Bible overnight in a backpacker lodge after landing at Auckland Airport: 'The Lord will guide you always; he will satisfy your needs in a **sun-scorched land,** and will strengthen your frame. You will be like a well-watered garden, and like a spring of water whose waters never fail. Your people will rebuild the ancient ruins and will raise up the age-old foundations; You will be called Repairer of Broken Walls, Restorer of Streets with Dwellings' (Isaiah 58:11–12, NIV).

These images, especially 'sun-scorched land', jumped out at me and spoke of rural northern Mozambique. *Confirmation!* I had many lasting images of broken ruins in those parts too, and this passage promised that God would guide me always, satisfy all my needs there, and strengthen my bones. *What a promise for a sixty-one-year-old body!*

For a short time, knowing God was calling to me specifically to Mozambique, I had a new courage and boldness. *How exciting!* Then the enormity of it all bombarded my thoughts. *Oh no, what have I done!?* I found myself doubting God's provision for me. Contrary to popular thinking, the cost of living for a Western person in Africa is considerably high. Few can live like the locals for a start, as it is a very hard lifestyle. Non-residents like me needed to live in a protected, safe situation initially. *Will there be enough support for me?*

I had to trust God would answer all my questions in time and

Nairobi, Kenya

not panic. After more prayer and sensing God's peace in the decision, I was ready to contact Kevin and Ginnie, World Outreach, my local church, and Ron and Lyndie in South Africa.

And I was excited!

Photos

Forestry Lookout tower 1972

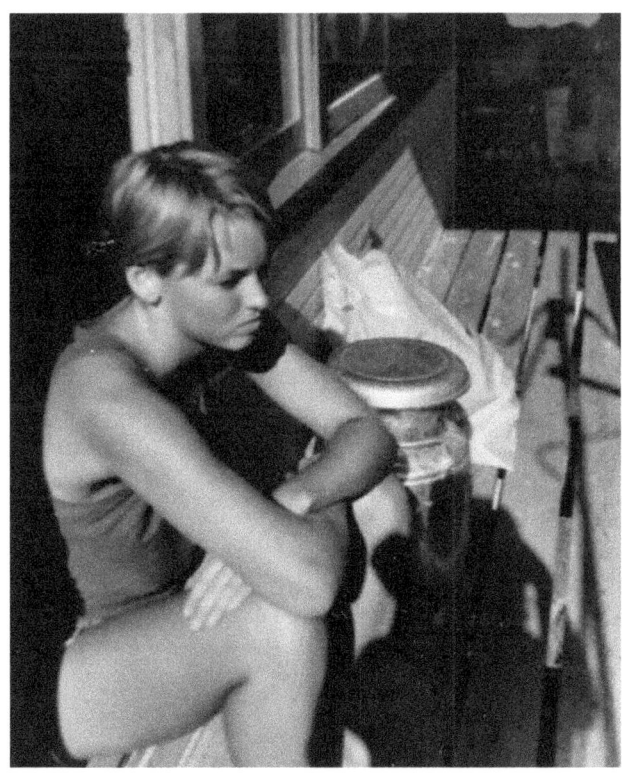

Lookout tower, discontent and dreaming of Africa 1973

Sailing from Mombasa, Kenya to remote Indian Ocean islands 1975

Our first house bus in NZ on the interisland ferry 1976

Photos

Children help with essential chores

Everything carried on heads and toys cleverly made with rubbish

Children from daycare sending puzzles and books with me

Puzzles well received by Mozambicans, young and old

Photos

Landrover trip to remote 'bush-bush' village for preschool

Arriving to upskill some local volunteers

Called to a Sun-Scorched Land

Shopping in the town market

Upstairs to the bread buns and dried fish

Photos

A remote Good Samaritan clinic

Young Mozambicans watch as a new preschool develops

Children enjoy school in En Gedi, Tanzania

Women refugees in Kibera, Nairobi learning new skills

Part 2: Portugal and World Outreach Internship 2014

The Proposal: Portugal First

Before leaving Mozambique to explore mission opportunities in East Africa, I met with Kevin and Ginnie to discuss a proposal in the event I returned. They helped define what I could be doing. They were willing to accept me on a one-year internship, providing I was formally accepted into the World Outreach family. This was positive, because I would not be limited to a long-term commitment (usually starting at three years) until I had already spent significant time there.

We discussed the language issue, and they suggested a short intensive course with a tutor in Lisbon, Portugal.

"Here are the contact details for Victoria. She usually recommends one year to learn Portuguese," they said. "That is, if you are accepted into the World Outreach family."

I wonder if she would be willing to teach me for only two months.

"Hope can also tutor you at Whitewater Farm, and the payment for that could enable her to do a discipling training course later." Ginnie and Kevin also advised gaining financial support for only one year from people and churches. This was more achievable than a long-term venture, with a shorter preparation time required.

Kevin showed me the new dorms being built to host future Bible study locals. I could have a one-bedroom apartment before the students arrived. They had a mattress available for me, but I would need to cover the cost of a fridge, bed base, mosquito net, dishes, and a minimum to set up. I had no need of a vehicle initially, which would be one less expense. Discussing local costs for everything allowed me to budget and work out how much I would need to raise in support before the trip was viable. It certainly gave me something to think about!

Now, having made the decision to return to Mozambique, it was time to put this step-by-step plan in process. It was all rather daunting, and the time frame seemed impossible. However, as different needs were explored, practical answers came about. By now, it was October 2013, and I had many preparations to achieve before arriving at Whitewater Farm in late March or early April 2014.

After contacting my key World Outreach leaders with my belief that God was leading me to Mozambique for an unknown time, things moved fast. I was excited but also nervous. World Outreach sent me a useful resource for missions as soon as I was formally accepted as an intern. I downloaded the step-by-step one-year guide. *This is helpful.* After the internship, I could apply to them for a full mission partnership. I was overjoyed that the process was coming together so smoothly and thankful to be going with a mission agency, as they offered so much in preparation, advice, and protection.

I needed a language boost before arriving. Victoria thought I could initially do a crash course to get me by.

"Can you start early February? I can squeeze you in at that

time," she asked from her classroom in Lisbon. "Let's see what we can do in eight weeks!"

"Yes! Perfect timing. I'll let you know my flights when they are finalised."

As I looked at the huge list of requirements to become a World Outreach missionary and enlist for one year as an intern with Kevin and Ginnie at Whitewater Farm, my heart and mind were faint. *And now Portugal, too!* I had to remind myself of verses I had memorised to counteract anxious feelings. *Remember, with God, all things are possible for those who love the Lord. Where He calls, He will provide.*

"How much time do you have to get this all sorted?" a close friend asked me.

"I have November, December, and January to get funds together and other items organised and approved. Then eight weeks of language lessons in Portugal, arriving in Mozambique in March," I said, trying to sound confident.

So Much to Prepare!

It was up to me (and God!) to raise one year's support, present a financial budget, get vaccinations and visas, and arrange malaria prevention/protection. A psychological health examination was required (World Outreach partners said it was to see if I was 'crazy' enough to join them!), and I had to organise a 'sending cell' of support people. The WO guidelines were comprehensive. Without them, I'm sure my mission trip would not have been as successful.

This was a team effort and a new experience for me. The sending cell support group was made up of people who would pray for me and the needs in Portugal and Mozambique. A chairperson organised monthly meetings focused on helping with my mission as it developed.

As well as providing moral and spiritual support, people volunteered practical help, like storing belongings while I was gone. My home church assisted with the financial aspects of receiving funds internationally while I was overseas.

Though my rental cottage was a gem, it was an added expense. At my age, resigning from a full-time teaching position that I loved and vacating my rental property was daunting. Without God's assurance of provision and protection and the many friends helping me, I would have found this an extremely anxious situation.

"You can store some of your belongings inside two cupboards at our place," offered some good friends, coming to my rescue. "Then you will have enough to set up house again when you return."

"You can use one of my bedrooms," said Kelly, "and store your bed and clothes here for when you come back for the six weeks during Mozambique's rainy season."

Other people offered to help with re-entry life, such as organising dental visits or places to stay while visiting other churches outside of my home area.

Wow, I am blessed with friends who own properties and are offering such valuable help.

Three major aspects challenged me: budgeting requirements, speaking engagements at churches to raise support, and overall IT skills. I had to learn to create PowerPoint presentations for raising support, set up a banking system with donors to access funds overseas, and email groups of people using 'bcc' to protect individuals' privacy.

"Help! How do I do this, Kelly?"

My friend from church, who had been the preschool manager at my childcare centre, came to my rescue many times as I struggled with the IT side of things.

"No worries, easie-peasie for me," she replied. "At least you know how to use the camera and writing programme to create learning stories for the children. That will be one less skill you need to learn when you send us your monthly newsletters."

This was an encouraging thought.

Based on my previous experience of visiting these African countries, I decided to take a small, inexpensive pocket-sized camera with me. Taking photos on my phone in public could be a temptation for thieves. I wanted photos for my own records and also for newsletters and PowerPoint presentations to share back home at churches. I was familiar with using this type of camera while teaching preschoolers. It was unobtrusive, easy to click, and produced some great shots—after deleting many!

I needed a diary to record events, and a journal for my Bible readings. Recording how I heard from God was part of my internship requirement, but it was a habit I had already established. Then there were notebooks for language study, too. I discovered that using a small notebook to record the currency exchange, cost of items and fuel, general greetings in Portuguese, local dialect, and names of key people was a very useful resource to have in my pocket.

I had to learn to step out of my comfort zone of doing things independently and ask for help in many areas. For example, I needed to have a brochure available at different churches for people to take home so they could think and pray about whether to support me. As that need arose, I found out about someone who created folded brochures for missionaries on a tight budget. I was very grateful for this person's help. Mine was her last job before she returned to Christchurch. *God's timing!*

I struggled initially with the courage to ask churches or groups for time to share about my upcoming mission trip. A home church of a handful of people and a church with two hundred people required different presentations. In all these aspects of preparation,

I asked God for help and to provide people to assist me.* These prayers were answered, sometimes before I even prayed. A sending cell was truly a valuable asset.

God went before me in my family situation too, smoothing anything that might have created anxiety in me. My son, an only child, had recently returned from three years of working in Auckland and was beginning a relationship with a highschool girlfriend. Both were in their early twenties. Her parents lived locally, and it was a great relief to be assured that they would keep an 'eye' on them and relay a message to me if anything went wrong.

At times, fear and worry clouded my emotions, but I was reminded of certain Bible verses I had memorised to help me overcome those feelings. It was supernatural divine help, as I had, in the past, used other methods with limited success. I had a huge measure of peace throughout the transition process, thanks to people I believe God had placed around me in this situation.

As I would have to deal with other currencies and time zones, helpful people showed me how to set up apps on my phone. I learned about the South African *rand*, the Mozambican *metical*, and the Portuguese *euro*. I was thankful for the currency converter app. I also had a language translator app in case I got stuck in a foreign country and needed to be understood. Times certainly had changed from when I first set foot on African soil thirty-eight years earlier, when a telegram was the fastest way to contact my parents!

An understanding travel agent, Bruce, came into my life and made all the flight connections between New Zealand, Australia, South Africa, Portugal, and Mozambique for the best dollar value. I found Bruce helpful, personable, and flexible with changing

---

* *In nothing be anxious, but in everything, by prayer and petition with thanksgiving, let your requests be made known to God. And the peace of God which surpasses all understanding, will guard your hearts and your thoughts in Christ Jesus.* (Philippians 4:6–7, WEB)

connections, depending on my situation with visas. I couldn't have organised the flights without his expertise and willingness.

I still needed to sort out a comprehensive medical kit, get all the required vaccinations and have them documented in my vaccine passport, book a three-hour psychological test, book accommodation in Portugal, and secure a space for my language lessons with Victoria. So much to organise!

Amazingly, it all came together after only a few months. Pledges of support from around sixty individuals and four churches meant my plans to set off by February 2014 would become a reality. My airfares were paid, and ten months of support had been pledged by people wanting to be a part of this mission venture. The most awesome outcome was the support and provision for language learning in Portugal on my way to Mozambique.

I was truly humbled and amazed.

Alan, a friend at church, commented on how fast the mission had gained support. "Your financial support came together faster than I have ever seen, and I have been on many other church mission-sending teams."

It was encouraging to witness a venture that showed God's hand in it all. As a fairly recent follower of Jesus Christ, building my trust in God's provision was essential.

Time to Go, and An Angel Escorts Me

Finally, the day came for goodbyes, bittersweet yet part of the journey. A few close friends and family members clustered around me in town. After hugs and blessings, I hopped on the bus to the Auckland hotel where bus transfers occurred. *Preparation time seemed to take forever and now suddenly it's time to say goodbye!*

From the hotel, I needed to find the downtown bus stop where the airport shuttle bus departed. Having packed everything I thought I would need for the next ten months in two countries—first Portugal and then Mozambique—I was laden with a large, heavy suitcase, a carry-on suitcase, a backpack, and my ukulele. I offered a silent prayer. *Help me find the bus stop, Lord!*

Making my way through the hotel, burdened with bags, I didn't have to wait long. Almost immediately, a hotel attendant came to my rescue, a large, strongly built Pacific Island man with a friendly face. After I explained what I needed to find, he kindly grabbed my bags. He told me the bus stop was across the busy downtown road, and while we walked there, he asked me where I was going.

I shared with him my calling to missions in Africa. He smiled, saying he and his family from the islands prayed for and supported missionaries. His smile and encouragement touched my heart. How remarkable that he was the one to help me cross the busy street with my heavy bags. After depositing my belongings and explaining when the next bus was to arrive, he walked off up the hill towards the hotel.

As I was pondering how extraordinary this encounter was, I tried to see him walking through the crowds. I could not find him. I looked and looked, scanning the road to see if he had crossed over to the hotel, but it was as though he had vanished! I felt it was an unusual encounter and wondered if he was, in fact, an angel sent in human form to help. My eyes teared up as I contemplated how much God loves me and provides for my every need, even just to get from one bus stop to another.*

Language Lessons in Portugal

Olá a Portugal! No longer married, I was a solo traveller now, being

---

* *I sought the Lord, and He answered me; He delivered me from all my fears.* (Psalm 34:4, NIV)

led by God's plan and purpose. My journey was not just for myself. I was representing supporters who wanted to assist Mozambicans in upskilling and raising the next generation with a knowledge of God's love.

Having lived in the warmer areas of New Zealand for many decades, I got a shock when I arrived in Lisbon in February 2014. *Gosh, this is colder than I expected.* A lovely Canadian couple called Jack and Kayla, with their young children, picked me up from the airport. I noticed they were wearing scarves and hats. We all had a laugh about my shortfall in packing warmer clothes! They told me that Victoria, our language tutor, often had to loan hats and scarves to students until they went shopping. I later found I also needed trainer-type shoes to handle the long walks on rough-hewn cobblestones from bus stops to my language class.

This was my second time in Portugal. When I sailed there with my former husband many years ago, I was restricted to a marina. This time, I landed by plane in a big city. My first impressions of Lisbon were the churches, blue and white tiles at bus stops, monuments and fountains, pastry shops, freshly baked bread, and an amazing integrated mass transit system. *I wonder why the people dress mainly in black.* I was surprised to see Catholic Bibles and religious books in the post office when I bought a stamp for my first postcard home.

My first email sent from Lisbon captured the moments in those first two weeks:

> Last day of February already! *Bom dia familia da igreja,* Good morning church family. (I think I wrote that correctly!)
>
> Wow, I am here in Portugal, having survived two weeks of intensive language lessons and culture shock, not understanding what is being spoken around me. My language

tutor, Victoria, is a real gem and is streamlining and simplifying (so she says!) what I need to know to grasp the basic foundations of learning Portuguese. It is definitely worth it to be here for this—she has been teaching language to missionaries for thirty years and has a wall of photos of them and their families. I even saw a picture of Kevin and Ginnie's family when they first arrived here to begin their language study with her!

The *Instituto Biblico Portugues* (IBP, a Christian Bible training school) is such a blessing to be staying at. They have been very thoughtful about making my stay comfortable, knowing I have arrived from summertime down under. There is even a Christian preschool/homeschool here for 12–15 children that I can attend anytime. I usually stay for the first hour or so, which involves listening to conversations, lots of laughing, and lots of singing. The teacher is a gifted musician and has recorded some CDs.

The Canadians, Jack and Kayla, have been studying the language for over a year and preparing for Angola. Martin from Germany has been here for five months and will arrive in northern Mozambique around the time I do. Two doctors from the UK are arriving soon to study with Victoria too.

Portugal is such a beautiful place, and the people are polite, friendly, and gracious with my attempts in using their language. I went to an evangelical Baptist church last Sunday, situated in a neighbourhood of mainly African and Indian residents. The Portuguese pastor's wife is from Seattle! They support a missionary woman in Mozambique who I met over there in September. Small world! It was a special celebration of their church, with a shared lunch afterwards.

It was interesting how that happened, as the church had only a very small area and no kitchen. After church, suddenly everyone was leaving, and my friend from IBP drove me to someone's house to cook up the chicken and beans for lunch ... I thought at this rate it would be dinnertime! An hour later, we raced back to the church, and everyone else arrived with their cooked meals to share too. Other people had rearranged the church to accommodate two long rows of trestle tables and chairs, and we all sat down to an amazing spread of foods and a special birthday cake. It was 5 o'clock before my friend and I arrived back after riding the bus.

The weather is getting warmer and has been sunny at times, thankfully. I am so grateful to be here and to have this opportunity to begin learning this difficult language.

Please keep me in your prayers, especially for:

- Keeping healthy and free from colds or flu (I have a had 24-hour flu but am better now)
- Adjusting to different foods and water
- Learning the language and keeping up with Victoria's homework!
- Patience and ability to learn various technological challenges.

Thank you for your continued support and prayers. I really could not do this without your involvement and commitment.

Blessings and love.

* * *

Once a week, my new friend at IBP and I joined a Bible study session with the Angolan and Mozambican refugees. The pastor loaned me a bilingual Bible, so I could help the refugees read and speak English while I was learning how to pronounce Portuguese.

Not only was I immersed in the language, but I developed friendships with people who followed Jesus and the Bible. A group of us went to a Hillsong UK worship service in Lisbon that was dubbed into Portuguese. *Wow, I know these songs in English!* My newfound friends helped me find a shop that sold bilingual Bibles. Now I had my own copy to use here for the next eight weeks and take to Mozambique, which helped enormously.*

I began to learn how to pray and sing worship songs in Portuguese. The church even asked me to join in with my ukulele one Sunday. *This is a big stretch for me!* The following week, this multilingual church congregation held some language classes using the bilingual Bible for pronunciation. I helped with the English pronunciation, while they helped with my Portuguese pronunciation. It was another fun and informal way to learn this challenging language.

Being an early childhood teacher in New Zealand, it was a bonus for me to spend time with the international school children learning language here at IBP. Joining in with their singing of Portuguese worship songs was such a privilege. Victoria was an excellent teacher, and the fact she could also speak English accelerated the learning process. She showed me some resources that past students had found helpful, and I managed to find handy pocket-sized dictionaries and other pictorial language resources in a few different shopping malls. I had homework every day. I was grateful to have my own room, which enabled me to focus during this eight-

---

* *Now to him that is able to do exceedingly abundantly above all we ask or think, according to the power that works in us...* (Ephesians 3:20–21, WEB)

The Proposal: Portugal First

week intensive study. *Graças a Deus!* (Thank God!) The lighting wasn't the best, so I had to wear my headlamp, which I expected would be good practice for Mozambique.

On the way to my IBP lessons, I got off the bus outside some *pastelarias* (pastry shops), so I practised speaking while ordering coffees and *sobremesas* (desserts). *Pastel de natas,* a small custard tart, became my favourite. It was just as well I was only there for eight weeks, as I would have had to shop for bigger clothes after the delicious Portuguese foods that I came to love! I wondered whether Mozambique, which had been a Portuguese colony in the past, would have some of these foods, particularly the lovely round breads and the barbecued chicken I learned to find with my nose while walking around the cobblestoned streets.

I developed more trust in the Holy Spirit's directions in surprising ways, even when crossing a motorway.* One weekend I walked to a nearby shopping mall. The route took me past tiled and plastered houses with house names beside wooden doors. A small farmlet with an orchard, chickens, and two friendly Jerusalem donkeys was at the bottom of the road. But then a busy motorway blocked my way. *How will I cross this?* I stood for a while next to the chickens and donkeys until finally spotting a bus driving over a bypass. *Aha! That's the way over.* Saying goodbye to the farm animals, I crossed the road to the mall.

The inside of the mall was decorated with huge mobiles, mosaics, and tiles. I was innocently taking photos of these colourful architectural aspects when an agitated security guard stopped me. I wondered nervously what I had done wrong. *"Desculpe!"* (Sorry!) One of the first words I had learned suddenly became useful.

He wanted to see my photos and indicated that I needed to delete them all. *How peculiar.* But then I remembered that only

---

* *Cast all your anxiety upon Him because He cares for you.* (1 Peter 5:7, NIV)

months before, while in Nairobi, there had been the Westgate Shopping Mall massacre. Malls were on high alert worldwide.

I honestly could not have learned and survived this whole experience without a relationship with God and knowing I had a team of supporters backing me financially, prayerfully, and socially. I was buried in homework and learning the technology side of things.

I realised I was missing social company. A welcome change occurred to my schedule with the arrival of Jan and Lori, young doctors from the United Kingdom who were taking a crash course in Portuguese for a short-term mission trip to Angola.

"We are off on Saturday by public bus to visit Sintra. Do you want to come?" Lori asked me one evening after a shared dinner in the communal kitchen.

"Sure, I'd love to get out and see some interesting places. What's there to see?"

"Have you heard of the Pena Palace? It's an extraordinary, whimsical palace with extensive gardens."

"Sounds great!"

They often invited me to ride the buses, trains, and ferries, and we went to some top tourist places I'd been reluctant to visit on my own. We had fun practising the language and laughed a lot. I was thankful they got me out of my serious study times!

Victoria had empathy for missionaries going to other countries and needing the correct documentation. This process was often difficult to understand when using one's native language, let alone a foreign language. She came with me to the Mozambique Embassy in Lisbon to assist with getting the correct visa to enter Mozambique. Once over there, I could apply for the longer-term visa called a DIRE.

Despite our best efforts, I was unable to obtain the visa. I had to contact my travel agent, hoping he could change my flights. I would need to return to South Africa before travelling back to Mozambique. I messaged prayer partners in New Zealand for help regarding this critical issue. Two Bible verses I had memorised helped control the feeling of anxiety compromising my peace.

My eight weeks in Portugal and studying the language went all too quickly, coming to an end in mid-April. I felt very privileged to have studied with Victoria. I had gained a solid foundation on which to keep building, using, and understanding this difficult language.

Boarding the international flight, I was excited in my spirit. In my heart, though, I looked fondly back at Portugal and the friends I'd made there. Hopefully, one day I could return to this delightful country and its people.

"*Obrigada amigas! Até logo.*" Thanks, friends. See you later.

South Africa, Visa Granted, and Mozambique—Finally!

It was fortunate that Saul and Sarah, the World Outreach field leaders for Mozambique, arrived at the mission house in Johannesburg at the same time as I returned from Portugal. I looked forward to getting to know them better. They had lived in Mozambique for over twenty-five years, planting churches, teaching preschool, baptising new believers, and mentoring new pastors. They had raised two sons there as well. Sarah attended the WO women's seminar on my previous visit, but I hadn't met Saul yet. Ron and Lyndie were there as well. I began to feel like part of the global family of Outreach missionaries.

I had some anxiety regarding the visa refused in Portugal, which would lead to a long-term DIRE visa once I arrived in Mozambique. Since Saul was fluent in business Portuguese, he came with me to the Mozambique High Commission in Pretoria. After what seemed a very short wait, we picked up the necessary visa in my passport and returned to the mission house. *Answered prayer!*

My anticipation for serving in Mozambique started to outweigh

South Africa, Visa Granted, and Mozambique – Finally!

my insecurities as I witnessed God's hand in granting the essential visa and bringing me into a supportive WO family. Again, I noticed most missionaries spent a lot more time in prayer, both spontaneous and scheduled, than was common back in New Zealand. I wondered whether it was because one's senses were more acute in unfamiliar circumstances. However, circumstances in Mozambique seemed so daunting that I think all believers here sought divine assistance in every way possible. I was privileged to join in with some seasoned long-term missionaries who had witnessed many miracles and God's hand in making all things work together for good. I had a lot to learn about my own prayer and faith walk.

Soon after, I boarded the flight from OR Tambo Airport in Johannesburg for The Big City, Mozambique, thankful for Ron and Lyndie's help. I spent the flight reflecting on what I remembered from my previous experience of arriving during a time of upheaval for the country. Mozambique was still affected by its traumatic past. Liberation from Portuguese colonial rule happened officially in June 1975, after many years of conflict, leaving the country in chaos.

I had experienced this firsthand. In July 1975, four of us sailed on a small yacht into the port of Lourenço Marques, now called Maputo, after spending three to four months in Madagascar and the Seychelle Islands. With no radio or communication systems aboard in those days, we were unaware of world news for months.

The port authorities informed us in Portuguese that we could not go ashore. Anchored out from the city, we were perplexed. None of us understood the language so were unable to comprehend much of what they said.

"Why won't they let us ashore yet? We have no water or fuel left and barely any food. What's going on? Something doesn't seem right."

Our intuition was correct. Things were not right ashore. By

some miracle, after two days, they let us go into town, but only for forty-eight hours.

I pondered, during my flight, how much had changed here since 1975, when streets were abandoned except for the FRELIMO army, mainly young men with machine guns at every corner. The shops were boarded up, looting was evident, and brokenness from the hasty Portuguese departure could be seen everywhere.

We were given a FRELIMO independence badge, which helped us understand a bit of what was going on at that time. As the banks were abandoned, we eventually traded our US cash dollars on the black market at seven times the bank rate. With literally stacks of local currency, we struggled to find supplies to help us continue to South Africa. We got a special bargain price for a box filled with big cans of cashews! I later learned cashews were one of Mozambique's chief exports.

Little did I think back then that I would return. Last year, during my 2013 visit to Mozambique, I learned that a Marxist communist takeover occurred in 1977, resulting in a resistance movement called RENAMO. Civil war continued for around twenty years. The schools of Mozambique were often used as bases for army activity, which contributed to an entire generation missing out on education. Decades later, the country still struggled with tension between these two political groups.

Long-term missionaries shared with me that, in 2000, Mozambique was one of the top twenty poorest nations. It suffered from diseases, droughts, floods, a health system inadequate to meet the needs of poor rural areas, unemployment, low literacy rates in remote areas, uneven distribution of wealth, and poor infrastructure in rural areas. *Complex problems!*

I learned primary schools were crowded in these northern areas, with only one teacher for sixty to one hundred children.

South Africa, Visa Granted, and Mozambique—Finally!

Young children entering school with a background in the Portuguese language had a head start in these large classrooms. Consequently, the bilingual *Preschool in a Box,* which Ginnie from Whitewater Ministries initiated with Tina's help, was well received in these isolated, poor villages. There was a high rate of illiteracy, and the adults we met were passionate about their children having every possible educational opportunity.

Flying into The Big City after a two-and-a-half-hour flight, I was struck again by the amazing lumps of smooth rock, a type of granite dome, or inselberg. A blast of humid air swamped me as I set my foot once again on Mozambique ground. A combination of green grass, dusty red roads, loads of coconut trees, and tin-roofed houses and buildings met my eyes. I was back! *I hope the immigration and customs officials understand my newly acquired Portuguese!*

Thankfully, my shrink-wrapped bags were of no interest to anyone on passing through the X-ray machine. This time, I had learned to say *"Não hoje"* to the many hands that wanted to help carry my bags. "Not today" seemed kind, leaving them with some hope for tomorrow. *I will need to navigate this scene with more understanding and less guilt and sympathy as time goes on.* Later, I added the phrase *"Talves outra dia"* (maybe another day).

To my relief, I saw my friends, Andy and Tina from Whitewater Farm, waiting on the outside balcony for me to reappear after customs and immigration. *Whew, I feel much more relaxed knowing a bit more language this time.* Having friends help with my luggage made me feel so welcomed.

As we headed into town in the twin cab ute, our first stop was the consulate. I was grateful to be part of a mission family that assisted me with legalities in a foreign country. Submitting documents and a passport for the long-term stay DIRE visa often took most of the day, they told me.

"We will drop off your documents first, then do the other jobs on the list," Andy informed me. "It usually involves a few hours of waiting around, as other people wait there too."

Jumping back into the truck, we set off into the crazy traffic of The Big City.

"Why are we stopping here?" I asked when we halted.

"Andy will stay in the truck while we dash to the outside cash machine," said Tina. "I'll show you how to get your dollars converted to local *meticais* to use in the markets."

I stood behind Tina, looking anxiously around, as she withdrew a pile of notes out of the machine. She guarded my back as I stuffed the *meticais* into my waist pack and hid it beneath my shirt. *I sure am glad to have friends helping me in this city!*

Once again, I was reminded that supermarket shopping was stressful, having to adjust to entering the shop between armed guards as well as fend off so many people begging. I didn't think I could manage this on my own. Years earlier, I worked in an emergency room at a busy hospital and learned about 'compassion fatigue'. One could be overwhelmed serving in such a needy part of Africa.

A variety of items were required back at Whitewater Farm. It was an adventure to hunt around a myriad of shops and locate items for preschool training, medical supplies in a malarial area, solar system parts, and truck or mechanical parts for machinery. Satisfied that the shopping list was fulfilled, but still waiting for the visa, we retreated to an air-conditioned hotel café that had hamburgers, ice-cold cokes, and french fries.

"Wait until you see their restrooms," said Tina. "Clean flush toilets with nice loo paper!"

What an oasis! I thought. We all enjoyed a brief respite from heat, crowds, and communicating in another language.

Our prayers for favour in the complicated official process

were answered, with my passport and documents passing between many desks and ending up with a lot of stamps. I received my DIRE that afternoon, permitting me to stay long term with proof of financial support and as part of an international organisation. We were all grateful and took it as a miracle—one of many to come in this great adventure of becoming part of God's army abroad.

Little by little, my independence was being smoothed out, just like those huge inselbergs.

Internship at Whitewater Farm

As we left The Big City, I leaned out the back window thinking, *I'm finally here for months, not weeks. It's hot, and it smells like Africa.* The highway took us past diesel-fumed buses, colourful stalls along the road, and huge cashew trees. People with brightly coloured plastic bowls of freshly roasted cashews waved at us to stop and buy. Some stood so far out on the highway waving their bowls that it seemed they were unaware of the danger. Finally, we stopped to buy some from a woman with a child who seemed desperate for a sale.

That small encounter at the beginning of my internship year reminded me of my reason for being here. My heart wanted to see the poor enriched and encouraged—especially women and children. By offering educational opportunities through a biblical-worldview curriculum, I believed I could help them grow into all God created them to be. Though I had initially signed up for one year as an intern, I anticipated continuing longer in Mozambique through World Outreach missions.

This was a step of faith. I had no idea what more was in store. How would I be a blessing in serving the needs of the people here and within the WO team on the ground? I think God spared me that knowledge, as He knew I would faint from fear and run away, like Jonah in the Bible.

Driving up to Whitewater Farm's entrance felt like coming home. I was slightly more familiar now with the culture and environmental conditions and looked forward to building on my growing language skills and the budding friendships that had begun the previous year. The exploratory trip had also prepared me for the financial costs and budgeting involved. Managing other people's donations effectively was a new concept for me, and I was grateful for WO training and preparation in this area.

After a week of settling in, Kevin, Ginnie, and I sat down to talk and pray together. I was feeling uncertain about what I would be doing.

Kevin asked me a strange question. "How do you eat an elephant?"

I wondered where this was leading. "I haven't the slightest idea!"

"One bite at a time."

As we looked at the World Outreach internship ministry plan, a sense of relief came over me. The framework helped identify my role, my short and long-term goals, and the tasks I could be involved with depending on my language abilities. It was comprehensive, including a spiritual care plan for developing intimacy with God in this foreign culture and making time for relaxation—all provided in bite-size chunks.

A booklet was supplied for me to write down these aspects, with spaces for reflections and further development. There was flexibility in this plan and times for coming together to review how it was going. I felt well supported in learning more about time management, not one of my strong points, and giving me a framework to communicate about perceived difficulties.

Following my 2013 exploratory trip, I had come prepared with a laptop full of Bible teachings, some favourite books, photos of family back home, and a drawing pad with coloured pencils. The sun crashed down at night and brought total darkness almost immediately. By 6pm, dinner was eaten and the dishes done, and usually by 7pm, there was plenty of nighttime left before sleeping. After learning a language and trying to figure out the culture all day long, I was ready to relax and not do too much mental activity.

We were expected to individually feed our spiritual life with God through regular Bible reading, prayer, and playing and singing praise and worship songs at appropriate times. *God, help me not be overwhelmed.* During the week, I sang worship songs with my ukulele. I committed the weekends to building my faith through reading or listening to Bible studies.

Part of my internship requirements included an expectation to attend the local village Christian church. Witnessing a community of believers vigorously sing and dance their praises to our same God in the Makua language in a mud-brick building was an eye-opener. English was rarely used in these churches, which was challenging in my first year. However, the longer I lived there, the easier it became. I was encouraged and thankful to God for His assistance in my language learning and for my bilingual Bible, an essential aid when asked to share an encouraging word in Portuguese.

Every Friday before breakfast, we joined all the workers in the courtyard of Whitewater Farm to sing Portuguese songs and pray. Other times, the English-language speakers would jump in the ute and travel an hour to another group of Christians from South Africa and Zimbabwe, who hosted an English church service with a luncheon in their beautiful gardens. I was so amazed to learn how God, Jesus, and the Holy Spirit were praised and worshipped through different languages and cultures. The love of Christ that we all shared created a universal feeling of belonging to the same family, whether in a mud hut or a beautiful courtyard.

We often prayed together before attempting any travel or activities. Not only did we face snakes, scorpions, malaria, and bad driving on treacherous roads with overcrowded taxi vans, but in the town's markets, opportunities for theft required us to have eyes in the back of our heads. We needed to be close to the Holy Spirit when our plans changed unexpectedly, which required trust and courage, especially when we ventured into the remote bush-bush areas.

Life was much the same as the year before, only not so dry. The fire season had passed. As always, yellow jerry cans of water at the front of the house served as backup for water from the taps. The delicious smell of woodsmoke reminded me I was back—but this time not to fight bush and grass fires! Later in the year, during the dry season, I would probably be volunteering to whack out small grass fires with a strip of old tyre attached to a long stick.

During the first few weeks of my internship, while the first of the dorm rooms were being finished for the Bible study students and other visitors, I stayed in the big house. Life required some adjustments, which I generally found exciting to adopt.

Some things, though, I struggled with and never really got used to, including the heat, humidity, and prolific mosquitos at night. Sleeping under the mosquito net was fairly comfortable; the net hung from a rectangular frame around the bed, so I could sleep without it touching me. No glass covered the windows, but on bright moonlit nights, the curtains needed to be closed, which unfortunately stopped the airflow.

When I moved to the dorm apartment a few weeks later, there were big windows on opposite sides of the bed, so the airflow was great. I didn't need to buy a costly pedestal fan yet. The missionaries who had been here longer had these fans, which had a remote control and were positioned inside the netting that hung over the bed.

"Why do you need a remote control on a fan?" I asked.

"You might end up with a chill or head cold if you leave it on all night, as the temperature cools down in the early hours. Keep the remote near your head so you can press the off button without waking up too much."

It sounded complicated, but malaria is a real danger in these parts. I coped with the humidity better this time, as I brought thin cotton nighties and other cotton clothing from secondhand shops back home. I became skilled at hopping into bed through the gap in the netting and closing it so no mozzies joined me. I was mostly successful. It was a restless night if one got trapped in there with me.

Drumbeats at Night

One night, the eerie sound of steady drumbeats woke me. They continued for hours. Over breakfast, I asked about them between mouthfuls of tea and toast.

Ginnie explained, "Witch doctors could be signalling the death of someone important or scaring away evil spirits. Animism, the worship of nature spirits and ancestral spirits, is still common here."

The local *feiticeiro* (witch doctor) generated fear in people and a need to control or appease the spirit world. I was very thankful to have the company of Bella, one of the older puppies, during the nights.

Whitewater Ministries had a holistic approach to serving people's needs. We not only introduced skills and opportunities to enrich their daily lives, but were messengers of the Gospel of Jesus Christ and the life-changing freedom it could bring—namely, freedom from fear. Other spirits did not welcome the Truth that Jesus Christ brings.

As time went on, I was to encounter more situations involving witchcraft. I was never comfortable hearing those drumbeats in the night. We believed in the power of prayer to overcome the dangers and obstacles we perceived.*

The wet season, from November to February, brought cyclones and flooding, with bridges washed out and roads washed away. Crops could be destroyed, resulting in a period referred to as the 'hunger season'. Mud and thatched-roof huts often collapsed, leaving people homeless. Most missionaries left for their home countries during these hot, humid months, as the country virtually came to a standstill. The infrastructure of stormwater drainage didn't withstand these torrential weather systems; either it wasn't there or was inadequate.

Missionaries returned during the dry season, February to November. Often the locals had suffered while we were away. We assisted them as much as we could with emergency food supplies. The dry season had perpetual blue skies with no clouds and a climate that was fairly hot but not too humid. I enjoyed this type of weather and found my hay fever and allergies disappeared.

Whitewater Farm was a close-knit community, requiring some codependency. As a new volunteer in a challenging environment, I valued that greatly. I was used to having my own vehicle and making independent decisions, but here, this was not wise or even possible. It was a learning opportunity, a time of sacrifice and surrender. I was very grateful when those with vehicles offered me a seat in the truck for shopping and relaxation excursions. My

---

* *For I am persuaded that neither death, nor life, nor angels, nor principalities, nor things present, nor things to come, nor powers, nor height, nor depth, nor any other created thing will be able to separate us from God's love which is in Christ Jesus our Lord.* (Romans 8:38–39, WEB)

prayer life and prayer partners helped me through the struggles of giving up luxuries I'd had back in New Zealand. An independent lifestyle is a luxury, but I was to learn later that it can also foster isolation.

Whitewater Farm, where Whitewater Ministries was located, was on the edge of the WiFi network, so our connection with the outside world was not reliable. We had to go into the nearest town to find the best spot to make phone calls and email newsletters. Since we depended on solar power for our energy needs, cloudy days required us to adapt our tasks. I learned to become efficient within this situation and regularly used my USB stick to back everything up.

A Diverse Community

The main house was the hub, with its big dining room and a lounge for the whole community to gather in for worship and Bible study. With a number of bedrooms set aside for visitors teaching at the Bible School, the house could accommodate large numbers of people. At that time, two Mozambican families lived in farm cottages, while other household workers, goat herders, and cashew farm workers came in from the nearby village. The main cottage near the big house was for support personnel—in this case, Tina and Andy, who complemented the team with their special abilities of preschool development, and a foreman for the farm workers.

Those of us with overseas support were fortunate to have money to buy chilly bins, which we kept cold with ice blocks from Whitewater Farm's deep freeze. The overall system could not support another electric fridge. A large, cool pantry for perishables meant we could enjoy our own types of foods, such as coleslaw salads. We were not accustomed to, nor could we produce, daily meals in the local style. With refrigeration, our diet could be more varied, and we didn't have to shop for fresh food every day. It also freed up our time to devote to other projects within Whitewater Ministries. Occasional meals of lasagne took on a whole new level of appreciation, as did Kevin's pumpkin pie for dessert!

The cashew factory also employed local people. An interesting community had been created between the cashew farm, Bible School, construction of future dorms for the discipleship training course, families who lived onsite and helped with daily chores, and men herding goats. It was a thriving, busy community that required a fair bit of organisation. The preschool venture had progressed from Whitewater Farm to a nearby village, then into remote villages where Whitewater Ministries had planted churches years before. I wondered if this was what Jesus meant when he told His apostles to share the Gospel with people close by, then in nearby places, and finally to the ends of the earth.

Families with children under the age of eight were keen to have preschool experiences in their villages. Few had a Christian background, and most were from animistic and Muslim backgrounds. Local Christ followers were involved after some training, with men and women volunteering time to enrich preschool children's education about the God of the Bible who loves them. A Portuguese/Makua bilingual programme provided a sensory-rich learning environment with practical knowledge through play.

After a shared dinner on Saturday evenings, I looked forward to a night of fun playing Mexican Train. This domino game brought all the farm residents together, as it was easy to understand without much language. It could get quite tense but often erupted in much laughter, the universal language.

I enjoyed this simple life and reflected on how I would not have liked living in a city with shopping malls. Although learning a new

South Africa, Visa Granted, and Mozambique—Finally!

language in a developing country, I found I was enriched in so many other ways.*

"What should we watch, guys?" I called to the others. *"Call the Midwives* or *Downton Abbey?"* On Wednesday nights, we would watch an episode of either of these BBC series. The smell of popcorn wafting in from the kitchen and ice clinking in cold fizzy drinks created our own movie night atmosphere. *Such a contrast in one day between English drama series and local Mozambican situations!* Surprisingly, I found it really relaxing. Reading books was enjoyable, but watching English-speaking DVDs relaxed my brain from continually trying to work out what was going on.

---

* *I lift up my eyes to the mountains—where does my help come from? My help comes from the Lord, the Maker of heaven and earth.* (Psalm 121:1–2, NIV)

Serving With Whitewater Ministries

As soon as I arrived at Whitewater Farm, I was again tasked with the daily care of feeding and walking the seven dogs. It was a relief to do something familiar. I grew to love them, thankful for their protection as I explored the natural environment. I spent happy days with these new doggie friends yet experienced sadness and tears as I watched some die of tick fever or snake bites. Their lives were often cut short due to the risks and lack of vet doctors in the district.

One of my first jobs in the morning was to collect cashew fruits and bring them back to the kitchen. It was amazing to learn what was involved before the cashew nut became edible. The fruit that grew was juicy, with the nut hanging off the bottom of the fruit. The nut had a toxic layer around it, which needed to be removed before it was safe to eat. Unfortunately, as Whitewater Farm had no fencing, people would come in the early dawn, collect the cashew fruits, and make an alcoholic drink out of them that could have dangerous side effects.

Soon after settling in, I joined Ginnie and Tina to find out how

I could assist in their pioneer Christian-based preschool venture. This presented cultural challenges for me. As my language was still quite limited, building relationships with locals was slow going. I hoped I could teach the volunteers how to use local materials to make teaching resources.

In the northern rural areas, Mozambican-style Portuguese was spoken without proper conjugations, as it was their second language. I was thankful for that! Business, immigration, and medical sectors spoke more formally. That's when I really needed others to assist me. I had brought my little notebook with Makua phrases from last year's visit, thankful I had written them down.

Soon after my arrival, we visited a village near Whitewater Farm to introduce the preschool programme. While others were setting up inside, I engaged with the children. "*Ihali/Salaama.*" The children laughed, taking notice. I proceeded with a counting game in Makua: "*Moza, bili, taru, sese, tanu, tanamoza, tanabili,*" etc. If nothing else, we were having fun!

Ginnie and Tina knew Portuguese, so I was more of an observer during these initial times of introducing the preschool vision. Feeling useless, I took comfort in knowing God had called me here. *Be patient,* I told myself. A sense of humour was invaluable! With a willing heart, prayer, and a growing humility in making mistakes, I came to believe one was never too old to learn something new.

Our Unique Routines at the Farm

All windows had bars and screens on them to discourage intruders, whether monkeys, snakes, or people. Scorpions still got in, as did malaria-carrying mosquitos. The ceilings in the big house had gaps between the boards, and years of bat guano drifted down at times, which produced an itch. The windows were all opened daily, and without glass, the house was continually dusty.

Some jobs were physical and required employing local people with strong arms as part of the Whitewater Farm community. The household and visitors' laundry was hand-washed, including big sheets. Keeping the carpet rugs free from fleas and dust was another labour-intensive chore.

I handwashed my laundry in cold water dumped into big plastic tubs. Thankful for this quiet time of scrubbing clothes, I could relax while listening to the early morning sounds.* Since the temperature got hotter soon after the sun rose, I needed to have my clothes, towels, and sheets washed by 7am. Sometimes I stomped the dirt out, cleaning my feet in the process.

Silvio, the houseman at the big house, was kind and patient, helping me with language and aspects of household chores unique to this environment. It was great to know that his job provided for his family, as adults with low education often experienced employment difficulties due to the civil war.

The farm made their own concrete tiles for roofing the dorm and Bible School. Piles of sand and bags of cement were mixed with water, then poured into moulds. The hot, dry climate hardened them. All buildings were constructed of concrete, with very little wood. Termites were voracious and could destroy the timber in a house in a very short time. The coolness of concrete houses in these climates was a bonus too. Stacking spare tiles and other building materials and rubbish away from my dorm room was essential, as they could harbour scorpions.

Last year, I'd noticed that Kevin had a few very large plastic tubs filled with compost stored up high on trestles, growing the house's supply of silver beet, tomatoes, and herbs. Being a keen gardener myself, I was pleased to see he had instructed the builders

---

* *And whatever you do, work heartily, as for the Lord, and not for men ... for you serve the Lord Christ.* (Colossians 3:23–24, WEB)

to attach a concrete raised bed to the newly constructed dorm units. I anticipated growing myself some veggies from seeds when I moved from the big house to the first finished unit.

Whitewater Ministries had started building these new dorm complexes near the Bible School the previous year. The self-contained dorms were primarily for local pastors-in-training with their families to stay in private accommodation but also catered for visiting overseas pastors and missionaries. Each unit had its own flush toilet and cold shower. What luxury! Next to the Bible School were large one-room halls for families and students from the bush villages to sleep in communally, using the firepit for cooking with a large dining room nearby.

We had benchtop water filters made either of clay from Brazil or stainless steel. The filter cones were expensive to replace, so we got good at scraping them every so often. The daily task of filling the water towers was accompanied by mixing up powdered milk for the day and putting it into the chiller. I was pleasantly surprised to see New Zealand milk powder sold here. I felt like I was adding a bit of New Zealand green grass to my tea or coffee!

When I arrived, the generator was being replaced with solar panels for all our electrical needs: lighting, a water pump for showers, the freezer and main house fridge, a small TV with a DVD player for our once-a-week evenings of movies and popcorn, while we charged our phones and laptops. We still had oil lanterns and solar shower bags for times when things didn't work as expected. The storage capabilities of the solar panels determined whether life would be with or without mod cons.

The phrase 'Go with the flow!' came to mind more than once. Fortunately, in my earlier adult years, I had sailed on small yachts around the world and had lived in house buses in New Zealand with my former husband. None of them had refrigeration. The yachts had oil lamps for lighting, and there were no cell phones to charge in those days. Little did I know how those experiences would prepare me to live in this simple lifestyle. I wanted to contribute more but believed with time and practise I would become more proficient in using my language skills. I took comfort in the fact I had been obedient to God's call to come, and kept sensitive to His still, small voice, learning to trust Him without knowing what was ahead.

I really enjoyed getting out and looking at the different vegetation. My soul found peace in God's creation, observing and noticing new plants or insects. In times of quiet reflection while walking the dogs, I was overwhelmed to think that the Creator of heaven and earth was here to help me in ways I couldn't imagine.

Taking pleasure in simple delights, I took to photographing single flowers I spotted in this semi-arid sandy soil and little butterflies, which were scarce too. A solitary flower growing in this insufficient soil, bringing its unique beauty despite the dry heat and sand, touched my heart. Late afternoon walks brought the sunsets, which were stunning as only African sunsets can be, so deeply orange and red. These were difficult to capture with my camera but became forever etched in my mind.

I was amazed at the many varieties of mango trees that grew abundantly and learned to spot the best mangoes that had just fallen from the tree. I didn't know then that eating too many mangoes would cause a delay in my departure some time later.

* * *

It was 4am, and the roosters were crowing. I could hear people setting off for work before it got too hot. Northern Mozambique is only 15 degrees south of the equator, so sunrise and sunset are abrupt with little twilight. The country does not operate with daylight savings so gets light about 4.30am with evenings plunged into darkness before 6pm. This influences how daytime chores get done, with people heading off to their gardens, or *mashambas,* early. By 7am, it is often too hot for hard physical labour.

Working in *mashambas* provided people with food, and sometimes the excess could be sold for cash to buy items like soap, or petrol for their motorbike. Children were often up around 5am, working until they set off walking to school—if they were fortunate enough to attend.

Although I was an early riser and up with the sun, I thought 5am a better time! Personal devotions, often with a cup of coffee or tea in hand, gave me valuable quiet time. I learned to love the early mornings with the smell of woodsmoke and the sounds of birds, humming insects, and occasional monkeys.

One morning, we had an early start going to the bush-bush villages. "How do I look?" I asked Ginnie and Tina, preparing to jump into the truck. I felt awkward wearing the long *capulana,* a type of sarong wrapped like a skirt covering my legs, as well as a scarf tied tightly around my head.

"Well, it will keep you out of trouble in the bush villages," replied Ginnie.

"But we wouldn't win any prizes for fashion, that's for sure!" added Tina, laughing.

Out in the bush-bush areas, we showed respect for the traditional customs, a small price to pay for the privilege of bringing a preschool programme based on the God of the Bible. The locals looked beautiful dressed like this, but I thought I looked silly.

I was advised to wear footwear that was light yet closed in when we travelled inland, as it was more protective. *Protective?* I thought, imagining snakes and scorpions.

What a Subsistence Lifestyle Looks Like

Living without electricity, piped in water, sewage collection, or stormwater drainage created a labour-intensive society. No access to modern refrigeration or freezers in this climate meant fresh or cooked food could not be kept longer than the next day, so food preparation and cooking was a daily chore. The locals relied on the dry, sunny weather to store and dry the crops they grew.

After the rainy season, the harvested crops were dried on top of the thatched roofs or on special drying racks. Rodents were prolific, so it was important to store and protect one's food supply. Little food storage huts were built next to the houses to store the cobs of maize after they had dried. If people could not afford to pay a mill to grind their maize corn, they would use a big wooden mortar and pestle. If they had money to buy large plastic containers from the Chinese shops, these could be a means of protecting their hard-earned food source. Sometimes large feed sacks were found and used.

I saw children take turns pounding dried corn or manioc roots into a coarse flour that would be cooked into a staple porridge-like food called *xima*, *ugali*, or *sadsa*, depending on what part of Africa you are in. This often accompanied *matapa*, a cooked dish of brown beans and greens, usually pumpkin leaves. Locals ate their main meal at midday. The meal, made fresh every day after working in the fields, was very filling. Dried beans were soaked in the morning, then cooked with other ingredients over a charcoal fire. The added aroma of smoke made them the best-tasting beans in the world!

As I learned more about the locals' lifestyle of subsistence farming, I understood what a sacrifice it was for them to teach in the preschools twice a week, even for only a few hours a day. But such was their passion to see their children have an opportunity to learn before attending school.

Whenever we drove along the highway to Whitewater Farm, we crossed a bridge over a wide, shallow river. Women and children followed the highway, walking with containers of water or dried laundry on their heads. Since very few people had water piped into their house or hut, a daily trip to the best and closest water hole or river was necessary. Children learned from a young age how to balance small jugs of water on their heads.

I looked down from the bridge as we crossed the river, amazed. "What a great way to do their laundry!"

"Yes, and notice how they can hang them on nearby bushes to dry," said Tina.

With temperatures in the thirties and forties, drying took a short time.

"People have to keep a sharp lookout, though," Andy added.

"What for?"

"Earlier in the year, a crocodile took a young child from beside the river!"

Every time we drove over this bridge from then on, I thought of that dangerous aspect of washing their clothes.

After one of the preschool sessions, Ginnie called out to me, "We've got time to go to the local market and shop for some fresh foods. The truck is leaving in ten minutes."

I grabbed bags to carry the produce and my *capulana* to wrap around my legs, then jumped into the ute full of people hitching a ride to town. Even though I'd been once during my visit the previous year, I was still shocked to see fresh goat heads on top of screened wooden food safes. The food safes guaranteed that the chunks of meat inside, from the owner's own goat, were not stolen, and the screens kept the flies off the fresh meat.

Other people sat on mats beside little piles of red peppers, tomatoes, or small, sweet onions. Although I liked coleslaw, I was finding the constant diet of it repetitive. I asked Tina, "Why are our salads always made with cabbage?"

"Lettuce doesn't grow very well in this soil or with an irregular water supply. Besides, the local people don't generally eat uncooked or salad-type foods. Remember that they have no refrigeration."

A rare carrot, apple, or freshly roasted local peanuts were a tasty addition for our unique coleslaw. I grew to love the sweet little cabbages.

The market was a maze of stalls. I followed my nose to the smell of fresh bread, walking cautiously up broken concrete steps littered with plastic debris. Spread before me were old wooden tables with uncovered loaves of bread, small and large, stacked in pyramids. Nearby, dried fish were heaped in piles, encouraging swarms of flies to land on the loaves. I loved these locally baked crusty bread rolls, but it meant a quick transaction while blocking my mouth and nose from unwanted flies and stinky fish smells. *A small price to pay for living in a non-touristy part of the country.*

The flies were fewer downstairs with the potatoes and onion sellers, allowing me to practise my growing market conversation. "*Bom dia. Quanto custa?*" (Good day. How much?) followed by "*Obrigada!*" (Thank you). *I am thankful no one speaks English here so I can practise.*

Preschool Here is Different

In the locals' daily lives, everyone had a job to do. Basic, repetitive chores were essential for their existence and their family's welfare. I marvelled at their tenacity and hard work despite the hazardous environment of disease, drought, and cyclones that could wipe out their mud huts or, even worse, their crops. And yet, they had a desire to provide an educational opportunity for their children before they went to school.

It was a huge sacrifice for these volunteers to take time to train and teach their young children. Without this passion in their heart, they wouldn't squeeze the time into their demanding lives. The adults had grown up during a time in history where school was not possible for them, so there was a lot of incentive for their children to learn what they didn't.

Early in my training, I asked, "Why don't we pay the locals to teach preschool?" The quick and short answer involved sustainability. It was a balancing act of honouring their volunteer teaching yet discouraging a dependent relationship. Creating a long-term solution required the venture to be self-sustaining; we would eventually return to our home countries, and they would have to continue within their own capabilities. The phrase 'a hand up, not a hand-out' came to mind. This initiative was about equipping people. While we were there, the teachers were rewarded each semester with bags of beans and rice, fabric for *capulanas*, and axes or hoes for cultivating crops. Their efforts were acknowledged and appreciated through these donations.

Ginnie and Tina planned to hold preschool seminars to support the training of volunteer teachers. The country's many public holidays determined the scheduling of seminars. Often families became involved, as many mothers had a nursing baby or a toddler. People walked or cycled long distances to attend, so Whitewater Farm provided accommodation in the bunk rooms. An outdoor cookhouse was built so the attendees could cook their own style of food. As this was a Christian-based preschool programme, we also scheduled in times of worship and prayer together. After all the time spent in preparation, the result was a memorable time of fellowship, fun, and family.

We started by using some of our own resources for teaching concepts to young children. During my visit the previous year, I noticed that Ginnie and Tina used balls, wooden train sets, blocks, pencils and crayons, and occasionally paper from their homeschooling days.

The preschool in the Bay of Islands, New Zealand where I was employed at the time of my first visit had been enthusiastic about choosing books and puzzles to share with their African preschool buddies. I brought some books with pictures of common foods and animals, more puzzles (including one with African animals), Duplo blocks, and beads with cord to string them on. These open-ended resources could be used to support numeracy and spatial concepts and would also assist with literacy. Clear plastic boxes with a rotating library of resources could be shared between other preschools to be established later if the first one was successful.

Since the preschool model was being developed to multiply in other regions, it was later decided we would show the locals how to make their own resources with materials at hand, empowering them in a sustainable way.

One surprising discovery I learned about rural adults was in watching their first experience with simple preschool puzzles. They were fascinated with putting the puzzles together. Placing five big-game animals into the right shapes proved challenging. I could see they had never done this before and was curious to find out what type of teaching occurred in the primary schools.

One day, after shopping for my fresh foods in town, I found the answer to that question. I could hear children chanting and repeating what the teacher said before I even saw the school. I learned later that classrooms could have up to seventy children and one teacher. Learning by repetition seemed the only feasible way to learn in under-resourced schools.

I wonder what our volunteers think of our sensory-type methods of teaching young children. Are we enriching their lives in new ways and preparing them for a better learning experience if they go to school? I could share my knowledge or experience in early childhood practices, but would it be beneficial or sustainable?

As time went on, I felt I had more to learn from this cross-cultural situation than just preschool education. God was doing a work in me too.

My First Visit to the New Model Preschool

Last year I saw how the preschool ideas were trialled at the farm with the local workers' children. Now it was time to begin a training preschool in the nearby village. Soon after I arrived as an intern, a ute was loaded with personnel, boxes of resources, rolled up woven mats for sitting on the floor, water with cups and biscuits, and two little wooden tables. We drove a few kilometres up the highway to a cluster of huts, where a multitude of children immediately greeted us. With many volunteers helping to carry the boxes of resources, we walked along sandy paths that wound past huts and sparse bushes with the odd tree. The colourful ladies in their bright *capulanas* and headscarves, balancing boxes of supplies on their heads as they led us to the only concrete building, created a lasting impression on my mind.

The year before, a local YWAM team, residents of Whitewater Farm, and parents of local children had helped transport the materials for the building: concrete blocks, sand, cement, water, and roofing iron. This first little preschool was solid and strong. Unlike the surrounding mud and thatch huts, it could withstand seasonal cyclones. A concrete wall defined a narrow storage room; however, without a door, the contents wouldn't be secure. I guessed, being early days, the building was still a work in progress.

On arrival at the new preschool, the first thing I noticed was that the small concrete building had empty door and window spaces. *Are the doors and bars coming later? How will our first session work with the usual spectator crowds?* I kept these thoughts to myself as we greeted the curious residents with *"Bom dia"* or *"Ihali salaama."*

We found ourselves with an audience of all ages of children and even teenagers crowding the windows and spilling in through the single door space. Before rolling out the mats, we stopped and prayed for God's help. Then we set up areas with the chosen activities and prepared to welcome the registered children. It was thrilling to see so many children and parents interested in this educational opportunity. At the same time, it was heartbreaking to see school-age children and teenagers who couldn't go to school for lack of money wanting to join in as well.

These early days of the preschool were exciting for everyone, which proved challenging. Boundaries needed to be established. One of the team suggested, "Next time we are going to bring a half-door barrier for the doorway!" We all agreed. The windows were high enough that the older, taller teenagers could look in and observe so we didn't totally exclude them.

Each child underwent a registration procedure and signing-in process. The team drew a line on the wall to measure the children's heights. Being taller than the mark on the wall was a visible way for the unregistered children to understand they could not join in. Apron-like uniforms—sleeveless tunics with ties on the sides—were made by a local tailor. Name tags were another organisational tool used to limit and define the participants. These also helped with our welcoming circle time, adding to the children's sense of importance.

Initially, we transported the preschool resources for the twice-weekly sessions. We needed to keep the resources secure from others who used the building. Along the highway were stalls of wooden furniture and doors built by craftsmen from local timbers. Eventually, we purchased a door with a padlock for the storage room from one of the stalls. The woven mats, two little tables, and boxes of resources could then be accessed by the preschool volunteers who lived there and set up in activity stations before we arrived. The local teachers would eventually run the preschool themselves, so they needed effective strategies put in place.

A large bushy tree grew close to the building. This area hosted a variety of activities; children cooked food there, then later used it as a toilet area. Ginnie was aware of the need for a community-built latrine for the preschool children to use. This was easier said than done and required much prayer.

This experience was so different to my training as a New Zealand early childhood teacher. I was learning so much about cross-cultural education and sharing simple yet profound good news about the God of the Bible. We prayed with the volunteers before teaching, inviting the Holy Spirit into our programme, and ended each session with a prayer of blessing and protection for all the children and volunteers.

Learning and Laughing Through Language

Learning to interact with people at the local market was an interesting and, at times, hilarious or embarrassing experience. Initially, I carried a tiny notebook with me to remind me of numbers and questions to ask, like *"Quanto custa?"* (How much?) or *"Muito caro!"* (Very expensive!). Simple yet useful words were *"mais"* (more) or *"menos"* (less). This convinced the sellers I had a better understanding of the language, and they would keep talking until my face revealed no comprehension. With patience and practise, I progressed to more vocabulary, even simple sentences.

One of my first attempts to ask for tomatoes met with a roar of laughter—the word for testicles sounds very similar to tomatoes! After that, I decided it was safer to simply point to the pile of tomatoes I wanted. For a time, I even gave up eating them.

Meanwhile, at preschool, I discovered another two words that sound similar but have very different meanings. Reaching into the back of the ute, I grabbed the floor mats and passed them to a local, asking, *"Você pode ajudar-me com as estrelas?"* It was one of my first sentences in Portuguese, so I was pleased with myself. However, it was met (once again) with puzzled looks.

Hope, who had come with us that day, came to my rescue. "You asked them to help with the stars! *Esteras* is the word they use here for mats or matting." *Estrelas* and *esteras* sounded so similar to me that it took many times to get the pronunciation correct. But the Mozambicans were always so forgiving, usually with laughter.

Back at Whitewater Farm, I gained more confidence in greeting residents and asking about their health and whether they'd had a good sleep. I was shocked the first time I heard one Mozambican worker reply, "*Constipação.*" Never had I heard such a personal detail about someone's bowels, or so I thought. I excused myself and found Ginnie to clarify the word's meaning.

Laughing, she said, "It's not being constipated, if that's what you are thinking! It just means they are feeling a bit sick with the change in the cooler weather and usually want some headache medicine."

Whew, I'm glad I know about that now!

Every day I prayed, asking God for courage to keep speaking Portuguese. Nothing long or fancy, just a simple, fast prayer. *Help me, God, to learn this difficult language!* Peace restored, I carried on with a light heart and big smile, persisting despite feeling awkward.

Learning essential vocabulary for money transactions and food items kept me busy. Using services such as banking, photocopying, and buying internet credit for my phone in the nearest town all provided opportunities to learn language other than preschool words.

My pocket-sized bilingual dictionary was a handy tool for remote areas like Whitewater Farm where the internet was not reliable enough to check with Google Translate. Other useful items were a small notebook and pen to write down commonly used phrases, greetings, money and time references, numbers, and names of people. I often wore a little waist bag on top of my *capulana*.

The Mozambicans were really forgiving. Portuguese was their

second language too, and they appreciated my efforts to try to learn. That realisation accelerated my learning once I got over myself! Eventually I learned to laugh with them. When my nervousness evaporated, the words came, and speaking became an enjoyable experience. I had to remember that my identity was based around the key truth that God loved me regardless of my performance in language learning. I needed to have patience with myself in the same way that, as a preschool teacher and mother, I was patient with little people learning to speak.

Part 3: First Year as a Missionary

Serving at Whitewater Farm

One of my most hilarious language blunders happened during the first week of dog chores. I strolled over to chat with the young couple who were looking after the seven dogs at Whitewater Farm. After the initial pleasantries of asking about their family and whether they'd had a good night's sleep, I got onto the subject of the dogs.

I had just completed eight weeks of language intensive in Portugal, so I conversed boldly, not preparing beforehand what to say. *"Então eu vou comer os cães. Você não precisa continuar."*

I was surprised to see shocked expressions on their faces. However, it wasn't until later, after they asked Ginnie if the dogs were still alive, that she explained my blunder. I had confidently reported that I'd 'eaten' all the dogs, so they didn't need to look after them anymore!

This type of goof chipped away at my pride. I continually made mistakes, sounding like a young child with basic conversation. It was a "sink or swim" situation: I either locked up in fear or forged ahead with a great deal of humour. I told myself, *Just get over the fear of making mistakes, because it's how we learn.* Easier said than done.

As I stumbled through more mishaps in speaking Portuguese, I was encouraged by a proverb that said pride can bring disgrace, but with humility comes wisdom. *I should possess truckloads of wisdom after this! Hopefully.*

Looking after seven dogs involved many chores. This gave me a chance to practise language with the families on Whitewater Farm and got me into the routine and rhythm of the place. These dogs were an essential part of everyday life. As well as being guard dogs, they spotted snakes and sensed danger while out walking in the bush tracks around Whitewater Farm. (During the dry fire season, these walks also provided an opportunity to spot smoke.)

One day, while I was checking the mango fruits on the trees for ripeness, the dogs took off running and barking ahead of me. Not much further ahead was a metre-long yellow snake! Thankfully, I could see it was dead; a tractor had run over its head that morning. I learned later it was a poisonous puff adder.

The dogs each had their job to do. A dog called Slim, three-legged and skinny but aggressive, performed the role of watchdog on a chain in the backyard. He shared this role with a huge Alsatian named Abrão, who stayed up all night with the night watchman out the front of the main house. Then there was Taz, a lovely collie-type dog, and Zac, a Jack Russell that hunted rodents ruthlessly in the houses. The two pups, Lina and Bella, were females of the same litter. In this part of rural Mozambique, there was no vet to sterilise animals. Part of my job was making sure the females had no boyfriends!

Without a vet to assist with diseases, snake bites, or tick fever, dog attrition was high. People usually started with a sizable number of dogs to maintain enough for security. Some were treated like pets, though. Whitewater Ministries, using donations wisely, had a recipe for making affordable dog food that did not involve buying expensive canned dog food from a city two hours' drive away. I learned to make this and dished it up only in the evening. After a ferocious scrap between two dogs, I learned to chain them up far away from each other when eating.

In the warm climate and with the closeness of the bush, we had to give the dogs regular flea baths. Water was precious, so we were conservative in the bathing of all the dogs. One of the farm workers assisted me with the bigger dogs, which resulted in more language learning, laughter, and wet clothes.

Taking seven dogs for a walk around the three-kilometre boundary of the farm every day developed a close bond between me and them. In those first weeks, I asked Taz the collie, "How could this dog job be useful in bringing God's Kingdom here on earth?"

Though I felt insignificant in my role, the Holy Spirit reminded me that developing patience and humility was essential in serving. Caring for seven dogs daily was an opportunity for these attitudes to grow. He helped me realise that tending to the dogs freed other people to do their appointed mission work. Furthermore, competency with my second language was essential before I could do much else.

Remembering that I was working for the Lord helped me keep the right perspective. I knew in my heart that God had brought me here for His plans and purposes. *Will I discover more about that in time?*

This seemingly menial job taught me how to move safely around Whitewater Farm. I fell in love with this environment. Struggling to converse in a foreign language was exhausting; these afternoon walks created a safe outdoor space to talk and pray to God as I struggled with the challenges of this unfamiliar lifestyle. Plus, these four-legged creatures that God created as 'man's best friend' protected me from snakes or two-legged intruders.

The Whitewater *Escolinha*/Preschool Model

After my language lessons in Portugal, I discovered rural Mozambicans spoke the language in some unique ways. The Portuguese word I'd learned for preschool was *pré-escola*, but Mozambicans in this area called it an *escolinha*. *Bebê* became *bebezinha/o* (baby girl/boy).

Ginnie, Tina, and Hope had made a start with this new *escolinha* project, based around concepts of *Preschool in a Box*, an international curriculum for rural areas. I could see that this programme needed to be culturally appropriate. The local volunteer teachers needed to be trained so they could continue when we weren't there. *I have much to learn!*

Though I loved participating in this cross-cultural programme, my limitations in speaking and understanding Portuguese created feelings of inadequacy. I needed to change the expectations I had of myself. Familiarity with the programme and remembering the songs from last year's visit were some comfort. I reassured myself that I had obeyed Jesus' first command in the Great Commission: 'Go'.

I appreciated the groundbreaking work from Tina, Ginnie, and Hope. We began our preschool sessions with a circle time, introducing everyone using their own names. In this culture, children were often not addressed with their real names, partly because of fear that sorcery would be used against them. Nicknames would be used instead. This presented a problem with the preschool registration process, which we had to overcome. Wearing name tags helped, a new concept for both children and volunteers.

We taught the days of the week through a Portuguese song,

using the shorter Mozambican version: *Domingo, segunda, terça, quarta, quinta, sexta, sábado, e agora outra vez* (Sunday, Monday, Tuesday, Wednesday, Thursday, Friday, Saturday, and now again). I found it easier to remember language through songs. The bilingual volunteer teachers were a great help in bridging the gap between Makua and Portuguese. In another regular song, we passed the Bible around and sang the days of creation. Tina and Ginnie also translated a song about how God sees each child as special and valued.

Soon after returning from Portugal, I learned a new song at a seminar for teachers in a coastal city south of The Big City. I had been hoping to learn something practical I could take back to our *escolinha* at the village. Walking from the seminar to our room, I met a young teacher who spoke English and Portuguese, as well as the local dialect. *How fortunate!*

"Is there an action song I could teach the young children up north in a rural area?" I asked her.

"Yes, what about *Head, shoulders, knees, and toes?* It's one we teach the children here."

It was close to the English version but slightly different, so I recorded the tune on my phone. I was thankful and amazed how quickly God brought that young woman across my path to answer my simple prayer. *Was this another 'human' angel sent to help me?*

When I returned to our model *escolinha*, I was excited to show the *crianças* (children) this new action song. We sat in a circle on the floor with our feet pointing inwards, as I thought this posture would be best to begin teaching an action song. Singing *Cabeça, ombros, joelhos, pés* brought many smiles from the children, who enjoyed this novel experience. We even changed the tempo, from *rápido* (fast) to *lento* (slow). It was satisfying to have contributed to this preschool programme using my developing language.

As I learned more about Mozambican history over the past fifty years, I surmised many children were malnourished not only physically but also emotionally, mentally, and spiritually. All too often, children became orphans through HIV/AIDS or malaria. If they were able to attend the government schools, they were helped enormously by knowing some Portuguese, the official language, which could only be learned at school. Generations of adults had not been able to go to school as children and therefore only spoke Makua. If our preschool experience could introduce this generation of children to some Portuguese before they started school, it would give them a good start in their education. More importantly, we believed they could benefit from knowing that God sees and loves them.

Teaching Volunteers to Make Resources

One of my jobs to help the team was making some resources for the activities. The first resource we needed was a calendar of the days of the week (*calendário dos dias da semana*). We thought having a board with pictures of different activities stuck on and rotated for different weeks would be helpful in organising the sessions for mostly illiterate adults.

Hope and I worked together, using coloured pencils to add colour to the seven days of creation. Tina had brought these pages with her, already illustrated with details for each creation day. During the process of colouring in the day, night, stars, plants, and animals of creation, we conversed in Portuguese. Conversed is a loose term, as our conversation was very basic and repetitive, such as "*O que é isso? Isso é ...*" (What is this? This is a ...).

We wondered how to display our brightly coloured creation days on the rough concrete walls. We asked Andy to drill holes for screws, as nails didn't work, then we tied a cord between two screws. Plastic clothes pegs came in handy to hang the creation days. We soon learned the screws needed to be removed and stored away after each session as they 'grew legs' and vanished before the next session. *Who would have thought two screws could be so valuable?*

The following week, Ginnie presented me with a box of old plastic cases that had previously held VCR video tapes. "These are too good to just throw away. How could they be used at the *escolinha*? Ask Andy if he can use his little angle grinder to cut them into flat sheets."

While I sanded the rough corners, my mind was busy with all sorts of possibilities. Borrowing permanent markers, I wrote large numerals on them. *Now what?* I looked around me for inspiration. Nearby were some plastic clothes pegs. *Aha, a lightbulb moment!* I told Hope, who was also helping, "We could show how many each number represents by attaching pegs to the plastic sheets, or the children could make a path of numbers to walk on."

This type of activity allowed teachers and children the possibility to be creative. Being creative in this context seemed new for them. *What will they think of it? Will they invent a game?*

One resource I'd brought was large pictures of children doing different actions. *The numbers can be used to tell the children how many times to do one of these actions, like jumping.* I was excited to develop a simple resource that could be used in teaching language and maths concepts. Putting up with the itching from sanding plastic was worth it.

Recognition of numbers while practising pencil control and fine motor skills was something that could benefit the preschool children. However, I became aware that paper, which needed to be purchased in a shop, was not a long-term solution. My mind pondered how this simple activity could still be achievable. *What about drawing in the sand or painting with water on the concrete walls? What about chalkboards? Would these ideas be possible in the bush-bush mud huts? Who pays the cost of chalk?*

I asked Ginnie, "Do you think making a template that we could laminate and reuse would work instead of paper?"

It was a good idea but wasn't feasible here. Another option could work, though. Rolls of clear plastic called Duraseal were sold in the Chinese shops. Each A4 paper with numbers or drawn shapes could be covered with this clear plastic. After using felt pens, the children could wipe the plastic-covered paper clean and reuse it.

Working with on-hand materials to create useful resources that would help preschool children when they entered 'big school' gave me satisfaction during my first year.

Ginnie and Tina prepared our first training seminar for families from the bush-bush villages. This was the first time the model *escolinha* would be used as a venue for training. The previous year had been used to create and develop the programme; this year, local volunteers would be trained. I learned how slowly ideas and projects took to materialise in a developing nation.

The families started arriving at the start of a national holiday. It was a tremendous effort and sacrifice for these fourteen men, women, and babies to travel and make time out of their busy life. Ginnie told me they all liked cake, so I made a few large chocolate cakes for the occasion.

The local volunteers at the nearby *escolinha* were by now able to teach and demonstrate the activities used during a typical preschool session, which they had learned earlier in the year. I was involved with providing resources, showing the families how to make items they could make later with the children in their village. I had to prepare notes explaining the activities. Hope came to my rescue when I got stuck.

Serving at Whitewater Farm

We provided sensory learning experiences to provide some understanding of how children learn through visual, auditory, and kinesthetic learning styles. Setting up learning stations for them to rotate proved a popular idea. Supplying books and puzzles created a chance for attendees to try them out for themselves.

It was necessary to make resources that illiterate adults could make and teach. I had been surprised, foraging around the farm, how many different seeds we found that we could use for counting. We had also cut shapes out of card and plastic and collected stones, pens, bottle caps, and the odd bit of rubbish. We traced these materials onto some easily found card to create a matching puzzle activity. I hoped this resource-making experience would show the villagers how to make games with materials found in their villages.

A second teaching and learning experience presented itself during this activity. A woman called Alina was struggling to hold a pen and trace around an object, and I wondered if she hadn't ever held a pen. Later, I learned that she'd had a stroke, losing some movement in one arm. Holding a pencil and drawing were unfamiliar activities, and she could not write her name or even read. She was clearly sad about that inability, but I thought, *Aha, here is a teachable moment!*

As I held the object for Alina to trace around, I explained in my simple Portuguese that we can assist young children or have a more capable child help them with an activity. It's important that we don't do it for them or be too concerned about it looking perfect. By offering to assist them, they are learning while doing the activity themselves and experience a sense of achievement.

Judging by the looks on the women's faces, I sensed this was a new idea and that they understood what I was trying to explain. *Wow, a teachable moment, cross-culturally too!* God must have supernaturally bridged the gap of explaining other aspects of education. How else could they have understood with my limited preschool vocabulary?

After the unit about Creation, we shared how God sees everyone as special and unique. Using a simple portrait drawn on A4 paper, I glued eyes, a nose, a mouth, and hair onto it with local resources. The dried brown bamboo sheaves were perfect for the nose. Whitewater Farm had a supply of crayons from the family, which we used. Another activity was making musical percussion instruments from cardboard rolls using little stones and seeds, then decorating the rolls. These resources complemented the Bible stories. Thinking ahead for sustainability, I wondered how they would supply paper for this activity when we were gone. What could they use instead?

Throughout teaching these activities at the seminar, I was learning how to use Portuguese words in a specific task. It was amazing how communication could still occur through nonverbal methods. Sometimes the cues I understood were embedded in my own culture and not necessarily universal, but laughter and a smile went a long way. I came to realise how much I used English language idioms. My brain would make direct translations as I thought of what to say, but this became challenging when I wanted to explain, for example, 'scarcity', and the phrase 'scarce as hens' teeth' came to mind. I learned to speak very direct, simple sentences.

Everyone seemed to have a great time in learning at this first of many seminars. The chocolate cake and roasted marshmallows added a touch of sweetness on departure day.

A Bush-Bush Seminar

One of our most interesting seminars was in a village about three hours away. A British Land Rover joined our transport team.

Heated discussions about which of the three vehicles were best in this rugged terrain—Toyota, Isuzu, or Land Rover—always brought laughter and bantering.

I enjoyed going out to the bush-bush despite having to wear a headscarf and *capulana* in hot conditions, hanging on for dear life in the vehicle, and using a hole-in-the-ground squat toilet—a position my knees objected to. I loved the open blue skies and waving to children as we drove past huge baobabs.

Ginnie and Tina planned the program, while I assisted by supplying resources to support the teachings. We needed to explain early childhood concepts simply to these preschool volunteers so they could understand how children learned and the different areas of development between birth and six years old. We modelled some activities, challenging the volunteers to figure out what stage of development they suited.

Our local teachers were again up to the challenge of travelling with us to teach the other villagers what they knew. It was a brilliant model of teaching, with the long-term goal of locals carrying on after we had left in the future.

I had been uncomfortable about being supported by donations from folk back home. Now I understood they were sowing into the educational situation here by sending funds to enable us to travel to these places. We were their hands and feet. Whitewater Ministries presented the volunteers with gifts of beans and rice, hoes or axes, and *capulana* fabric to make into uniforms. This meaningful gesture showed them their commitment was valued.

I was having a firsthand experience of lifting rural children out of an impoverished situation by a team effort, local and international. God's love for them seemed a new concept. By sharing practical skills and knowledge, we put words into action. The parents were grateful for any educational opportunity for themselves and the children. Nearly everyone valued a better education for their children, even out in bush-bush villages of simple mud-brick and thatched-roof dwellings.

Organising the preschool resources with Hope, we used a mixture of Portuguese words and pictures to list the contents on each box.

Thinking of the logistics, I asked Ginnie, "How will these resource boxes get to the villages?"

"If one of the Whitewater Farm vehicles is going out there anyway, the exchange can be made. Also, one of our local volunteer residents has a motorbike. He is being trained to be the preschool coordinator and will take the boxes out to exchange them."

We always prayed about how things would work out from our ideas, and God provided an answer just as we needed it. It was a faith-building time for me. In my early morning prayers and devotions, I sang my favourite song, which included the phrase 'I won't be overwhelmed'. *Help me, God, look to You.*

I marvelled at Kevin and Ginnie's ability to manage not only practical farm projects but so many Kingdom-building activities at Whitewater Ministries.

Latrine Building

The tree used by children, including our preschoolers, as a toilet area provided a situation for local partnership to solve. We missionaries could have easily dug and built a latrine for them. However, the goal was for the local preschool team and the parents of the enrolled children to provide for this need.

I was observing the importance of bringing local ownership and responsibility into a situation to avoid the historical response of outsiders coming in, funding, and doing the entire project. It was a demonstration of a 'hand up, not a handout' as opposed to what had happened so often in the past.

Communication was critical for language and understanding cultural practices. For a successful outcome involving partnerships, it was vital to have good communication between English, Makua, and Portuguese speakers. My role was to pray for God's help and share the situation in my newsletters home for partners to pray about.

We were grateful for the few volunteer teachers who could bridge the language barrier of Portuguese with their mother tongue, Makua. Much prayer went into this project from our side of the situation. Eventually, a hole was dug and covered so the children could squat. Before the end of the year, construction of walls, a little door, and a roof of sticks and brush had been completed.

The preschool hosted a celebration of this community's success in supporting the construction process of a private latrine for the children to use while at preschool. The latrine was a benefit to the nearby residents as well. In a community so poor in natural resources and time to work on such a project, this was a significant achievement, and for people to work together was an answer to prayer.

My New Home Completed

With the first single unit almost completed, I would be able to move in soon. Kevin called out to me one morning. "How are you with painting? You could paint the bars in the windows with anti-rust."

I was keen to help. "Sure, I did lots of painting during my yachting days."

Soon after the paint dried, Ginnie found some curtains to keep out the bright full moon. With only a fly screen and no glass in the windows, plenty of dust covered everything inside when the wind blew. I borrowed a mattress and a steel-framed bed with a mozzie net and found locally painted artworks to hang on the walls, making the room feel like home.

The roof tiles were made onsite from concrete. Wood was avoided in construction as insects had a voracious appetite. Only the doors were crafted from wood, using farm trees that were pit sawn by hand into planks. A simple steel bar crossed over the double doors to become a secure lock. Kevin and Ginnie allowed me to keep one of the younger dogs, Bella, as a companion and guard at night, since the dorm complex was a long distance from the main house.

"Here, you might need this as well." Kevin offered me a loudhailer that could send an immediate call for help, as cell phone coverage was patchy.

With these precautions and a developing faith and trust that God would hear my prayers for protection and courage, I mostly slept soundly at night. The drums sounding their messages could still wake me up to wonder what was happening, but now only with curiosity, not fear.

I used a hose and water pump to water my small, thriving garden of silver beet and tomatoes in the goat-enriched compost. Cloudy days meant no solar charging and low battery power, so I depended on the yellow jerry cans carried by farm workers on those days. Practising my newly learned language, I asked, *"Pode ajudar-me? Por favor, este jardim não tem água"* (Can you help me? Please, this garden not have water). Embarrassed by my clumsy language, I was thankful they understood.

I was grateful I did not have to walk to the spring and carry buckets of water on my head as the locals, with excellent balance, did regularly. Naturally, I shared some of the produce with those who helped me with watering. Hope's father was a keen gardener too, so I shared some New Zealand seeds with him. Though my gardening vocabulary grew with these interactions, I was still impatient with my slow progress.

Since the farm's solar system could not handle more refrigerators, Ginnie offered use of the main deep freeze to make my own frozen water bottles so I could keep foods cool in a big chilly bin. I got used to making up just enough powdered milk for my cups of tea and coffee for the day. My treats were muesli, yoghurt, cheese, or nice apples from occasional trips to The Big City.

I stuck laminated photos of family and friends to my wall,

which was a cheerful sight. Playing my ukulele, praying, reading the Bible, and reviewing language lessons from Portugal kept me busy and focused on looking ahead, not behind. For the most part, my days were busy, and I felt a sense of purpose, even when I wasn't always sure what exactly that purpose was. It was a relief to know God had led me here and was continuing to be an ever-present help and guide.

In the mornings, I often sat in a comfortable wooden chair outside the dorm that had a place to put a cup of tea. It took me a few weeks to sit out there at night. My first night outside was incredibly dark, but the stars overhead were sparkling and glorious. I felt privileged to be there, close to God and marvelling at His amazing creation. One of the psalms states God determines how many stars there are and that He knows them each by name. *I cannot begin to fathom the immensity of God.*

Out there with my hot drink, listening to the night noises and soaking in the presence of God, I watched the night sky of stars and planets move overhead. Spotting my favourite constellations always made me feel connected to heaven, no matter whether I was at sea or on a mountain top, here in Africa or back in New Zealand.

Wildlife Outside and Inside

One morning before 7am, during my mundane chore of scrubbing clothes in a tub of cold water, I saw another yellow and brown patterned snake slither along on the ground. *Yikes, that's too close for comfort!* It was a puff adder, like the dead one a few days prior. This one looked longer than a metre. I was immediately reminded of when Jesus reassured his disciples that they had authority to trample on serpents and scorpions and that nothing would hurt

My New Home Completed

them. I paused, pondering whether I should jump up and trample on it.* However, I was content to watch it slither away.

Shortly after that little excitement, I moved something on the ground. Underneath was a scorpion with its tail raised to strike. I had heard that the smaller variety has the biggest sting. After those encounters, I made sure the area outside around my living quarters were swept clean. However, I soon discovered more scorpions hiding inside under buckets and brooms. Eventually, my living quarters became scorpion-free most of the time.

A few weeks later, before going to the weekly prayer time in the garden area, I heard chattering and crashing in the trees. *What is that?* Jumping out of bed, I looked out the window. A troop of monkeys were in the row of trees and bamboo just outside! They were after the mangoes and anything else ripe in the gardens. I had never seen monkeys so close to human habitation. They moved quickly through the treetops and kept us entertained for a while, delaying our prayer time. The dogs all added their barking, so it was a noisy start to the day. They kept coming for a few weeks and then moved off to the next seasonal food supply.

I watched the quick flights of the bats coming and going from a hole in the top of the main house they could get through. Thankfully, there were no bats in my attic! I prayed there would be no predators around at night and kept a big torch with me just in case.

---

* *He replied ..."I have given you authority to trample on* **snakes and scorpions** *and to overcome all the power of the enemy; nothing will harm you."* (Luke 10:19, NIV)

Baptisms

Travelling south to another area, Tina, Ginnie, and I attended a regional literacy seminar, where we considered strategies for teaching in largely illiterate, remote rural areas.

Locally based missionary pastors were training their indigenous pastors in the next step of becoming followers of Jesus Christ. After our conference, we took a bus with other teachers to witness the baptisms of three young men. I felt privileged to witness this.

We had permission from the resort on the Indian Ocean beach to access the water. Crowds of local people and tourists witnessed the baptisms. I pictured a passage in the Book of Acts where three thousand people were baptised after hearing the disciple Peter share what Jesus taught! Even though only three baptisms took place that day, it still was significant in my mind, bringing alive New Testament events in modern times and unifying cultures and people groups around the world.

On a personal level, the day reminded me of my own baptism

Baptisms

on a beach nine years earlier in the northern area of New Zealand, with believers and campground tourists looking on from the shore.

A few months after my arrival, Kevin asked if I wanted to travel in the old Land Rover to a remote village where a church had been planted. It could take two to three hours to get there, depending on the conditions. Ginnie had to stay at Whitewater Farm for other ministries occurring that same day.

Two local pastors Kevin was training accompanied us. They would be baptising five men. I was advised to take my bilingual Bible and handy wipes to keep my hands clean. Other items were important too: a sun hat and mozzie repellent, a diary, and a camera. There was no need for a cell phone, as the reception was poor. I knew by this time to wear my *capulana* and cover my head with a scarf.

After a mug of hot coffee and a breakfast of buns toasted with little fried bananas, we were ready for the day.

Kevin told me, "Take a muesli bar or snack. It needs to be quick and easy to chew."

"Why is that?"

"Lunch can take a while to prepare for all of us. They rely on wood for fuel and clay pots to cook in. Plus, the baptisms will be before the actual church service. And if we need a snack, we don't want to attract attention in a community of hungry children who notice everything! Also, don't forget your water bottle, as their water will most likely cause stomach upsets for us."

"What about eating their food?"

"The food will be okay to eat, as it will be cooked. It's delicious!"

I was so excited to be part of this inland mission trip. From the highway, we crossed the railway lines to head into open country lined with roads that soon became tracks, some of which had been washed out. This was Land Rover country—unless one owned an Isuzu or Toyota 4x4, of course. I had to hang on for dear life as we twisted and turned through ruts, streams, and narrow bush tracks.

Arriving at the church after several hours of driving through narrow bush tracks and dry riverbeds was an unforgettable experience. I had always loved watching *National Geographic* programmes of these sorts of adventures, and I was pinching myself. Finally, I was living the dream! Even more special was the fact it was to a place with followers of Jesus Christ.

The church was quite large, with neatly plastered mud walls, a thatched roof, hand-hewn beams, and narrow benches. Two new pastors, one young man from this village and one from a coastal area, would be doing the baptisms. Another nearby church community joined us for this momentous occasion. There may have been between fifty to eighty people, and the large mud-brick church accommodated us all easily.

A couple of women cooked over stick fires with clay pots balanced on bricks, stirring the food with long wooden spoons. I wondered what was for lunch—but more importantly, where the baptisms would take place, as we had not crossed any rivers.

We walked single file on a narrow track through the *mashambas* (fields) of sesame, maize, and cotton for fifteen minutes to arrive at the baptism site. The women wore bright, colourful *capulanas* with their heads covered in scarves, while the men and children had on their Sunday best clothes, some with zips broken or buttons missing, yet very clean. We turned a corner in the path to see a small brown muddy-looking hole where the baptisms would take place. I had a sobering thought. *Do they drink this water too?* I was thankful for my bottled water in the Land Rover.

The five men getting baptised were very solemn, one of them

Baptisms

much older than the other four. One pastor was wearing a white shirt and tie, as it was a special occasion. However, as he turned to dunk the young man, I noticed the back of his shirt was ripped in a number of places. *Is this his best shirt?* Kevin had some words of knowledge and encouragement, which were translated into Makua for those who didn't know Portuguese.

I was curious why no women were getting baptised and found out later that women were baptised at another time of year.

The young pastors doing the baptising had been students at Whitewater Farm's Bible School. They had made huge sacrifices to study and train to be pastors. Some had to travel two days by bicycle on sandy paths or to walk many kilometres. To see their commitment despite challenging conditions was inspiring. People here in remote Africa answered the same command that Jesus told His disciples in Israel over two thousand years ago.*

When we returned from our walk through the *mashambas* to the church, I noticed some white plastic chairs at the front, facing the believers on wooden benches. Though I knew it was their custom to honour visitors, I didn't feel comfortable in that position. My mind was full of insecurities. *What am I doing sitting in the front? I haven't even been to a Bible college. I'm just a follower of Jesus ... Help me, God, to know when to share an encouraging word.*

Peace filled me with God-focused thoughts. Months of practice helped me read in Portuguese confidently. When my cue came to share a word from the Bible, I felt only a few butterflies in my stomach. *Thank goodness the English text is beside what I'm reading in Portuguese!* One of the younger men translated it further into Makua. It was an amazing experience to be part of a global church of believers.

---

* *Those who accepted his message were baptised, and about three thousand were added to their number that day.* (Acts 2:41, NIV)

The church was filled with dancing lines of women and men and vibrant voices singing Makua or Portuguese songs. They used handmade musical instruments. A bit of metal fastened to wood made a remarkable set of percussion instruments. The metre-long xylophone created out of local hardwood sounded great, and they had also made a drum with skin stretched over the top of an old, hollowed log, and a few sets of shakers out of bottle caps and wire. Being with multicultural believers of Jesus Christ, praising our Lord in their culture and language, was very moving.

Communion consisted of orange-flavoured Raro drink and bits of bread. *Oh no, we are sharing one cup!* Afraid to offend them, I glanced at Kevin for guidance. He sipped a tiny bit, not touching the edge. Thinking of that muddy water source, I prayed for protection from any impurities.

Finally, after a few hours of exuberant singing, preaching by the young pastors, and testimonies from the men who got baptised, it was time for *almoço*, or lunch. Again, we were honoured, eating with the other pastors inside the church off the only little wooden table. Thankfully, we still had our plastic chairs. The rest of the community sat outside on the ground and ate communally. Children peered through the windows and doors to see us eating.

A plate of *xima* was served to the local pastors, as they preferred that to rice. Kevin and I were served an enormous platter of rice with a few small, chopped pieces of chicken in gravy. They wanted to honour us for coming by serving rice even though it was a luxury for their community. The chicken (or rooster, as it happened) had also been killed in our honour. It was humbling to be fed after a long morning by such a materially poor community. They were indeed rich in hospitality.

Relationships Help Grow Language

After my initial goof of declaring I 'had eaten the dogs' instead of 'was feeding the dogs', I continued to visit Ida and her young daughter, Nuza, in one of the farm cottages. I joined them one day at their vegetable plot (*mashamba*), which was close to the Bible School dorm room where I had just moved.

While we were picking leaves and onions, Ida showed me a big brown bean pod that was a bit hairy. She told me it was no good to eat and started itching her skin. Nuza was three at the time and still learning language. When I asked the name of this plant, she pointed to the trees and made motions like an animal. *Do I understand her correctly? A monkey?* With much laughter, I pulled out my little pocket dictionary, amazed to find out these were called 'monkey beans' or *feijão de macaco*.

Ida pointed to my windows and showed me that when the wind blew and the beans were dry, the little hairs would travel into my house and make me itch. *So that's what is causing me to scratch!*

After the gardening lesson, I got busy wiping and sweeping up those little monkey bean hairs and then closed the cloth curtains. What a relief to have understood something so important in my daily living situation. More importantly, it built on our friendship.

Soon after, Ida invited me to spend the morning with her and Nuza as they prepared the main meal of the day. Again, we visited one of their farm garden plots and picked tomatoes, pumpkin leaves, and small yellow potatoes. The dish we planned to make, *matapa*, was a mixture of *couve* (in-season greens), ground raw peanuts, onions, garlic paste, and tomato paste. This would be eaten with *xima* (maize flour), small chunks of waxy potato, and brown beans. In addition, goat meat from the farm would be chopped into little unidentifiable pieces complete with little bones.

As we walked back to their cottage, we picked up sticks for the fire needed to cook the main meal. On the concrete slab in front of Ida's door were three burnt bricks, a well-used wooden mortar and pestle for use while standing, a large woven tray, and a pile of large fresh banana leaves. A large aluminium pot held beans soaking in water, which Ida placed on the bricks for the wood fire to cook. These beans, cooked over an open wood fire, tasted the best ever!

I was curious why Ida didn't use charcoal, as locally made charcoal was frequently the primary source of fuel to cook on. Big bags of charcoal could be purchased alongside the road. Ida may have been out of charcoal or even money to purchase it, which was why we gathered wood for cooking. I wondered about the long-term effects of gathering wood and making charcoal and whether it was contributing to the encroaching desert around us.

The forests in Mozambique, Whitewater Farm residents had explained when I arrived, were threatened by three activities: inefficient use of the timber resource through charcoal making, using wood for cooking, and building wood-framed huts that were regularly destroyed by seasonal cyclones. People living in poverty in this area were mostly illiterate and struggling for survival, so conservation practices were unknown. The surrounding areas lacked trees and had mostly sandy soil. I was beginning to understand some of the complexities of African problems. No wood meant no fire and no cooked meals to eat.

While the beans cooked, we shelled a big bowl of small, farm-grown peanuts. Some of these peanuts were sold commercially, and some were shared out amongst the local residents on the farm. We made a pile on a large woven tray, rubbed them, and blew off the little papery skins. About an hour later, we had a bowl of shelled and skinned peanuts that we put into the mortar and pestle and pounded into a flour.

Throughout this time, we sat chatting on a thin woven mat on concrete, and I learned more Portuguese. As numbness crept in, I also learned that my sixty-plus-year-old body did not like to sit on flat ground on a mat too long. I soon found a little block of wood to perch on!

Ida stood to pound the many cloves of freshly peeled garlic in her large mortar and pestle. This made a paste that she added to oil in a pot with finely chopped sweet red onions. The big banana leaves were used as clean areas to prepare the food on.

Ida gave three-year-old Nuza little jobs to do, like scooping out seeds from the papaya. When she gave her the only sharp knife to cut the papaya into little pieces, I gasped, quietly horrified that this little person was in charge of a very sharp knife. *Is she safe using that?* My eyes must have flashed in alarm because Ida assured me that, under supervision, children learned to handle knives. If they got cut, it only happened once, and then they learned! This was considered a minor risk and was how very young children were taught. I remembered my first time seeing a three-year-old girl with a small tin of water balanced on her head following her mother along a busy highway. The phrase *'Not wrong, just different'* came to mind.

The thinly sliced sweet onions, garlic paste, and tomato paste went into another pot. A short time later, chunks of fresh, slightly ripe papaya were added. Meanwhile, Ida had rolled up the bunch of green leaves and soaked them in a pot of cold water. She threw out that green water, saying it took the bitterness out of the leaves. *Am I understanding her correctly?*

After adding the greens and ground peanuts, the last to go in the pot was a handful of dirty-looking chunks of locally harvested sea salt, then everything cooked down into a green mash. The brown beans cooked some more, with the smoke from the wood adding the unique flavour. Meat and potatoes completed the dish. When they were ready to have *almoço* (the main midday meal), the *xima* (maize flour) was cooked with water over the fire.

Ida had produced a labour-intensive yet filling and nutritious meal that was simply delicious. *So this is what subsistence living looks like, growing all their food for survival and cooking it.* I was aware this was a common lifestyle for Africa's rural poor, but to experience a large part of their day was sobering.

Without refrigeration, there was no storage for leftovers, so the main meal had to be prepared daily. Lunch leftovers were eaten in the evening. When Marcos came home from working on the farm, they sat on the floor eating together and then, after a short nap, resumed working. I was surprised how much they would eat, with the plates being piled high with food. They worked hard physically, getting up at 4.30am when it was cooler, so they needed a big meal.

It was an eye-opener to see how much of their life was consumed by repetitive hard labour. Yet they still wanted to volunteer for the *escolinha!*

Relationships Help Grow Language

Growing in Confidence

Midway through the year, I became aware that my Portuguese language exposure was less frequent than I needed. There were many English speakers on the farm, and the farm workers only spoke Makua. If Portuguese was needed, the more experienced residents often did the talking. *If I could stay in town longer, maybe my language would have a better chance of improving?*

The remoteness of Whitewater Farm had challenges for my transportation needs. Reliance on being a passenger in one of Whitewater Farm's utes, often on strict time schedules, meant I couldn't linger in the open-air markets or town shops to practise speaking Portuguese. Alternatively, I could take a taxi. However, I observed the *chapas* (taxi vans) flying along the highway, crammed full of people and travelling at an alarming speed. Horrific crashes along the busy highway were a sobering sight. After a few months of taking *chapa* rides to town for language lessons, I felt hesitant to continue.

Ginnie came to me one day with a suggestion. "Carlos, Whitewater Farm's foreman, is bilingual with Makua and Portuguese. He could help you after his jobs as long as you pay him and prepare your own lessons. This could be a solution for both of you, as Carlos needs some extra money."

"Anything that could improve my language sounds good to me!"

Carlos spoke zero English, but by this time, I knew enough Portuguese that we could understand each other to some degree. The resources I'd brought from Portugal were invaluable, as they helped to structure the lessons. For a few weeks, it was a productive time, meeting for forty-five minutes after 3.30pm.

Sadly, things changed. Carlos wasn't always at work. His phone was often out of credit, so communication wasn't possible. Our meetings became infrequent. Fortunately, one of the best books I'd read before going into this long-term cross-cultural situation was *Foreign to the Familiar: A Guide to Understanding Hot and Cold Climate Cultures* by Sarah A. Lanier. This book defused a lot of misunderstanding and frustrations from unmet expectations. However, it didn't help with my language learning. I had a growing inner conviction that I was destined to be in Mozambique for longer than a year, so I wanted to pursue language learning for the longer term.

After some months, I got to drive the trucks around Whitewater Farm roads. With growing confidence, I drove for some Mercy Mission trips that were close by and to preschool sessions up the road. Even though I was an experienced driver, the erratic traffic on the roads and the off-road conditions still required prayer before, during, and after the journey.

An emergency soon put me to the test.

"Quickly, a mother with a baby dehydrated by vomiting and diarrhoea needs our help," Ginnie said. She asked for volunteers from those who weren't involved in the baby-feeding programme. It was not possible for the mother and baby to go to the hospital; it was too far away, and the baby was too sick.

"I can drive, but I need someone to show me where to find them," I offered.

"Take Andy off the building site, as his other role is in Mercy Missions, and he's trained in first aid," Ginnie suggested.

The location was through many tracks in between multiple huts, and only local knowledge could find it. Hope knew the area, so she volunteered to accompany us too. Reassured, I still sent a bullet prayer to God. *Help!*

Andy grabbed an electrolyte solution and the metal drip holder. Driving off the highway and weaving the truck through closely packed mud huts was challenging. Without Hope to guide us, it would have been impossible to locate the mother and baby.

The mother attended Hope's church (*igreja*) with her children, so we all prayed for healing while Andy hooked up the electrolyte solution. Looking at the modern health equipment inside this dark windowless mud hut, I thought, *What a contrast of cultures!* Andy's Portuguese was better than mine, while Hope could converse in Makua with the mother and explain everything. But we all were united as we prayed in our various languages, believing God heard our prayers.

Again, with Hope to navigate, I was able to drive out and return to Whitewater Farm. We got word shortly after that the baby had recovered. Basic first aid and prayer were simple solutions to a family living in poverty, and I loved seeing God's quick answer firsthand!

The following week, I drove a mother and her baby to the local hospital for treatment. I had visited it before with other missionaries, but this time I noticed more. The hospital appeared rundown, crowded with relatives that lived in the rooms. Most family members were outside, cooking their loved ones' meals, as the hospital provided no food.

I hope I don't need to go to the hospital while I'm here! But soon after my delivery of patients to the hospital, I became not just regular sick, but super sick. I was shivering all over, could hardly move a limb, and was feverish with chills. Thankful that I was not alone, I barely managed to message Ginnie for help. She brought Andy, trained and experienced in tropical healthcare.

The thermometer showed a high fever, and with the intense shivering, they thought I could have malaria. *What? How could that be?* I had been taking daily malaria-prevention medication. Suddenly, I remembered that when I visited Marion on the coast for three days, I had forgotten to take my meds with me. The mozzie net didn't cover me very well, resulting in buzzing bugs around me every night.

Ginnie knew from her fifteen years of experience in this country that the malaria test at the hospital wasn't always accurate. Besides, it was nearly dark. She and Andy suggested we assume it was malaria and immediately take the anti-malarial drug for treatment. Fortunately, thanks to generous donations, I'd been able to afford an emergency supply. The rural poor people here could not pay for it, so they were sick for weeks or died from it. I was in bed for days, hardly moving and totally exhausted, sipping water or a warm broth Tina made for me.

At that time, no vaccine was available for malaria and only preventive measures could help avoid it. Mozambique was a high-risk place for malaria, with the northern and coastal regions most high. USAID reports that in 2015, malaria accounted for 29 percent of deaths overall and 42 percent of deaths in children under five. It was a serious disease that was prevalent in our area. Fortunately, the antiviral that I took, along with the prayers for healing, got me over the worst of it, but it was a couple of weeks before I fully recovered.*

There was never a dull moment, and there were always different ways to serve in this large team. Along with my language sessions, preschool planning, resource making, and dog chores, I might help to prepare a meal for visiting pastors or missionaries or bake a chocolate cake for the Bible School graduation. Weeding the lawn, picking cashew fruits off the trees, practising my ukulele, or finding someone to talk or pray with kept me focused and busy.

Each month, I wrote informative newsletters with photos and

---

* *The Holy Spirit answered me, "Do not fear! For I am with you; do not be dismayed, for I am your God. I will strengthen you and help you."* (Isaiah 41:10, NIV)

prayer and praise points for my supporters and churches. This required time to download photos from my camera into orderly folders on my laptop, so I had to be efficient in recording the events and finding the right photos. Emailing them in batches required a trip to town, as the WiFi there was better than at Whitewater Farm. We would have a catchup and cup of tea with WO field leaders Saul and Sarah, who had a house in town.

Making business trips to The Big City for immigration reasons or shopping at a small supermarket stocked with South African goods meant a day filled to the brim with items on long lists to find and people to catch up with. A visit to the Bible Translation Centre was interesting, with multicultural short- and long-term missionaries coming and going. A Child Safety seminar by World Outreach informed missionaries from the area on this growing concern. A couple from Malawi who operated a Christian school travelled three days by bus to attend. It was so encouraging to see and hear other people's stories of teaching and sharing the Gospel of Jesus Christ in their location and culture.

Encouraged by a New Zealand Missions Pastor

At times, Whitewater Farm hosted pastors from New Zealand to support the missionaries in the area. The overseer/pastor for missions in the Assemblies of God (AoG) visited while I was there. *This is really timely!* I was sensing a crossroads situation.

Pat introduced himself and made time for us to chat and assess my internship experience. I felt immediately at ease with him, especially after we discovered our somewhat similar journey before we had surrendered our lives to Christ. We opened our meeting with prayer, seeking the wisdom of the Holy Spirit.

"So how's it all going here?" he asked.

I shared my triumphs, struggles, and doubts about language

learning, along with my heart about being here. I believed there was more for me but had doubts about my abilities. "I even wonder if maybe I'm getting too old!" I admitted reluctantly. Pat told me about his parents being missionaries in Uganda for many years and even going back in their eighties to serve and teach. *Twenty years older than I am now!* His experience, guidance, and examples of other missionaries' struggles helped me to see a better perspective of myself.

By the end of our meeting, I felt encouraged to continue, listening and praying about my future in Mozambique. *I am so grateful to be part of a church and mission movement that offers mentoring along the way.*

Marion's Good Samaritan Health Clinic Opens

On my trip the previous year, I visited one of Marion's Good Samaritan clinics with its gardens for growing trees, herbs, and vegetables for various herbal remedies. This year, Marion invited me to attend the opening of a new inland outpost. She loaded up the little Datsun truck with her healthcare workers (*socorristas*) and nearby Mozambican friends. The team brought sacks of food and huge pots to cook the lunch of beans and rice.

On the back of her little pickup was a new bicycle for the health workers, who needed to access really remote residents. As this village was in the bush-bush, we had a 4.30am start. The night before, I set out what I needed to wear and carry: my *capulana*, headscarf, water bottle, camera, notebook, and handy wipes.

The rugged red dirt road through green fields of sugarcane and pineapple plants provided dramatic scenery. I saw occasional baobab trees in the distance. The sight of these giant, solitary trees, looking as though they were growing upside down with their roots to the sky, filled me with awe. They were an impressive sight and

Relationships Help Grow Language

probably served as landmarks when travelling dirt paths through flat land without any major landmarks, except for these trees appearing like sentinels.

Finally, we arrived at a little village. Children ran alongside the truck and waved in excitement. The residents of this mud-hut village greeted us with a generosity of spirit and delightful smiles.

A special table with four plastic chairs was set up for Marion, me, the district's government health official, and Papa Camilo, who opened with prayer. The celebration began with traditional Makua singing and a shuffling type of dance. Young men kept the beat on wooden drums, and boys used bottle-cap shakers. The *socorristas* performed a short skit in Makua (as few people here knew Portuguese) about the Good Samaritan story from the Bible. They each wore a red T-shirt with *Medicina Natural* on the front and a verse adapted from the Bible on the back: *Deus nos amou, assim também devemos amar-nos uns aos outros*. In English, this translated to 'God loved us, so we should also love one another'. They wore these as their uniform when on duty as healthcare workers.

The official opening of a Good Samaritan outpost health clinic represented hard work and dedication. Over a period of two years, the *socorristas* learned how to make natural remedies and treat simple wounds and abscesses as well as how to study God's Word so they could pray for people if requested. The remedies needed to be within the budget of these very poor subsistence farmers. Every clinic had an orphans' feeding programme, as many orphans were malnourished. The healthcare workers appeared confident and excited to be part of this community-based healthcare venture. Hospitals and doctors were either not affordable or simply too far away.

The little concrete-block clinic, with its red tin roof and white walls with red trim, was the most substantial building in the village. The cross of Christ, an outline of a hand, and the Portuguese translation of *The Good Samaritan, Natural Medicine Relief Port* were painted in red on the walls. Inside the clinic were simple wooden shelves with bottles of remedies and small bags of dried herbs to purchase.

Marion had mentioned that she hoped to include a one- or two-day seminar for teaching the *socorristas* in these rural clinics a simple programme for orphans. This would include Bible stories, songs, and an activity to enrich the children's lives who were not able to attend school.

Marion had brought a few herbs to plant near the clinic as a start to their gardens. The children watered these symbols of hope. I wondered how the plants would ever survive in this arid, parched soil. The Good Samaritan's main clinic, hours away, would supply them with herbs and roots that were dried and prepared for the recipes of tinctures and syrups until their own plants were established.

I felt so privileged to see this inspiring, practical outreach. I pondered whether I could be part of training *socorristas* for the orphans' programme. *Is this God's best for me at this time? Is it something I could help with?* At this early stage of my language, I had doubts, but my spirit seemed to tell me otherwise. *Yes, in God's timing!*

Taking the Jesus Film to the Bush-Bush

A few months after the bush-bush baptisms, a pastor invited Kevin to share the Gospel by bringing the Jesus film in the Makua language to his own village. I was thrilled to be invited. Joining us were three Mozambican women with their young children. They had trained for six months with YWAM (Youth with a Mission), an interdenominational Christian evangelistic mission organisation.

Kevin explained that we would drive for a couple of hours

through areas washed out by flooded streams and over remnants of dirt roads. These paths were mainly used by locals on bicycles and foot traffic, as well as women carrying firewood, water, or huge bundles of dried grasses for roof thatch on their heads. Children either pushed handmade toys made from salvaged rubbish or carried small items on their heads too.

It was another 4.30am start, cool and just getting light. The Land Rover's roof was packed with an outdoor movie screen, tents, food, chairs, and some basic technical equipment. Slim, short adults and children squeezed inside the vehicle.

After a few outreach day trips to the bush-bush, I knew to pack certain items. However, this was my first overnight adventure, so I added a head-torch, mozzie repellent, and a hooded sweatshirt for the cooler evening air. Ginnie loaned me a thin roll-up foam mat for sleeping on the ground. My 'sleeping bag' was a cotton duvet cover. Most importantly, I packed my pocket-sized Portuguese dictionary, a notebook with Makua phrases I had collected, and my bilingual Bible.

As I faced the prospect of a rugged Land Rover journey, a night of sleeping on the ground in a tent with three women and children, and using the bush toilet (a hole in the ground), I was reminded of a promise in the Bible—when God calls you to a particular task, He will also provide the strength for it. I prayed fervently that God would provide for me what I required and, more importantly, that hearts would be receptive to the Jesus film.

As we arrived at Pastor Cola's village, we passed his little mud-brick church. I was surprised to see a simple sign painted over the door: *Igreja Evangélica Assembleia de Deus* (Evangelical Church of the Assembly of God). The words had been carved into the smooth mud plaster and then painted with a whitewash. There had been Catholic churches in years past with the Portuguese colonists. However, the sign notified visitors this was an evangelical AOG church. I found that interesting, as my sending church was also of the Assemblies of God denomination.

A group of men were outside Pastor Cola's house, ready to unpack and help set up the outdoor theatre on the dusty, red ground. The wooden benches, woven reed chairs, and white plastic chairs we had brought were set out and the white screen tied up between a metal pole frame. Kevin got busy unpacking and connecting the technical equipment. The Acer laptop would be the source of the Jesus film, using an amplifier and generator. Shy children stood around, watching. It was such a contrast to see twenty-first century technology while, in the distance, women stooped over clay pots set over smoky fires, much as they had done for centuries.

Many helpers climbed up onto the truck and set up the four-person tent. I needed my foam mattress close to the tent door. During the night, with my small torch dimmed, I would be checking out the stars as I made my way carefully to the bush 'loo'. I didn't want to trip over anyone going out of the tent.

The women sharing the tent would sleep on the ground on straw mats (*esteiras*), without pillows, covering themselves with thin *capulanas*. I rolled my clothes into a pillow and was thankful for Ginnie's foam mat. I put my head-torch nearby. Happy with my preparations, I watched Kevin and Pastor Cola finish setting things up for our cinema night.

As soon as it was dark, the movie displayed on the white sheet. Dozens of people, who had walked from neighbouring areas, watched it intently. It was dubbed in Makua, which I found interesting to follow. After the movie, there was a time of prayer and reflection, with heads bowed.

Many women and young girls had worked steadily to cook a meal of beans, *xima*, and rice. One scrawny rooster was caught when we arrived. Its head was chopped off and it was cut into tiny pieces. I felt humbled that they shared what little they had with us.

Relationships Help Grow Language

Someone gave thanks to God in Makua, and finally by 8.30pm, we ate a delicious, filling meal. The open fire, stars shining overhead, and shared meal brought us all together, despite language and cultural differences. It was a wondrous moment, forever etched in my mind.

A light fog rolled in, hiding the trees and bushes around us and bringing chillier air. Kevin explained, "The locals call this the *kisimba*. With the dry fire season approaching, it creates a light dew on everything before the sun burns it off in the morning."

"Thanks for inviting me to come," I said. "It's been an unforgettable experience to see how the Gospel is shared with technology and film. What a long day! I'm ready for bed."

I waved to the others. "*Até amanhã. Deus abençoe você.*" (See you tomorrow. God bless you.) Then I realised they wouldn't understand what I said since nearly all were Makua speakers. I think they understood my sentiments, anyway. My tent companions were already fast asleep after the warm meal.

I had located the toilet during the daylight hours. I noticed it was rather small, but then I wasn't an expert in these structures in the bush. At night, it seemed particularly small. I had to crawl in, locate the hole, and crawl out again. Thankful for my supply of wet wipes, I cleaned my hands. Back in the tent, I resumed my sleep.

Even though I was up with the roosters crowing, someone was already boiling water on the smoky outdoor fire for a big pot of tea. This time, I drank it their way, with a few spoons of sugar stirred in. We had brought some bread buns to share. Normally they would eat leftovers from the night before or a dried manioc root, filling but not so nutritious. Breaking off some bread, I shared it with the children who were up early. Their eyes conveyed that this was a treat for them.

When the others were awake, I commented on the little brushy, covered toilet. The women collapsed into laughter. I was embarrassed, but after being here five months, I had learned to laugh with them. It turned out that the little hut had been abandoned by adults and was only used by young children. The newer ablution area with a shower and toilet was partially completed, with mud-brick walls and a curtain door. But because there was no roof on it, I'd thought it wasn't in operation yet. As I looked at the tiny hut in the daylight, I gasped. *No wonder I was crawling on my knees!*

Showing the Jesus film in such a remote area became a cherished memory. Pastor Cola was very grateful for this visual Gospel in their mother tongue. *What will be the outcome of this?* After planting the seed of truth about Jesus Christ with that viewing, Pastor Cola might see its 'fruit'. Whatever we bring, God can use it for His plans and purposes.* We don't have to be super talented; we just need to be willing to follow where God leads.

I learned that my ability to cope with more than one overnight stay in the bush was limited. But how thankful I was to have been part of that mission adventure.

October/November: FIRE Season and Mangoes!

Clear blue skies for months eventually resulted in a hot, dry season with tinder dry grasses and brush that took only a spark to set alight. We were always on the lookout for any sign or smell of smoke, as acres of dry bush surrounded Whitewater Farm. The cashew and mango trees and the 120 goats were a source of employment and income for the local village. A major highway cut through Whitewater Farm, so a cigarette tossed out the window of passing vehicles could spread rapidly, especially with any wind.

---

* *Go into all the world and preach the gospel to all creation. Whoever believes and is baptised will be saved.* (Mark 16:15–16a, NIV)

Near the end of September, around midday, I spotted smoke and raised the alarm.

Kevin shouted, "Hop in the big water truck and follow the men."

The younger men swatted the brush and grass fires with old tyre flaps nailed to long poles. The rough vehicle track around Whitewater Farm became a firebreak to work around. Being on the edge of internet reception, we weren't sure how quickly our messages would reach our prayer teams: "Please pray for a lack of wind, for rain, or for the *kisimba* with its damp dew to smother the grasses during the night."

We kept fighting the fires all day until we finally put it out at 6pm. Through the night, we continued praying that it would not come near the buildings or cashew orchards. We woke up to see foggy dew covering the dry scrub like a wet blanket. On my lips immediately came the words, "Thank you, God, for hearing our prayers."

One fire was memorable, but for another reason. Instead of driving the water truck, I was swatting little grass fires with tyre rubber nailed onto a sturdy stick. By late afternoon, the men had contained the larger fuel areas, and the fire was under control. Excitement and laughter came from the men, who said they had caught a large *lagarto* (lizard), indicating its length was about a metre long.

As dinner approached, they came over to the main house with a bowl of the cooked lizard in a broth. I was shocked to notice the scales were still on it! I bravely tried a taste, but I can't say I liked it. They laughed, surprised that I had eaten some of it. They considered it a delicacy.

Later, I shared with Hope that I had tried the *lagarto*. Amused, she told me that local farmers ate rats too. However, she specified they were not the rats found in town or around people's habitations.

The locals built special tunnels in their *mashambas* to trap bush rats, then roasted them on a fire. These provided protein when people couldn't afford fish, chicken, or goat meat. I saw these rats for sale alongside the road on long skewers, roasted and butterflied out on the poles. I never tried them, but I thought they might have tasted like rabbit.

The mangoes were also ripening in this hot, dry season. Whitewater Farm had a vast variety of large mature mango trees. I got to know the different varieties, eating my favourites. Every afternoon, I took the dogs for a walk around the property, a couple of kilometres of sandy tracks. Whenever I discovered perfectly ripe mangoes on the ground, I peeled them with my teeth, munching on them with juice running down my chin.

Little did I know I was slowly developing an allergy to them. After a few weeks, each time I ate mangoes, my lips got swollen and numb. Then one eye swelled up slightly. When my tongue and throat got itchy, I realised I had a serious problem! After this discovery, I found other in-season fruits to enjoy. The big lychee trees were very old but still bore fruit, while 'blackberries' hung from the branches of a mulberry tree. Desserts were only baked on the weekends when there was time, so I combined mulberries with apples for a fruit pie. What a treat!

Preparations for Leaving

Although my internship was coming to a close, I sensed my stay in Mozambique was not yet at its end. I prayed for direction and clarity and sought guidance from seniors in the World Outreach mission field. We considered several options for 2015 with a focus on me developing better Portuguese, as it was essential for relationship building and sharing the Good News of Jesus Christ.

Ginnie suggested, "Why don't you return to Portugal for five months of intensive language training?"

"That's a possibility, as my permanent residency visa for Mozambique doesn't expire until the end of April next year," I replied. "If I stay in Mozambique, though, I could attend a local six-month YWAM discipleship training course, building language skills as well as providing Bible studies with evangelising and discipling in the upper northern areas." *I also need to renew my full New Zealand teacher's registration, so that when I permanently return from the mission field, whenever that might be, I can have employment again.*

Kevin pointed out that I would need to apply for a three-year WO full mission partnership when I returned to New Zealand during the wet months of December and January. So much to think about!

Initially, I thought I was to assist in the preschool situation in Mozambique. Little did I know that the *escolinha* training would provide broader opportunities ahead. Many times, I wondered if I was doing enough. I was exercising patience, listening, and obeying the direction I believed God was leading me. Mostly, it was step by step, bit by bit.

My idea of being a missionary overseas was changing too. Near the end of my season at The Farm, after the internship review with Kevin and Ginnie, I met with the WO leadership teams for debriefing. They encouraged me to consider other possibilities since I had a teachable attitude and had come a long way since the start of the internship.

Kevin commented, "You were made for missions!"

I wasn't feeling very 'successful' and even wondered what that meant or looked like. I found myself despairing as to my effectiveness when I compared myself to other people's ministries. I still felt inadequate as a single older woman. My mind was telling me I hadn't led anyone to accept Jesus as their Saviour nor baptised or discipled anyone. I was also disappointed that my language wasn't as fluent as I was hoping for.

However, deep within my spirit, I knew God had not given up on me. I believed He had brought me here through extraordinary provision. Despite my doubts, I remembered that His Word said His ways are higher than my ways. I knew He loved me despite what I did or did not do! His Word spoke to me and reassured me, so I had the peace that surpasses all human understanding.

I stumbled across a Bible verse that spoke wisdom about not comparing oneself to others. The sensitive and wise counselling from the WO leaders in Africa suggested a more positive reflection of my progress. Maybe I was too critical of myself and unrealistic of the outcomes in only one year. Maybe God was doing an inward 'work' in me.

Through their eyes, the leaders helped me see some progress since my arrival. I was part of the team; I had upskilled locals in preschool skills; my language was improving; I was driving the Land Rover; and I was praying with others and ministering to sick people out in villages. Comparing all that to my total dependence on others when I arrived, I was indeed developing. I loved being here and felt I was to stay longer, but I didn't know what that would look like.

After listening to my concerns and hearing my heart, the WO leaders presented me with an exciting third option. A woman called Anya who lived with her family in a nearby town had schooled Sarah and Saul's sons in Portuguese when they were growing up here.

Saul told me, "We know Anya well and will take you to meet her before you return to New Zealand. How about this weekend?"

Anya was a mature Portuguese-speaking woman who had taught language to missionary kids and Peace Corps workers over the past twenty years. She did not know English at all. Her brother and his Makua wife sometimes lived with her if their traditional house was damaged by seasonal floods or cyclones. Anya had raised her sister's children in years past and now looked after her brother's children.

Andy and Tina offered to take me into town. They had shopping to do, and we all had newsletters to send via the internet. *How amazing is that? Things are moving into place quickly!* This exciting possibility was another example of God working things out far more abundantly than we can ever ask or imagine.

We parked outside the rundown concrete building. Huge

rubbish heaps piled up, blocking the road access. The only rubbish collection for the town was done infrequently by a tractor and dump truck, with a handful of men with shovels.

A smiling Anya met me, her shy three-year-old nephew hiding behind her skirt. I liked her immediately.

Discussing details with Sarah there to interpret meant there was little chance of misunderstanding each other. Anya was willing to take me on and assist with my day-to-day language lessons. *Woohoo!* I would pay her rent and live there in my own room as part of the family. I added separate fees for language lessons five days a week to my budget. Anya would do all the cooking with recipes from her family's Portuguese restaurant. *Another woohoo!*

Anya had furniture I could borrow for as long as I needed it. The single wooden bed with woven rope only needed a new foam squab, which I could purchase. Anya showed me drawers, a desk for me to study at, and a huge wooden wardrobe from her family. My bedroom faced into the courtyard area and was furthest from the street noise.

Cedru, a Makua house worker, attended to most of the chores. Anya's family had employed Cedru full time for decades. I noticed buckets of water in the bathroom next to my bedroom and wondered why they were there. The porcelain bathtub, toilet, and sink looked rather worse for wear. Anya, with Sarah translating, explained in Portuguese that once the Portuguese left in 1975, no water was piped in. Water needed to be fetched by Cedru in large containers when the courtyard tank ran empty.

Power was intermittent as people illegally wired into power lines that often got overloaded. WiFi was sporadic, and the windows had no glass, only screens and bars. Anya cooked on a charcoal stove in the courtyard since her gas stove had been stolen in years gone by. Though this house wasn't a mud hut, running it was still labour intensive.

Preparations for Leaving

The building was close to the markets. *After my daily lessons, I can practise around town. It will be a total language immersion experience!*

A large courtyard filled with rusty old vehicles, including a 1954 VW bug and a tractor, was part of the premises. Wandering goats found their way inside and nibbled at anything. The family used to operate a Portuguese-style bakery next to the restaurant, but it was now derelict.

In past years, Sarah had trained Mozambicans in preschool teaching and had a vision for continued training of preschool volunteers, a new healthcare programme for young women, and discipling in Bible studies. Anya suggested to Sarah that they hold the workshops in the old restaurant part of the building.

This presented a fantastic opportunity for me to return, continue with preschool training, and build on friendships already begun. But one of the amazing things they suggested was the possibility of me buying a motorbike so I could visit a preschool on the other side of town.

Sarah asked me, "Would you like to be part of training up some volunteers to start an *escolinha* there next year?"

In a heartbeat! Saul and Sarah had previous experiences of travelling by motorbike in the area and wanted to purchase a bike next year for one of their pastors to visit remote areas. They offered to help set me up with a bike as well if I could raise the funds to purchase one by the time I returned. *Should I tell them I've only been a passenger on motorbikes? I wonder if they can teach me how to ride too, Lord!*

I was really excited about this solution for me to continue what had been started during the past year. There would be far more language practice and cultural learning in this situation. I looked forward to continuing my journey with excitement and a growing optimism about what God was leading me into for next year. *But will my sponsors be on board with this?*

I was so thankful for World Outreach missions, Whitewater Ministries, and Kevin and Ginnie, who had taken me on as an intern. With all my heart, I believed God was still leading me and had more for me here. I was learning to trust Him for my direction and provision, albeit with some lingering doubts. *Will He provide for everything, even funds for a motorbike?*

Packing Up for the Rainy Season

The rainy season, also known as the hunger season, often brought flooding and cyclones. The local population usually hibernated inside their houses. It was a lean time of year for food, as the crops hadn't yet produced.

The weather became cloudy and sudden huge thunderstorms drenched us in the afternoons. The first week of thunderstorms brought with it a tragic end for three people known by residents of Whitewater Farm, who were struck by lightning and killed. *Life can change quickly. I wonder if they were believers in Jesus Christ.*

The cloudy weather also brought a decrease in solar energy storage; this meant the water pumps wouldn't always work and lighting was dim. Once again, the yellow jerry cans were filled with water from the well, ready for when the pumps failed. We prepared our candles, matches, and torches. Cell phones were charged up and used with caution, as the electricity supply could vanish at any moment.

In November, we worked together to finish jobs around Whitewater Farm and retrieved the resources for the preschools, which would be closed during this time. Ginnie organised their packing and storage. I drove the Land Rover truck with two young men to load up plastic boxes with locked lids to keep rodents or insects out.

Preparations for Leaving

A few days later, I took one of the young women teachers to pick up the tables and gate.

The fleas in this hot, humid weather were also increasing. Carlos and I bathed all the dogs and their bedding. We washed the verandas and the dogs' mats and towels. Fleas can be so debilitating, and the dogs were a valuable part of life there.

As we were washing the dogs, we had a visit from the local police. Every year or so, they located all foreign people on long-term visas. We presented our passports with the DIRE visas and other documentation and also blessed them with free Gideon Bibles.

Roadblocks frequently stopped us in various districts, and officials checked our documentation. Giving little Gideon Bibles with a friendly smile and sometimes a prayer eased our transit through many areas.

Saul and Sarah came by with their truck and helped me transport my belongings from Whitewater Farm to Anya's home in town. I was thrilled that the dream God had put in my heart as a teenager to go to Africa and help people was continuing to grow. Loading up the truck with personal items and moving them into my next residence was such a practical promise from God. I could return to my New Zealand community of supporters and intercessors with renewed enthusiasm and a developing plan for further mission ventures.

Carlos and Ida would stay behind with other residents to look after the property and dogs while we were all back in New Zealand, England, or Scotland. After finally saying our goodbyes to our Mozambican friends, we piled into the truck with our baggage to head to The Big City. It was a quiet two-hour journey. We were shattered mentally and physically from packing up.

After dropping the truck off at the Bible Translation Centre, we arrived at the airport by taxi early enough to treat ourselves to a local meal of BBQ chicken, rice, and ice-cold Cokes. Well-fed and rested, we hugged and prayed for our safety back to our countries of origin. For most of us, the following eight weeks would involve preparation, gathering supplies, reconnecting with supporters, renewing friendships, and visiting family before returning for another year in Mozambique.

Home for Christmas and a Surprise Visit

What a relief! I exited the arrival terminal at Auckland Airport, finally home on New Zealand soil after four airports and many hours. My good friend Kelly greeted me, loaded up the luggage, and drove north to her house, where she gave me a bedroom to call home.

I was astounded by the deserted state of the countryside after my time in Africa. "Where is everyone? In Africa, a person could suddenly appear out of the landscape, or there'd be some signs of houses with smoke rising. It looks like a big park or reserve here."

The rolling hills were green, lush, and peaceful. The sun was bright and clear. Fat cows and sheep were well-fed and clean. *There's absolutely no rubbish to be seen anywhere!* After living in a country with systems still developing, I had a new appreciation for things like sanitation, reliable power, stormwater drainage, and orderly driving.

I was grateful to have a place to sleep and put my luggage. After a rest from jet lag, I reunited with my son and his family and organised time for Christmas festivities. I also visited my previous preschool to ask if they needed relief work over the holidays. I enjoyed being back with the children and was surprised that my colleagues had shared with the children about Mozambique. They wanted to help the Mozambican children by donating more puzzles and books to take back with me next year.

Preparations for Leaving

My colleagues asked me, "Do you want to organise another nativity play as part of our Christmas celebration with whanau?"

Wow, two years in a row! I felt privileged to arrange the Christmas story about the birth of Jesus in a non-Christian preschool. We had permission from the owners, manager, and teaching staff. What a contrast between working in a New Zealand preschool and training volunteers in poor mud-hut villages. I enjoyed speaking English again too.

All too quickly, I needed to prepare presentations for various churches and homegroup supporters of the plan ahead and my new need, to have a motorbike as my own transport. *How can I overcome my fear of speaking to large groups of people?* I did not have the courage to argue with God as Moses had when he said, "Please send someone else!" *Lord, please give me courage to speak!*

The PowerPoint slideshow of 2014 and my vision for 2015 came together more easily than I anticipated. By now I had learned more IT skills. Speaking was another matter. I could have benefited from some training, but there was no time. I had some faithful people praying, though. Despite feeling nervous to speak in front of crowds, I amazed myself as I answered questions and presented my request for $2,000 for a motorbike. If it was meant to be, God would prompt someone's heart to contribute.

Despite witnessing how God had answered my needs over the past few years, I was still thrilled and somewhat shocked after church one evening. God had prompted two women who didn't know each other to give $1,000 each towards the motorbike. They both wanted to be anonymous donors. I was amazed. Although I still had no idea how the bike would be purchased in Mozambique or when I would learn to ride, I had experienced God coming through each time I stepped out and asked Him in faith, providing just what I needed for the next step.

I was also kept busy filling out forms with World Outreach to apply for a three-year mission partnership, including the psychological test. I arranged for my travel agent to book the necessary flights, connecting through various countries. More immunisations were required as well. My teacher registration renewal process would need to wait until another time.

Then it was Christmas Day. It was so great to spend it at Kelly's house with my son Ross, Kels, and little Ava, with a hammock to swing on and curious cows looking at us over the hills. I was overwhelmed with the abundance of fresh fruits and vegetables available during a summer Christmas.

A surprising donation came that enabled me to visit my USA family for my birthday. One of my brothers generously deposited funds for me to return to the west coast of the USA for a short visit over the New Year's period.

I hadn't seen my mother or any of my siblings for some time. My father had passed away a few years earlier. This visit was a precious time with them all, especially my mother, whose health was deteriorating. My parents had always encouraged me to follow my dreams, to travel and go where I was led. Africa was a long way away. I was grateful that another brother and his family lived close to our mother. It gave me a sense of peace to return to Mozambique.

But first, I needed to return to New Zealand to prepare for another year.

Back to New Zealand to Prepare

One day, while visiting a friend near a marine store, I felt led to purchase a small solar panel that could fit in my suitcase for someone who lived remotely without electricity. I also bought some easy-set mouse and rat traps, as my new residence in town was close to the open market and next to a rubbish dump. With children's books and puzzles adding weight to my suitcase, I invested in a kindle for reading e-books instead of taking more hard-copy books.

For medical and political reasons, I had been advised to change my travel insurance to one that included evacuation coverage. I could not have handled this so calmly without a firm faith that God was with me and wouldn't leave me, that He would always provide for me and would go before me. My faith held strong, and I was grateful for intercessors praying on my behalf.

After sitting the psychological assessment, I was pronounced a stable person and received the full three-year mission partnership approval from World Outreach. *Woohoo, I'm in!* I felt incredibly blessed, honoured, and excited to embark on this continuing mission journey.

I spent more lovely quality time with my son and his family before my return to Mozambique. I was so grateful for many friends who helped me with recording DVDs onto an external hard drive for the long evenings ahead. I was also given an emergency first aid kit and a camera that took good photos in low light. The preschool donated durable books and puzzles.

Many people in New Zealand sent prayers and gifts for other people halfway around the world who they would never meet. I felt privileged to be the person whose hands and feet provided the link and thankful for the grace, favour, provision, and protection of God.

Despite the sadness of leaving friends and family behind, I felt a growing excitement as I embarked with heavy luggage and four airports ahead of me. *What will God show me next?* I prayed for favour that my luggage was within the weight allowance and that it would all arrive safely!

Photos

Church family and friends farewell in Kerikeri

Arrive in Portugal and my first purchase is a scarf!

Bilingual Bible studies at a Lisbon church

Daytime lessons and challenging homework

Photos

My new home as an intern with Taz and Bella

Preschool seminar making resources with teacher volunteers

Teaching an action song in Portuguese to children possibly destined for school

Kevin's Team showing the 'Jesus' film to a remote village, using a simple white sheet, a laptop, and a large battery

Photos

Seasonal heavy rains bring devastation

The road washed away in front of Saul and Sarah's house

Called to a Sun-Scorched Land

Remote AOG mudbrick church

Baptisms in a muddy pond

Part 4: The Return and In Town 2015

Back to Mozambique

With eight hectic weeks of preparations behind me, I breathed a sigh of relief at the departure gate of Auckland Airport. *Once on the plane, I can really relax.* I'd arrived with a full number of bags, hoping they were not overweight. When I found the total exceeded the weight limit by 1.5 kg, I asked God for favour, believing He answers the smallest prayer requests.

I felt like a polar bear waddling up to the check-in desk, wearing many layers of clothes to decrease the weight in my suitcases. I presented my bags to be tagged and sent on their journey. By some small miracle, they were within the 30 kg allowance. I breathed a sigh of relief.

I was grateful for my prayer partners in my mission-sending group in Kerikeri. Prayer definitely minimises anxieties and is a source of courage. Travelling with prayer support proved far better than without it, as I had in my early days of travelling and sailing oceans before becoming a Christian. While visiting a friend in Auckland, I was encouraged to learn that another prayer network, the Ground Crew mission support group, had also added their prayers.

I looked around for my friend Kristie's mother, Tami, who I was escorting back to South Africa after her visit to see Kristie in Kerikeri. This was a last-minute arrangement and an answer to Kristie's prayers for someone to assist her mother. As Tami was getting more forgetful, I needed to ensure she made the transfers at two airports, plus request wheelchairs at each destination.

Flying via Dubai was a long but pleasant journey. We arrived in Johannesburg tired but otherwise healthy. Tami's family, who lived there, picked us both up from OR Tambo Airport. Once I had settled and recovered from jet lag, I left my heaviest bag behind with Tami for a few days before travelling on to Mozambique. This was a real blessing for me. Again, God had organised things before I knew I needed them!

Before my return to Mozambique, I had been invited to explore a unique method of teaching literacy to non-literate people. I had met Anna the year before at a literacy conference in Mozambique. After seeing my interest in teaching literacy, she suggested I visit her place near Nelspruit, South Africa.

Anna and a colleague had pioneered a method for teaching literacy to people whose language was only oral. Not only did this teach them the letter and sound relationships in their own heart language, but it also helped them learn Portuguese, the official language. They could then connect with a Bible translated into their own heart language.

Anna and her husband welcomed me into their home with their two dogs, took me to their local church, and showed me their small aviation service. They told me many stories of their adventures flying mission teams into disaster areas over the border and to remote areas to teach literacy to Mozambicans, who would then teach others.

While I was there, two pilots arrived from New Zealand to assist in the latest disaster in southern Mozambique. I felt privileged to hear firsthand from a global team volunteering in emergency flights with donated medical and food supplies. *Here I am on African soil, witnessing people doing rescue work just as I had watched on TV programmes!*

I learned as much as I could from Anna in this short time, as Sarah and I had discussed the possibility of teaching literacy up north. All too soon, I needed to return to Johannesburg, collect my luggage with its preschool resources and solar panel, and fly on to northern Mozambique.

* * *

The flight was short, and as I exited the plane in The Big City, the walk across the tarmac was blisteringly hot. I felt like I was in an oven. Being February, thunderclouds and rain pushed the humidity up. I hadn't been here during this time of year. In wet weather, rain bucketed down and rapid flooding occurred. This was the hunger season too. Crops had been planted but nothing was ready to harvest. Often the floods would wash the seedlings away—or worse, the houses.

This was my third time entering The Big City Airport, so the customs and immigration processes were more familiar. To my relief, my friends Sarah, Andy, and his wife Tina waved from the outside balcony after the formalities. They rescued me from the baggage guys, who were desperate to help me. I was so thankful to have friends to welcome me and assist in the overwhelming heat and noise of locals shouting and pushing for attention.

Since we lived two hours away, a trip to The Big City involved trips to the supermarket, to immigration, and often to shop for vehicle parts or other practical items. This trip, we shopped for food not found in our town and also for two important items I would need at Anya's house. One was a water filter, as the water from different sources around town might result in tummy bugs. I chose a clay water filter tower from Brazil, which would keep the water cool. The second item was a fan on a pedestal with a remote control. At Anya's *casa* or house, my bedroom had only two small windows facing the courtyard, with absolutely no wind movements. The fan would sit inside the full mosquito net hanging from a rectangular wooden frame.

After buying tinned foods, muesli ingredients, yoghurt, apples, and the unique South African sausages, we headed north. I kept some local cash, *meticais*, ready to buy fresh roasted cashew nuts from people selling them alongside the highway. Young men would throw caution to the wind, launching out into the middle of the road with their plastic bowls of cashews. I certainly wasn't in New Zealand anymore! When we spotted women with children selling nuts, we stopped. We didn't know their circumstances, but we felt this could be their only source of income.

Temporary Housing

Anya thought it would be better for me to wait to move in with her until her brother and wife moved back to their house. When I got to know their personal issues, I understood why she wanted to make my reception trouble-free.

Saul and Sarah's house was very close to Anya's place on the main street. I settled into their spare bedroom with my collection of suitcases and the solar panel. Saul helped me obtain a SIM card with phone credit, then drove to Whitewater Farm to collect my other belongings stored there from last year. Andy kindly made me a wooden frame to hang the mosquito net over the bed.

Saul and Sarah, as regional field officers of World Outreach, were involved with missionary activities in this semi-remote area of northern Mozambique. They had church-planted and trained pastors in the district for over twenty-five years, raising their two sons on the mission field. In past years, Sarah had also trained a local man for kindergarten work. She helped him establish his own preschool in town, with one hundred children from mainly government employees who could afford the fees.

Their concrete block house did not receive piped town water, nor did it have glass in the windows, only screens. Dust covered the inside of the house daily. Laundry had to be done by hand, water collected in containers from around town, and other menial tasks done.

To help with the workload, Saul and Sarah employed two helpers, who were a special part of their family: Arnaldo for outside work and Rénia for inside work. Both were committed Christians, as were their families, and they attended one of the local *evangélico* churches. They were very grateful for the work as, for different reasons, they would have been begging because of their circumstances.

Rénia had been with the family for many years, living with them in different locations around Mozambique. She worked very hard at keeping the house spotless and the red clay floors polished and gleaming.

Arnaldo was a long-time friend of the family who used to play with their sons. As a child, while climbing onto some roofs in town, he fell. Through a severe concussion, he became paralysed down one side. When he became older and married his wife, Saul and Sarah employed him full-time.

Arnaldo and his wife had a mud-brick hut in town. Through his steady employment, he was able to put tin on the roof so that when the rains came, the house didn't fall down. They could also afford to send their twin girls to school. Arnaldo and I conversed about our faith in simple sentences, which always ended with *"Graças a Deus"* (Thanks be to God). Arnaldo made the best coconut milk from fresh coconuts that fell on the property.

I became closer friends with Saul and Sarah when I moved into town. They often held Bible studies or prayer meetings at their house. Visiting preachers or missionaries came to stay with them too. The cross-cultural studies I did before coming onto the mission field helped me recognise one key aspect: interdependence was essential. People looked after each other in multiple ways for their mutual survival. I observed this in the relationships around me while living in town.

Floods

Torrential downpours in the afternoons brought rivers of water throughout Saul and Sarah's gardens and carport. One day, while away visiting our Whitewater Ministries friends at their farm, the heavens opened, dumping an enormous amount of rain that trapped us temporarily. Finally, it eased, and we drove slowly back, looking at the sides of the highway where some houses had partially collapsed.

We turned the corner to find a shocking sight. I gasped. "Where's the road in front of your place?"

There was a hole in the road big enough for a truck to fit in and a small water pipe left dangling midair. Because the stormwater drainage had not been completed, a huge portion of the mainly sand road had been swept away.

"How could this happen?" I asked.

They explained that not only did it take time to manually dig the drains, but the long pipes meant to channel the water away were temporarily stored on the side of the road. Often the pipes grew legs and disappeared to someone else's project before being installed.

We couldn't get the car into their driveway, so all visitors had to park down the other road. It would be weeks before the town council did anything to fix this road, so we diverted the water from ongoing rainfall to bypass their house foundations.

Over the coming weeks and months, the passersby decided this massive hole was a convenient place to dump their rubbish and anything else. So another stinky rubbish pit started, like the one at Anya's. After a while, somebody threw a cigarette in, and it became a smouldering pile, probably melting the black water pipe that had been left dangling across the gap. No water came from it anyway, as the town's water pump was clogged with river sand. No one knew when a replacement would come. When the wind blew, the stinky smoke became a nuisance, especially while hanging out clothes to dry. Whether at Anya's for lessons or at Saul and Sarah's, the smell of burning, stinking rubbish followed me for months.

Saul visited the council and asked for help in fixing the problem but, unless he was willing to give them a substantial 'donation', his plea fell on deaf ears. We prayed for patience and God's intervention. Our prayers were heard; one day, a dump truck, a tractor, and a dozen men with shovels came to fix the mess. This was a praise the Lord moment—or, as Arnaldo said, *"Graças a Deus!"*

Prayer Walks for Exercise

I missed my long walks around Whitewater Farm with the dogs. Walking in town was not as enjoyable. I often attracted attention as a foreigner, and the speed at which I power walked amused the locals. *Why do they walk so slowly?* Sarah also missed someone to walk with for outdoor exercise, so we teamed up for walks early in the morning. On these walks, I heard many stories about the people, how they lived, and the struggles they had with sickness and poverty. As we grew in confidence with this exercise programme, we began to get up at 5am to walk around the town and surrounding villages, praying.

"No one would know we are praying in the Holy Spirit's prayer language. They would assume we are just talking," Sarah commented one morning.

When we walked around the back roads after heavy rains, we saw how devastating it was for those who had houses made from clay bricks dried in the sun with thatch roofs. Saul and Sarah only had a big hole in the road outside their house; other people suffered greater hardships. Many huts and houses had partially or totally fallen down during this last period of rains.

There were such a lot of losses that it was overwhelming to imagine how we could help. This was a common occurrence, apparently. Saul and Sarah, with limited WO donations for emergency help, could only help people in their church. They employed Pastor Tino to find out who amongst the congregation had damages and needed help the most, then provided money to buy plastic tarpaulins and food.

The government received foreign aid during these frequent cyclones and floods, but often the funds and food did not make it up north to these remote areas. People were grateful for the missionaries based in the area. Needless to say, wisdom was required in how best to help them.

Language Lessons Begin in Town

Anya and I started my language lessons, which were two to three hours in the afternoons when the children were asleep after *almoço* (lunch).

"Maria-Patricia is too long to say," I said. "How can we shorten my name?"

She laughed. *"Avó? Mas você não é muito velho. Tia está muito melhor!"* (Grandmother? But you are not very old. Aunt is much better!)

I referred to my pocket dictionary to check the new vocabulary she'd used and agreed. We decided I should be respectfully addressed as *Tia Maria*. I smiled to myself, remembering this was the name of one of my favourite alcoholic drinks as a younger person.

Anya had found some old family furniture from her childhood days stored in the abandoned restaurant. Her parents had brought the furniture from Portugal many years ago. She and Cedru moved the furnishings into my room while I was back in New Zealand, then waited until I returned and viewed the bedroom to see if it would be suitable for my needs.

The small handmade wooden bed frame with slats and sides was a challenge. Anya wondered whether I would be comfortable enough on it, explaining I would need to buy a new single foam mattress. The bed was to be for Cris, her young nephew, when he was older. For now, Cris slept on a woven mat on the concrete floor next to Anya.

I can do this, I thought, remembering I had slept in narrow berths while sailing on yachts. I was much older now, though! However, I didn't want to spend unnecessary funds on a bigger bed, which the town did not sell, anyway. Looking at it another way, I realised that its small size gave me more space in the room. *At least it is long enough for me to stretch out.* I had a desk for studying and writing newsletters home on my laptop. A large ornate wardrobe and matching drawers filled one corner. One dim overhead lightbulb hung from a long cord that looked ancient on the highest ceiling I have ever seen. I had experienced how unreliable electricity could be in this part of the country the year before. *I guess I'll need my head torch to read at night!*

Preschool Plans

Just before my arrival at the beginning of the year, Sarah had been visited by Lisa, a solo mother and the daughter of one of the pastors Saul had trained. Lisa and her friend Irene, also a young single mother, wanted to teach a five-day-a-week preschool session in her father's *evangélica igreja* (evangelical church) just out of town.

Sarah and I had previously discussed the possibility of me assisting with this *escolinha* programme as my language developed with Anya's help. Lisa and Irene were already offering brief sessions for free. When Sarah and I observed Lisa's method of teaching children aged under six, we could see that with more training, she could offer a better learning experience than the repetitive chanting from her own primary school experience. *Wow, what we talked about last year is already happening!*

I was excited to continue to train volunteers in early childhood education with a Christian perspective. God's idea of having a motorbike was part of the plan, as this *escolinha* was on the outskirts of town. *I don't know yet what those plans are, Lord, but help me trust you and follow where you lead me!**

Sarah would assist me less and less as the year progressed, assuming my proficiency in Portuguese improved. Anya's language lessons would focus on preschool concepts and phrases. *I pray I can learn quickly.*

---

* *Trust in the Lord with all your heart, and lean not on your own understanding. In all your ways submit to him, and he will make your paths straight.* (Proverbs 3:5–6, NIV)

Back to Mozambique

Exploring the Town

My mornings were free to explore the town. While staying at Whitewater Farm last year, I had little opportunity to look around since I shared a ride in other people's vehicles. Time was limited to what was on the shopping list. Now that I could wander around more, I found a variety of interesting shops on the main street and hidden in the depths of the market maze. Simple things like finding a small jar of mayonnaise brought moments of joy, especially when I could converse a bit more with the shopkeepers.

The bigger shops sold ice-cold Coca Cola or liquid yoghurt drinks, and sometimes I was fortunate enough to find frozen chicken. The shelves in the little shops held tinned fruit, beans, dried spaghetti, tins of tomato paste, Five Roses tea bags, curry powder, tinned tuna and sardines, cooking oil, toothpaste, and toilet paper. Around the outside of the market, one could buy huge bags of charcoal to use as fuel to cook the daily meal. I found a young boy selling long-handled spoons hand-carved from local hardwood, useful for stirring *xima* (maize meal) cooked over a fire. I wondered if these would make a special gift for my supporters. I would try to remember them for my return to New Zealand in ten months.

Many stalls displayed colourful fabrics for *capulanas*. In the remote rural villages, women were expected to cover their legs to their ankles with a matching headscarf for modesty. Along the roadside shops, tailors sat outside, ready to sew anything on their treadle sewing machines. Some things I couldn't find though, such as handy wipes, South African rusks, and the Joko tea I was growing fond of. I saved these products for the big supermarket shopping list.

Andy reminded me there was another type of bakery other than the market's open stalls with bread buns. "Do you like donuts, MP?" he asked. "They arrive at the shop that sells frozen chickens.

Real donuts with the hole in the middle and sugar on top. You have to get there quickly, as they sell out."

"Really?" Maybe by living in town, I could be in the right place at the right time for a fresh donut! Sure enough, one day I was at that shop when they arrived. What a treat! Plus, I got one of the few frozen chickens to contribute to a shared meal with Saul and Sarah.

As a resident in town, I was frequently faced with people begging for money. When just passing through, it was sometimes easier to give a one-off donation, but this became unsustainable when seeing someone daily. I was reminded of the wise quotation, 'Give a man a fish and you feed him for a day. Teach him how to fish and you feed him for a lifetime.' I asked Saul and Sarah how to approach this situation now that I'd moved into town.

Their strategy was specific for their situation, but it also helped me understand the complexities of money and wisdom in sharing it. To financially support families who suffered either housing disasters or food shortages, Saul and Sarah opened a bank account for the pastors they had discipled and trained. It was then the responsibility of the pastor to decide who needed assistance. This took the pressure off the foreigners to provide the funds directly, which encouraged a type of dependency. It was difficult to assist the pastor's family directly, as it created jealousy and there was a cultural expectation to share amongst relatives.

That was wise counsel for a larger situation like theirs, but what about mine? Saul and Sarah encouraged me to continue to say, "*Hoje não, talvez outro dia*" (Not today, maybe another day). They assured me that as I became more familiar in town, people would get the message. Sometimes, though, I had another response, especially if prompted by the Holy Spirit. If a child asked me, I would give him some bread buns. The well-fed ones quickly stopped asking.

Back to Mozambique

I had another question. "What am I going to do with this small solar panel system?"

"Leave it with me," replied Saul. "I will be in the outer villages in the next few months, and I'll see who would benefit from having it."

I was beginning to see that blessing someone in the bush-bush could be a difficult gesture for me to achieve. I prayed about the solar panel at times but couldn't see what to do with it. I was to see God work things out in time.

I never got used to the amount of rubbish strewn about the streets. I discovered more huge piles of garbage, other than the one beside Anya's building. Stinking rotten produce left over from the fruit and vegetable market and even dead animals sat decomposing for weeks on end. Plastic was everywhere. Invariably, someone would throw a cigarette onto the garbage piles, and they became stinking, smouldering messes. A couple of times a year, men with shovels or a tractor would scoop it into a dump truck and take it away someplace. But in the meantime, we all had to live with it. No public toilets were in town, either. Everyone, both men and women, relieved themselves near the rubbish piles and vacant walls.

The town looked broken and neglected. All the commercial buildings lacked paint after years of neglect caused by war and being in a forgotten district far from the capital. Though the wires overhead suggested electricity, the supply was fragile. People illegally hooked into it near the market, causing outages. The main street had some concrete drainage but nowhere for water to go. The side streets had haphazard cobblestones, incomplete paving, and no stormwater drainage. Whole streets could get washed away. Repairs didn't seem to be a priority. *How do the local people live with this ugly sight?*

Finding Bread Buns and Beef Meat

Freshly baked bread buns were high on my list to purchase. One early morning while having coffee with Anya and Cris on the screened veranda, I saw a young man walking fast into town. It wasn't the speed of his walk that got my attention, though. He carried a large table on his head with bread buns neatly stacked on top! *Where are those loaves baked?* As soon as I finished my coffee, I raced to the market to buy his fresh bread. *Yum, nothing like warm, fresh buns!*

During my afternoon language lesson, Anya told me people can build a clay wood-fired oven in their village or next to their house. *Wow, so the piles of bread loaves in the market are baked at different places by many local bakers!* The small round buns and bigger loaves were all hand-fashioned and irregular shapes. I loved that bread, crusty on the outside and dense yet soft on the inside. *That was one good legacy left by the Portuguese colonists.*

Fortunately, I liked goat meat, the most common red meat available, which made delicious curry. I wondered if beef was ever sold. My imagination ran wild with thoughts of a fly-screened box big enough to hold it, picturing the head of a cow on top, similar to the goat meat being sold. That thought, though grotesque, made me giggle.

The day I forgot to take my camera was the day I found out how they sell beef meat. An amazing sight presented itself to me behind a crowd of people on the footpath. A whole cow lay on a cobblestoned part of the path, thankfully away from the dirt. The seller was its owner. He had a big hatchet that he used to carve and chop chunks of meat off the beast as its blood drained down the gutter. A European-sounding man asked for the eye fillet, pointing to it down the length of the beast's back. The owner tried not to understand his sign language. Finally, he said, "*Não*," shaking his head, and explained it was to be shared amongst everyone. *Good on him!* The chopping up of the beast continued, people came and went, and the meat, bones, and even hooves disappeared quickly. The European man went home empty-handed.

Finally Moving to Anya's

After spending a short time at Saul and Sarah's, I was ready to move. Friends helped to relocate my things from Whitewater Farm to Anya's house, loading them into the ute and carrying them into my bedroom.

The pitch-black evenings, starting around 6pm, made for long evenings indoors, which I spent reading or watching English-speaking DVDs on my laptop. After a long day of total immersion in Portuguese, my brain was exhausted. DVDs like *Downton Abbey* and *Call the Midwives* provided entertainment before bedtime.

My small chilly bin cooler that I'd used last year kept ants away from my weekend food, such as homemade muesli. The rest of the week, I mostly shared meals with Anya and Cris or visitors. Anya had an old deep freeze that rarely worked as a freezer. In the mornings, we would place bottles of water that we filtered ourselves in it for chilled water for mealtimes. When the power went off, everything stayed chilled inside it.

Once a week, I feasted on a single square of mint crisp chocolate from the South African shops while watching DVDs under my mosquito net at night. Anya thought I might like a hot drink in the evenings, so she asked Cedru to boil the water outside over the fire, filling a huge thermos on the kitchen table. As soon as it was dark, we locked doors against *ladrões* (robbers) and snakes, rats, lizards, or stray animals that might wander inside. I found this hard to get used to, as I liked to view the stars at night sometimes. Small sacrifices.

During the four to six weeks of settling into Anya's family life, I learned language for three hours a day. This included reading passages from my bilingual Bible for practising pronunciation, which developed into a lovely time of sharing our faith. As my language and understanding grew, I learned Anya believed her prayers weren't being answered. She felt that her time at church was boring and dry.

I joined them on Saturday nights at the local Catholic church, when the service was in Portuguese. Sunday services were in Makua, which Anya did not speak. This was the church she attended as a child. She wanted her nephew Cris to come to know the God of the Bible, particularly as his Makua mother believed the local superstitions and frequented the witch doctor.

I learned to write out prayers for healing and comfort in Portuguese as situations occurred. I held in my heart Anya's desire to know God more and to find some answers for coping with her past and present troubles. *Please give me your listening ears, Holy Spirit, and help my language progress!*

For years, Anya had baked birthday and special occasion cakes for people to earn extra money. She had a weird electric baking oven that looked like a flying saucer. If the power was off, Cedru would help her bake a cake in a cast-iron camp oven with charcoal on the top and bottom. Anya and I both loved cooking, baking, and eating different foods, and this was a valuable bridge towards learning the language and sharing within a family context. We swapped recipes, which I had to translate into Portuguese. Anya would talk me through a recipe, such as her *arroz doce* (rice pudding), while I searched my little dictionary for the words I didn't know. I wrote out a recipe for brownies, as she had heard about them from some Peace Corps volunteers in town. The problem was buying the cocoa powder, as it was only available in The Big City.

We had many laughs as I tried to learn cooking words. I talked while writing out the recipes. When I said and wrote '2 *avós*', Anya and three-year-old Cris burst out laughing, much to my chagrin. Anya explained I had said 'two grandparents' instead of 'two eggs' (*ovos*) to mix into the cake. As she gave Cris an empty coca cola bottle, I wondered if it was to be a plaything for him. But no! She propped Cris up on a chair and he used the bottle to mix the ingredients in a green plastic bowl. *What a clever method for mixing a cake!*

I wanted to surprise Anya with a fresh apple and cinnamon cake. Apples don't grow in Mozambique so are transported from South Africa. By the time they make it to the local market, they are bruised and old. Oh, for a crisp fresh royal gala apple from New Zealand! I described the cake to Anya, explaining that it came with a special ingredient, *canetas*. Again, laughter filled the kitchen as she held an apple and a *caneta* (pen). Searching my pocket dictionary, I found the word for cinnamon was *canela*. We made only one cake, which we enjoyed, but as a commercial venture in baking birthday cakes, it was too expensive. I enjoyed Anya's curiosity and willingness to learn new recipes, and she enjoyed sharing with me too.

Anya's past Peace Corps friends had shared an Italian meal with her, but she didn't know how to make it. I wondered where I could buy mince to make the Bolognese sauce. Anya told me Cedru would use goat meat from the market and use a hand grinder to turn it into mince. Cheese was unavailable, but dried spaghetti noodles were sold locally. Tomato paste was available too.

"Have you ever had garlic bread?" I asked.

Anya crushed garlic with the mortar and pestle, adding a pinch of salt. The garlic was fresh and pungent. I added it to some sliced bread buns in foil to roast over the hot coals. Success! We all enjoyed a spaghetti Bolognese meal, complete with garlic bread. *Muito bom!*

Every day, the challenges of conversing chipped away at my pride and fear of making mistakes. My independent attitude had to take a back seat. With dependence came vulnerability, and I learned to lean on God more and more. I discovered I liked to bring humour into a situation, but it took some time before I was able to make a joke that was understood by all. The reward of daily practice and persistence, with patient teaching by Anya, was friendships.

Anya and Cedru cautioned me not to go to the night market. As a single foreign woman, I could be an easy target for pickpockets or opportunists. However, I reassured them in my best Portuguese that I wouldn't venture into the inner market alleys and would only be gone for a short time. I wanted to see how the night market operated, and I wasn't disappointed! It was an amazing sight, forever etched in my mind. I left my camera behind, as I didn't want to draw attention.

Long tables held individual piles of fresh, slippery-looking fish of all sizes. Between these piles were paraffin lamps, sending up plumes of black smoke but giving a warm yellow light. *I don't recognise any of these fish!* Locals seemed surprised to see me there on my own. They thought it was funny when I asked questions in my pidgin language. Finally, I bought what looked like tuna steaks and took them back to Anya as a treat, or so I thought. She said she preferred the frozen bony imported trout from the shop. *Oh, I didn't expect that.*

Since I was living in Anya's house, I wanted to eat what they ate. Anya cooked mainly Portuguese-type foods rather than Makua meals, believing I wouldn't enjoy them much. However, I was keen to try a typical Makua meal, so Anya prepared one. She barbequed the small bony fish and served it with *xima*, okra boiled with green mango, and stewed tomato. It certainly looked colourful on the plate. However, there were more bones than fish and the slimy okra was challenging. She was right—it was not my favourite meal. I was thankful when, the next day, she marinated chicken in freshly crushed garlic and barbecued it on charcoal with rice and a raw cabbage and red onion salad. This was more to my liking and hers, as she had been brought up on Portuguese-style meals. We had a laugh over it all.

The meals Anya cooked depended largely on the seasonal availability of certain foods. When I saw large avocados for sale in the outdoor markets, I assumed she would use them within the main meal as part of a salad or spread them on the morning breakfast bread.

"What are you going to make with the avocado, Anya?" I asked her one morning.

"Cedru has grated fresh coconut this morning. I will squeeze it and add the coconut milk, then the dried coconut, mixing it together with some lemon juice. Then I will put it in the freezer to chill for our lunchtime *sobremesa* or dessert."

Wow, I would never have thought of eating avocado like that.

Anya told me she only considered avocado a fruit for dessert. I found it was surprisingly delicious and refreshing in the hot, humid climate.

We ate breakfast, or *mata-bicho,* on the screened-in veranda, where we could observe the early morning traffic without being

Finally Moving to Anya's

noticeable ourselves. We had a simple meal of fried bananas, sweet and sticky, placed inside freshly baked buns and washed down with strong milky tea. Even Cris had a cup of sweetened tea that he spooned into his mouth. I got to observe how hardworking the women were while I ate my breakfast. They had already been up for hours, as daybreak was at 4.30am. Invariably, they were transporting filled buckets of water, flour, bunches of bananas, or buckets of small stones on their heads, very often with a baby or toddler strapped to their back with a *capulana*.

Leftovers from *almoço*, the main lunchtime meal, were eaten in a small quantity in the evening. I was shocked to see that the leftovers, which could be chicken, rice, and vegetables, were left out unrefrigerated till evening on the main salon table. Food poisoning sprang to mind! But I discovered it was actually safe, and I never got sick. Perhaps my silent prayers over the food also offered protection.

On the weekends, I made my own muesli with the occasional freshly chopped apple (a touch of home-life), then joined with other team members for a potluck and games evening.

A few years earlier, intruders with clubs had taken Anya's gas stove. The old dog, Rosso, sustained broken bones from being clubbed as he tried to protect it, and he now walked around with a crooked leg. Vets were in the bigger towns, but Anya couldn't afford the fees anyway. Dogs were treated as guard dogs or just strays, not pets. No one was there to sterilise them. They were frequently skinny, flea ridden, and standing on three legs from scratching. I was glad my series of rabies vaccinations would last me a lifetime. This decision was to prove worthwhile, as a few months later, I would be faced with a rabid dog.

I was thankful for Cedru, who helped with domestic chores such as fetching water when the outside tank got empty and with the maintenance and security. I discovered in our conversation that he was my age. Many of his generation had died in the civil war or through working extremely hard during their lives. I did not see many people of our age around town. He was considered very old (*muito velho*).

Cedru rode his old bicycle early in the mornings and late at night along the highway from another settlement, possibly fifteen to twenty kilometres away. He supported a large extended family; many older members had died of disease, and he and his wife had taken over raising the orphaned nieces and nephews.

Travelling along the only highway seemed a hazardous activity, as it was difficult to see cyclists on the highway with big trucks whizzing by and no verge on which to escape traffic. I soon bought Cedru a bright yellow high-viz vest from The Big City.

Cedru had never been to school, but he was incredibly innovative and hardworking. Nothing was wasted. He even mended a plastic rubbish bin by melting holes with hot needles and stitching the cracked plastic together again. He mended Cris's little jandal by melting the parts over hot charcoal and joining them together. His generation, who had seen shortages and were cash poor, learned to be inventive and adaptable. I had a lot of respect for him.

Even though Anya and her family lived in town, we had a similar lifestyle to the locals out in the villages. Water had to be collected and stored in drums or buckets, and cooking took place outdoors using charcoal. Food storage was minimal, so meals had to be prepared every day. But her home was in a commercial building built of concrete blocks, so there was no danger of it falling down like the mud-brick and thatch huts. *I am thankful for that and for my private bedroom!* Her brother and his wife's family often needed to move in, as their house collapsed from the rains.

The bathroom appeared to contain a normal bath and toilet. However, the toilet was actually a long drop inside the house. When running water in the town's pipes had ceased because of the war or lack of maintenance, the base of the porcelain toilet broke through into a cesspit. This was next to my bedroom and smelled unpleasant, at times. We bathed in a bathtub using buckets of cold water and a cup. I had the luxury of doing my laundry in plastic tubs inside the courtyard. In the hot dry season, clothes dried super-fast on a line tied between some sturdy structures, high enough so the free-ranging village goats didn't nibble on them!

Anya's Brother and His Family

Anya's brother Zé moved back into her house with his young family soon after I moved in. Their house had suffered damage during the flood that eroded Saul and Sarah's road, with a couple of walls caving in. Attempting to converse in my newly acquired language, I asked about their house. My first mistake was not having Anya there to monitor the conversation. In this culture, the unspoken expectation was that if one person had more assets, other family members were entitled to have some of them. As a foreigner, I was expected to provide a handout.

The next day I discovered that in my conversation with Zé and Esa, I had 'agreed' to give them money to rebuild their house! My heart was indeed to help them, but financially, this was not possible. It took some help from Anya to explain that other people supported me, and I did not have enough money to rebuild their house.

Anya seemed protective of her space, happy to raise her brother's children but wary of Zé and Esa living under the same roof. In the past, they had expected her to pay for all the food and to cook and clean for them as well as look after their children. The boys' father was struggling with his own challenges, unable to help care for them. When Zé was sober, he was kind and gentle. But I saw that, in reality, he focused on buying alcohol, with his behaviour changing for the worse. I was sad to witness the detrimental effect of alcohol on this family. *If only there was an Alcoholics Anonymous programme here, as it's such a big problem in town.*

Esa was training to be a primary school teacher. Being a local Makua, this was impressive in many ways. However, it was Anya who raised her children. I also observed Esa tying little amulets around the children's wrists and ankles to ward off evil spirits. The boys' Makua mother and grandmother followed animistic practices, consulting their local witch doctor for charms, potions, and incantations. Anya explained to me that these amulets were the ones she untied and threw away when the children were in her house. This was another cause of tension between them.

Soon after moving into Anya's household, I felt overcome with homesickness for my own family and culture. The demands of being totally immersed in a language and culture vastly different to mine were very challenging. I was thankful to be part of the World Outreach mission family, with friends here who spoke English and who had been in this country for many years. They helped me through this period by showing me how important it was to socialise with them on the weekends, with potluck dinners and games. We had lots of laughs, and it was relaxing to be with others who had the same language and sense of humour. We also spent time together in prayer and Bible studies, learning God's truth and perspective.

The Giant Lizard and Fat Snake Battle

A drama happened late one afternoon, minutes after Saul and Sarah had picked me up to go to Whitewater Farm. Anya heard a loud commotion outside, with people shouting and throwing rocks under the tree next to her veranda. She looked out the window to see a long lizard (*lagarto*) and fat snake having a battle. Zé estimated the *lagarto* was half a metre long and the snake was two metres long. The snake disappeared in the grass next to our courtyard, or *quintal*, where the rubbish was piled.

As they recounted the story, I thought, *Oh no! In our courtyard?*

Anya said, "Wait, there's more! One of the local 'crazy' ladies came and picked up the lizard by its tail and walked up the street with it, swinging it around."

The lizard lashed out at a man sitting on some steps outside a shop, scratching his arms and legs. He screamed as blood poured out from his wounds, and an ambulance arrived to take him to hospital. That was as unbelievable as the overall event.

I was so annoyed to have missed it. Africa ... full of strange but true stories!

Motorbikes and My Big Red Honda Hero

"Well, today's the day!" said Sarah. "Are you ready to go to The Big City and look at buying our motorbikes?"

Andy offered to take us in his ute, as we didn't know yet how many we would buy or how to transport them back to Anya's main street residence. Besides, Saul and Sarah only had a station wagon. When we arrived at the Honda showroom, Saul did the negotiations. He got a discounted price for three bikes plus made a deal to get all three transported up to our town in a big truck, a two-hour journey. I was thrilled to have a red motorbike but worried that the electric start model was out of stock. *I hope I can kick start it!*

By the time we finished our other business and shopping, it was getting dark. The highway was not well lit, and potholes seemed to appear out of nowhere. Huge trucks roared past people on bicycles and pedestrians with pots of water on their heads. The darker it became, the more dangerous it seemed. All the way home, we prayed for the truck's safe delivery of the three motorbikes. Saul had asked Anya earlier if the bikes could be stored in the unused restaurant and locked securely. The truck arrived at 8pm, and we all worked quickly to unload the bikes onto the large concrete veranda out front and get them inside away from tempting eyes. *Thank you, Lord!*

In the morning, I saw our three big, strong Honda Hero bikes from India, heavy-framed bikes suitable for rough roads or sandy tracks. The bonus of a 97 cc bike was that we would be exempt from having to get a full motorbike licence, or so Saul thought. The 50 cc Chinese bikes were cheaper but were always breaking down, and being lightly constructed, they suffered wear and tear issues.

Tino, the local pastor for the *Igreja Actos* (Acts Church), needed to learn how to ride too. The following week, Saul and Sarah instructed Tino and me how to kick-start and change gears. I had some humiliating trials with kick-starting my bike, entertaining local onlookers. *What's another humbling experience?*

Anya's residence bordered the sandy side street where the dump was. Within the first week, the bike slid out from under me in the sand at a slow speed. *Ouch!* My leg was burnt. My prayers for healing the burn intensified, as I feared any infection or complication. Saul and Sarah gave me helpful advice for burns while praying with me for complete healing, and a speedy, positive result came. *No more wearing shorts for me!* I was pleased to have leather 'fashion' boots from New Zealand that worked for bike-riding too. I could not believe how many locals wore jandals, t-shirts, and often no helmet while whizzing along at great speeds, seemingly oblivious to the consequences of crashing.

I struggled to kick-start my bike, as it had high compression. Often I was exhausted by the time it started. However, I didn't give up. I knew this was part of God's plan in whatever or wherever He was to guide me. As He had called me, the Bible assured me He

Finally Moving to Anya's

would provide all my needs, including courage, strength, and protection.*

We needed to complete paperwork at the local police licensing office before being licensed to drive. Before we all set off there, we prayed in Portuguese for God's favour, as Tino only understood Makua and Portuguese. Saul negotiated through the complex paperwork for both Tino and me. Official requirements were difficult at the best of times. I was thankful God provided the help each step of the way even before I knew I needed it.

We had to physically present the bikes to the inspector, so Sarah rode my bike with me as the passenger. I wasn't ready to go solo yet. When we arrived at the office, the admin person insisted we go to The Big City to register the bikes and complete a written and driving test because of their size, even though Saul showed them they were less than 100 cc. I learned later that the admin person was asking for some sort of 'gift' to facilitate the licensing. This was a common practice but one custom we didn't follow.

We prayed again before the trip to the city. If we saw a roadblock ahead, we offered little Gideon Bibles or a can of Coca Cola and a friendly word. Sometimes we asked the officials manning the roadblocks if they wanted prayer. None of the vehicles I travelled in were searched or pressured for bribes with that approach.

Back at the licensing office, I sensed an impasse between Saul and the registrar. Another police officer came in, and Saul explained his understanding of the situation. Later, Saul said he heard the police officer say to the registrar, "Why not just give it to them?" I wondered if he was an angel in disguise!

After an urgent email message about the potential difficulty in

---

* *... but those who hope in the Lord will renew their strength. They will soar on wings like eagles; they will run and not grow weary; they will walk and not be faint.* (Isaiah 40:31, NIV)

getting the bikes registered, our prayer partners back in New Zealand petitioned God for favour in the situation. Finally, we all got our licences endorsed by showing only our international driver's licences and passports and providing photos to attach. Many stamps and seals later, we were on our way to learning how to ride the bikes. I could never have done all this on my own. *Graças a Deus!*

Two Ramps, an Iron Gate, and the Kitchen Padlock

Back at Anya's, Cedru had purchased a bag of cement and constructed two ramps so I could enter the courtyard through the rusty iron gate and ride my bike around the bricks and other debris into a little kitchen room. Anya advised me to buy a padlock for the door. It was challenging to navigate this obstacle course, but it was essential that I keep the bike hidden and locked away. Anya even suggested hiring a night guard to make sure nobody stole it. I thought that seemed a bit of an overkill, but a large gas stove had been stolen from her house. In the end, I assured her I felt we had enough protective measures and that God's angels would guard it too. *My biggest challenge is riding my bike through these obstacles. Outside the gate is an enormous sandy hole too! Lord, help me.*

My Honda Hero was more than adequate for me. Cris's father had a smaller 50 cc Chinese bike, like most of the local people. When his whole family piled onto it with bags of charcoal, pumpkins, or chickens, their bike disappeared underneath them. *They should really have my bike, as it's bigger and stronger. Maybe when I don't need it anymore, I can gift it to them.* However, it was early days yet, and I knew this bike was the best choice for me at the time.

My first ride on the open road was again as a passenger. I was thankful that Sarah, a very experienced bike rider, drove us to Whitewater Farm, as the big trucks whizzing by were intimidating. Going along the town's broken and potholed roads with its crazy drivers was also a challenge.

I practised shifting gears and managing my bike around the dirt roads of Whitewater Farm, gaining confidence. For many years, I had been a mountain biker, so I kept telling myself it was just a bit of an adaptation. I wasn't skilled or confident enough to drive on the highway yet, and I still had problems with kick-starting. I even had strangers come to my rescue in town and start it for me. This was a little nerve-wracking, as any of them could have driven off with my bike. However, they proved to only want to help. I was grateful for this and relieved to meet kindness in these young men.

A Change of Motorbike and on the Highway

After a month of trials and tribulations with kick-starting the motorbike, Saul contacted the bike shop. One electric-start bike had finally arrived from India, and it was the same colour as mine—red! So we again borrowed Andy's pickup and transported bike number one (still in pristine condition) back to The Big City to exchange for bike number two with the electric start. It cost a little more but was necessary. The exchange restored my dignity and confidence. It was so easy to just push the button and focus on shifting gears and getting around town. *Hallelujah!**

Our next excursion was to ride to the church on the edge of town that Saul and Sarah had planted many years ago. I was thrilled to make that drive on my own, following them on their bikes and even visiting the crocodile park on the way back.

---

* *My God will supply every need of yours according to his riches in glory in Christ Jesus.* (Philippians 4:19, WEB)

Tino's daughter Lisa, bringing her young son Issac, had begun to teach at the *escolinha* in the church during the week. Twice a week, I headed there on my motorbike to support Lisa and her friend Irene. Anya was an essential part of this situation, as she helped me prepare sentences specifically related to the preschool context.

Now confidently astride my electric start Honda Hero, God's promises for His protection in town and beyond were soon to be proven. My first solo ride out to Whitewater Farm was a near disaster before I even got to the highway. I had been riding independently around town and the outskirts for a few weeks without incident. This one afternoon, there must have been an angel or two protecting me. Just outside of town was a narrow bit of road with many stallholders selling fresh vegetables and gasoline in one-litre plastic bottles on both sides of the road.

As I slowed to navigate potholes, an oncoming truck refused to budge from the middle of the road. It seemed I was going to land in the front seat of his truck. What happened next was quite incredible. I found myself pushed over sideways and, with the abrupt edge of the road meeting the sand, landed off to the side of the bike. But no burnt leg, this time!

Brushing myself off, I thought it was a miracle that I hadn't been run over, and the bike was undamaged. The truck just continued on its way. *I'm sure there is a Bible verse that says God will command His angels to guard me, lifting me up so that I don't hit a stone!** I thanked God not only for His protection but also for my electric start button. I was soon on my way to Whitewater Farm again—though a bit shaken, I must admit.

---

* *For he will put his angels in charge of you, to guard you in all your ways. They will bear you up in their hands, so that you won't dash your foot against a stone.* (Psalm 91:11–12, WEB)

Bible Studies

Our spiritual life here was individual and corporate, both essential aspects for wisdom, guidance, strength, and comfort. At times, we joined other mission groups in someone's home to watch Bible teaching videos. Weekly sessions on spiritual warfare, the power of the Holy Spirit, and specific videos for women were, we hoped, relevant, informative, and transformative in our daily lives.

Praise and worship songs on my laptop inspired me during my private devotional times, lifting my spirits and helping centre me on the character of God—who He is, and His love, protection, provision, and guidance. Daily, I journaled and recorded my Bible readings and any revelations the Holy Spirit showed me. At times, these were astounding and faith building to reread.

Corporately, we attended both local and English-speaking churches and joined with other global missionaries in fasting and praying for breakthroughs. Exercising at Anya's to praise and worship songs, as well as my early morning prayer walks around town with Sarah, boosted my connection to God. *My prayer life is certainly receiving a major upgrade!*

Three Different Churches

Within the first four weeks, I attended three culturally different churches, where we all praised and sang to the Lord and read from the Bible. The first was a church in Sanhoje, a small settlement beside the highway that Saul and Sarah had planted and mentored in years past. We arrived with others, everyone wearing our Sunday best. The church was located on the highway and was a typical mud-brick building. Long run steel roofing protected the walls to some extent. Women in colourful *capulanas* cooked over a wood fire with clay pots and long-handled wooden spoons. My nostrils filled with a favourite smell: brown beans with small bits of potatoes and meat over a smoky fire.

Everyone welcomed us and was appreciative that we were attending their Sunday church. Their custom was to put plastic chairs up the front for the visitors. We faced the congregation, who sat on wooden benches, men on one side and women with children on the other. No matter how many times I was put in this position, I was never comfortable with it.

Vibrant singing and dancing to welcome the Spirit of God began with groups of young men, followed by older men, women, and children. There were clay walls, windows with no screens or glass, and a dirt floor, but what mattered was this enthusiastic worship by all in their native Makua. At times, we joined in with Portuguese songs. The preaching was in Makua, but a young man jumped up to the front to interpret it into Portuguese for our benefit. My bilingual Bible, plus some translation from Sarah, helped my understanding. I really learned how precious the Bible translators' jobs were in getting God's Word into heart languages for people to understand the Gospel.

Two weeks later, we attended the English church at the 'Zims' church fellowship about an hour's drive away. I had gone there the previous year. This was our only opportunity to worship corporately with people who spoke our language, though we came from a mixture of countries—Zimbabwe, South Africa, England, Germany, and, for myself, New Zealand and the USA. We appreciated fellowshipping with them.

We were spoiled again with a South African *braai* (barbecue) with lots of salads, puddings, and ice-cold drinks. The view from the partially covered veranda was stunning, and with the swimming pool and tropical plants around it, it was a little oasis for us. Sometimes we took Bible study notes home to follow up at our own pace.

Finally Moving to Anya's

Saul and Sarah suggested I share something about myself and my family at their regular *Igreja Actos* or Acts Church in town. I wrote out a few sentences of introduction and checked it with Anya before I shared it. Anya, after laughing a bit—actually, a lot—asked me why I had been tired for thirty years! It turned out the word for "married" (*casada*) was similar to "tired" (*cansada*)!

"*Muita obrigada, Anya!*" (Many thanks, Anya!) She had saved me from yet another embarrassing moment.

Plans and Ideas for the Year Ahead

Sarah was developing an idea she'd had for a long time, involving the front room of the building Anya owned where the family had their restaurant and bakery in pre-war years. We sat in the abandoned room one afternoon, having a brainstorming session about a Christian drop-in centre for Bible studies and preschool training with a biblical curriculum.

"We could stock some reading material in Makua and Portuguese," Sarah proposed, "or it could be a resting place for women with small children in town. A safe toilet-stop, some simple food available, and art supplies for the children. There's also a desire by young people to learn English. We could tutor them and expose them to the Gospel."

"What about an after-school Bible-based programme for school-age children too?" I said.

Our excitement growing, we got busy sweeping, mopping, and cleaning the space. Cedru helped move the old restaurant equipment into another storage room. Anya was pleased that something positive was about to begin in her family's street-front building after its years of neglect.

Sarah suggested I could support Lisa and Irene in the day-to-day operations of the preschool in the *Igreja Actos*. She saw an opportunity to further my involvement with the *escolinha* education using ideas from the curriculum developed last year by Tina and Ginnie at Whitewater Ministries. She also offered some thoughts about holding a seminar for young Makua women needing health education, confidence building, and maybe something to assist them in considering a career. *Sarah and her husband have lived with the people here for over twenty-five years,* I reminded myself. *I don't need to compare myself with her!*

My daily lessons were still focused on preschool vocabulary and situation-based conversations. *Practise, practise, practise.* As Anya and I read my bilingual Bible together for pronunciation, we prayed and shared Bible verses and discussions about our faith, which grew as our relationship developed. It was a satisfying aspect for both of us. *What is God doing in Anya's faith walk and with her brother and family? There are aspects I cannot see, but I believe God is working. What more can I do?*

Preschool Volunteers Training Together

Whitewater Ministries offered a preschool model seminar at Whitewater Farm for the three villages in which Kevin and Ginnie had planted churches years before. These villages had Christian men and women who wanted to be *escolinha* volunteers, helping to prepare their community of children for school. Ginnie suggested the same training opportunity for our young women at *Igreja Actos*. Sarah and I assisted Ginnie and Tina with teaching modules during the seminar. It was perfect timing to upskill and encourage

Lisa and Irene early in the year, as their only experience with teaching was rote learning at primary school.

What also excited me was that the model *escolinha* next to Whitewater Farm had some teachers keen to impart what they learned last year. This long-term project for local Mozambicans to learn and take ownership of their preschool system was becoming a reality, creating an opportunity to teach Lisa, Irene, and rural villagers. It was a step towards transitioning from dependency on outside organisations to active participation in their own children's future education.

Whitewater Farm offered transport to the women with babies, as the other two villages were too far away for them to walk to. Some of the men cycled there, which on sandy paths needed commitment! They slept in the dorm building on mats placed on bed frames or else on the floor, where they were accustomed to sleeping, especially with babies. It was a huge sacrifice for them, but they were passionate about their children getting an educational opportunity. We all ate communally from donated food cooked by the attendees.

My role was teaching the attendees to make resources from materials at hand, which they could take back to their villages and then make more of. I had some phrases I'd used last year at a similar seminar, so I could talk in Portuguese while demonstrating what to do, using a notebook to assist me when I forgot words! I explained how to make a puzzle for children to match the objects to the drawn shape, and briefly explained how mathematical concepts can be learned by young children doing puzzles. "Let's go outside and collect some seeds, rocks, plastic, or anything else that can be traced," I suggested.

Excited, they set off for half an hour and returned with some interesting objects to trace onto cardboard. *They are really enjoying this new experience.* Proudly, they added these puzzles to their village's box of resources.

Ginnie and Tina taught the five concepts of learning for young children, providing a background as to why preschool programmes were different from primary school learning. We had fun teaching the attendees how young children primarily learn through their five senses of seeing, hearing, smelling, touching, and tasting.

For the physical aspects of learning, we enjoyed teaching how children learn through movement and games. It was satisfying to teach the *Cabeça, ombros, joelhos, pés* (Head, shoulders, knees, and toes) action song in Portuguese that I'd learned from a Mozambican teacher last year. Learning the days of the week in Portuguese through song also proved engaging.

We showed them how to teach the weekly calendar by providing materials to make their own *calendário*. One resource developed by the *Preschool in a Box* team was a set of large numbers illustrating each day of creation. The attendees coloured them in with crayons we provided. Later, on a town trip, we laminated the sheets for each resource box. These four resource boxes of books, puzzles, and other teaching aides could be rotated between each village preschool over a month, like a library.

It was a challenge for each village to find a secure yet easy-to-collect storage place for when the sessions were open. The preschools were held in mud-brick buildings with thatched roofs; the only common area was the village church (*igreja*). There might be wooden doors and windows, but there were no storage areas to secure the resources. Each village decided how best they could secure these boxes while on loan. Saul and Sarah had a wooden box they no longer used, which they donated to Lisa and Irene's preschool. My donors bought them a padlock to safely store their resources in the church building.

The *escolinha* programme introduced the God of the Bible as well as practical skills and understanding of new educational concepts. Our prayer was that eventually the volunteers would feel inspired to introduce ideas that reflected their culture into their own learning centre. It was an ambitious training programme but one in which we all had some experience and could contribute to help it be a successful, satisfying experience.

I was learning how to adapt early childhood concepts within this cultural environment, including in very poor villages. All the volunteers came with a faith in Jesus Christ and a passion to give every child in their village an opportunity to learn Portuguese for school ahead. Each session began with prayer, singing, and praising God simultaneously in three languages: Makua, Portuguese, and English. *I wonder if heaven sounds like this!*

Loaded up with knowledge, experience, and resources, Lisa and Irene could now begin a preschool experience based on the Whitewater Ministries model. One of the first items to discuss related to a small fee to cover snacks for the children after their two-hour session. This was an essential part of the programme. It was always difficult to enable the venture to be self-sustaining, as in the long run, we could not promise ongoing funding.

The programme would be bilingual to prepare the children for school, which was only Portuguese. Because Lisa and Irene were solo parents, they also needed to work in their *mashambas* (gardens) to produce their food. The songs and resources that they made at the Whitewater preschool seminar would help them get started.

My preschool back in New Zealand contacted me with some surprising news. As well as working there part-time during their holidays, I had been sending them newsletters, showing photos of the children in Mozambique. The teachers and children decided to

Plans and Ideas for the Year Ahead

fundraise for Lisa and Irene's preschool at *Igreja Actos*. I asked Lisa and Irene what they most wanted for the children. They requested fabric for little tunics (*batas*) to serve as a uniform for each enrolled child. *This money came at just the right time!* We took them shopping to a *capulana* shop with a tailor who could sew twelve tunics.

"It's shopping day in The Big City tomorrow," Sarah said, advising me to come over early. "Bring money from your preschool sponsors. We might find some resources for Lisa's *escolinha* too."

We found a stationery shop in The Big City to buy some more paper and staples. But surprisingly, I discovered a glass cabinet filled with brightly coloured cardboard books for young hands.

"Hey, look!" I cried out, "Here are some books with pictures of animals, fruits and vegetables, colours, and numbers, and it's in Portuguese!"

"Perfect! Just what we need," replied Sarah.

How amazing that we found these items! Thank you, Lord, for guiding us to them. We were very grateful, and I had enough donations to buy them.

It was exciting to see the link between these two preschools so far away geographically and so different culturally. I wanted to do a live video chat between the two groups, but we had time-zone differences and unreliable internet. Instead, I took photos and emailed them for the teachers to share with the children in the Bay of Islands.

One morning soon after opening the *escolinha*, Lisa introduced me to a little girl who was crying. She explained that the child's mother had died last year, and her father had died last week. She was being looked after by an aunt, who brought her to the church's preschool because she was crying so much. Life was difficult for people here, and it was comforting to know that in some small way, we could help this young orphan. She came to a few preschool sessions. Eventually, they found other family members or neighbours to raise her in another village.

This was a common occurrence, as malaria, HIV/AIDS, tuberculosis, and cancer took their toll on adult family members. The shortage of doctors, nurses, hospitals, and basic medical treatments impacted people. The remoteness and lack of roading or money to afford taxi buses also contributed to the neglect of healthcare in this region.

What we contributed was a drop in the bucket, but I hoped God would use that and multiply it in ways we could scarcely imagine.

Finding Beauty in the Brokenness

After a few months of living in town, I began to be challenged by what I had to look at day in and day out. I found myself overwhelmed by the litter, brokenness, and ugliness everywhere. Mountains of rubbish piled up in various places, blowing around the streets. Plastic littered the paths into the markets. There were no bins, and no regular collections seemed to be available. *Where else can it go?* Big piles sat for months and months, growing bigger, decomposing, and smouldering with random fires. Along with the bad smells, depending on the wind, rats strayed into our courtyard. I struggled with the flies, heat, and humidity. When I first arrived, I hadn't noticed the squalor so much, but as time went on, it affected my outlook more and more. I hungered for beauty.

One morning as I went to the bathroom, I noticed something strange in the long drop toilet. Muddy, claw-like markings were on the side of the porcelain bowl. Puzzled, I asked Anya what it could mean. She immediately exclaimed it was from a rat climbing up from the cesspit. The marks were excrement, not mud! She yelled to Cedru that a rat was loose inside the house. I immediately shut the door to my bedroom, which was next to the bathroom. *I hope I'm not too late!*

Anya put Cedru on the lookout for one or more rats inside. She also had a hungry dog that could sniff them out. Rat traps were a luxury and unavailable in this town. Cedru had a strategy, Anya explained, which was to trap the rat in a corner and donk it on the head with a shovel. If that failed, he would chase it outside to the courtyard. I decided this was a good time to go for a walk. I learned later it was indeed donked on the head by the shovel and fed to the hungry dog. *Whew, not in my room then.*

The rusty water tank in Anya's courtyard looked like a huge commercial cylinder scavenged from some other engineering purpose. It collected rainwater off the rusty metal roof. For half a year, I fetched water from this tank to wash my clothes, sheets, and towels in plastic tubs and buckets. At times, Cedru climbed a broken ladder to check how full the tank was. Once, as he leaned over the rusty edge, he saw a dead animal and a bird floating in the water.

I understood now the necessity of filtering our water for drinking and was pleased I had been able to invest in a clay filter urn for my water. Though it took some time to drain through, after seeing those dead animals, I was thankful to have it. Observing Cedru's filtering system for Anya's household, using old cloths and funnels and then storing water in plastic cola bottles, I made a mental note that when I left, I would gift Anya my clay urn.

For some reason, at this time, I only noticed the worst part of my surroundings. At breakfast, we sat at a chipped, wobbly table on rusty, tattered chairs, where we could see through the dirty screen and broken wooden louvres to life outside. Anya said it was unwise to show the outside world that you had nice furniture, as you could become a target for *ladrões*. *Ah, so that's why she doesn't fix anything or paint the outside walls.*

Sometimes, depending on how the wind blew and whether the rubbish pile was smouldering, we were unable to sit there for breakfast and retreated to the courtyard—which wasn't much better since it was full of rusty old vehicles that had belonged to Anya's late father. One tractor in particular could have been useful, but whenever Anya found a buyer, her brother would demand a higher price, resulting in the buyer losing interest. So it sat there for years, gathering more rust. The roaming goats liked it for climbing on, though.

The previous year had been my first full-time year in Mozambique as an intern for World Outreach. I spent it at the beautiful cashew and mango farm where Whitewater Ministries was based. Whitewater Farm, located outside of any urban town, was beautiful in natural scenery and well kept. Any rubbish was processed either by burning, burying, or recycling for other projects, so evidence of rubbish or litter on the ground was nonexistent. My move to Anya's was my first encounter with living in a town that sold multiple things wrapped in plastic. Single-use plastic bags blew around the streets.

How fortunate I am to be able to go home to New Zealand for two months after enduring this for only ten months. I wondered how people here in town could still smile and laugh in this environment. It didn't occur to me that perhaps this was the least of their troubles.

I was of no use to anyone if I kept looking down instead of up. Remembering a verse, I prayed, *I will lift my eyes to the hills (wherever they are). My help comes from the Lord, the Maker of heaven and earth. Help me to fix my eyes not on what is seen, but on what is unseen.*

Overwhelmed and depressed by what I saw daily, I turned to God again and again in prayer. *Help me, Lord, to change my perspective of living in this broken, smelly place. Where is the beauty*

Plans and Ideas for the Year Ahead

in this place? Help me see things and people as You see them. Help me find my joy again. Amen.

An answer came to me a few days later. One afternoon, I looked out of my little rusty screened and barred window at the blue skies and puffy white clouds with fresh eyes. I reflected on how this must be, in a small way, like someone in a prison cell seeking a bright spot to focus on. This was a pivotal moment. I was immediately thankful I was not in a jail cell but could walk outside anytime and that I had eyes to see a rare flower or the blue sky. I sensed God challenging me to find Him in the beauty amidst the thorns every day in this town and beyond.

A few years back, when I was in a hard place, a favourite teacher at the time had suggested that I keep a daily gratitude journal. This helped me enormously at the time. I decided to look for everyday things to be thankful for. That morning, I opened my emails to read an encouraging message from a friend who was praying for me. She shared her favourite Bible verse and the need for gratitude. She didn't know my struggle at the time, but the Holy Spirit did!

I wrote the verse on a piece of paper and stuck it to my wall: "Rejoice always, pray continually, give thanks in all circumstances; for this is God's will for you in Christ Jesus (1 Thessalonians 5:16–18, NIV).

As I ventured out of my bedroom after that revelation, I noticed more smiling faces amidst the hardship. *Thank you, God. I can see!* Beautiful faces of children walking and talking. Laughter in the markets between mothers carrying babies on their backs and heavy baskets on their heads. These women would have been up since 4am, working in their fields in the dawn's light, feeding children and preparing them for school if they could afford it, walking to collect water in containers they carried on their heads, walking to the river to wash the family's clothes, and going to the market to buy food to prepare. Their chores were endless, yet some of these women's eyes sparkled with glimmers of hope or joy that came from deep within. The eyes of others looked dim and defeated.

I gained a deeper respect for these hardy, resourceful, resilient people. The challenges of people living in a town, compared to residents in a rural area, presented different problems. The rural population lived in vulnerable mud huts that might fall down in the frequent cyclones, or droughts or floods could cut their food supplies short, but the townspeople also struggled with their living situations. When I thought about where I lived in New Zealand, it was like paradise. *I will be more grateful back home, especially for reliable infrastructure and basic services!*

A small green blade of grass in the cracked concrete path with a tiny blossom peering from the edges of the path brought joy to my heart. Watching children with little backpacks going off to school, I noticed an act of kindness by an older child looking after a younger one as they walked. My heart smiled. That morning, my 'inside eyes' saw some hope for the future here.

I visited the private preschool where the owner/teacher was a past student of Sarah's early childhood training programme. Just over one hundred children attended, whose parents were mostly employed by the government. The preschool provided a hot lunch cooked onsite. This was a privileged type of preschool that cost a substantial amount in fees. The chosen helpers for the day handed bowls of cooked food to the other children carefully, almost reverently. I noticed such gratitude on their little faces as they all ate a hot, filling meal.

Every day, I noticed something or someone that shone a special light of loveliness amongst the brokenness. Darkness can never put out light.

I wanted to share the hope of Jesus, but without language and relationship, it seemed an impossible gap to bridge. Instead, I offered people a warm smile. At times, this touched their hearts, pleased they had been noticed. Smiles seemed so insignificant, but they would have to do until my language developed further.

I remembered that when I asked God to clarify where I was to go in Africa, it seemed he had spoken to me of Mozambique, a sun-scorched land, with promises of satisfying my needs there and keeping me strong. This encouraged hope to grow in my heart, despite being in this setting where I saw brokenness everywhere.* I asked God to help me see when and where I could extend His love through me, a cracked and broken vessel.

I felt so inadequate but was learning, day by day, how to be open for the Holy Spirit to reach people with God's love. I prayed daily that God would shine His love through me to reach others, that I could help them in any way, and that somehow, through His grace, I could offer them hope and a new life in Jesus.

Watching our Faith Grow

Although conscious of my shortcomings, I remembered how much God loves me and that His Holy Spirit is alive in me. I wondered, though, *How will my small attempts make a difference in anyone's life here in Mozambique?* The story of the loaves and fishes displayed how God can multiply what little we bring into a situation. *Surrendering my needs and wants to serve other people requires me to give up on myself. Help me choose acts of kindness.* This sounded simple, but at times, it was a struggle.

One afternoon, when I had returned from the market and Anya had finished her chores, she suggested we all take our chairs outdoors and sit on the main street veranda to watch the passersby.

---

* *... while we don't look at the things which are seen, but at the things which are not seen.* (2 Corinthians 4:18a, WEB)

She didn't want to do this on her own. My body and mind were exhausted. I would have preferred to rest and then rejoin her and Cris for dinner and games, but the Holy Spirit prompted me to lay down what I wanted to do.* Resting could come later.

Anya explained she was terrified of her nephew randomly being abducted for evil purposes. *Oh?!* Having me there on the veranda as well added some security for her. I saw how she enjoyed watching people on the street pass by her front porch. She told me her family would do this in the afternoons before the war changed everything. Many people stopped to chat with Anya, and I realised how well known her family was. I was pleasantly surprised at the renewed energy I experienced from putting her needs above mine.

Anya's life, like so many, was not an easy one. She had a complicated past, with family members suffering traumatic events. After the death of her sister, Anya raised three of her sister's four children as her own, though they still had links with their Muslim father. She took them to church and told them about the God of the Bible and that Jesus loves them. They were now young adults. Now, her brother and his Makua wife expected her to raise their two boys under the age of five too. Just sharing in the simple experience of sitting with young Cris on the front porch and watching the world go by brought Anya visible joy. *It was worth my effort in taking the time to join her, despite feeling tired.*

Silently laughing at myself, I wondered why it took going to Africa for me to become less self-centred. Was I learning to respond with obedience to the Holy Spirit's promptings? *Or perhaps it isn't about me at all, but God is using me to show Anya his love and concern for her heart's desires. Okay, I'm over-thinking things again!* I had no idea, and didn't really need to know the details either. Going step by step every day and leaving the rest to

---

* *Even so, faith apart from works is dead.* (James 2:26b, WEB)

God seemed the best approach. Jesus said to love God and love your neighbour. *Why is that so hard?*

Anya wanted to lead by example and go to the local church for her nephews so that the God of the Bible and Jesus would be some sort of foundation in their spiritual upbringing. The next weekend, it worked out that I could accompany them. By now, I understood more of Anya's family background and how the church held a special connection to her Portuguese roots and family memories. But she despaired sometimes. The church was so dry in its teachings that she found it hard to connect with God.

Pondering Anya's sadness in believing God did not hear her prayers, I brought her concerns to the Lord and asked Him to reveal how I could help her come to know that He really cares for her. Jesus said we would have tribulations but to fear not, as he would be with us through these times. How could Anya come to believe this? I was not sure what I could do, as my language wasn't sufficiently developed. However, I found some Psalms I hoped would help heal her heart.

I read the Bible aloud for fifteen minutes at the start of our lessons, with Anya correcting my pronunciation. She felt that this was a connection we could develop in her understanding of prayer and God.

Through our relationship, shared prayers, and God's grace, I saw Anya's yearning to see God provide more for her increase. *What's next, Lord?* I believed God would multiply my efforts to yield a much larger outcome. But how and when? Anya was an influential and well-known person around town with an extended family, including Muslims and Makua members. There were nine mosques in this little town, and only a handful of Christian churches. With a deeper revelation of Jesus and how much God loves her, I believed Anya could influence the network around her.

Each evidence of God's provision, no matter how big or small, developed greater faith in me to trust Him in answering my prayers. God was doing a work in my heart too.

When three-year-old Cris became feverish and sick, our lessons came to a halt. Anya knew it was malaria, a common illness here. As she cared for him physically, we focused on praying for him. I helped her find Bible verses that could bolster her faith and asked her for help creating a general prayer template in Portuguese that could be applied to anyone. I thought this could be useful for us both. To our amazement and gratitude, Cris recovered rapidly, according to Anya's experience of malaria. My confidence in God answering our prayers grew.

One afternoon, Anya was wondering about baptism, as she was baptised as a baby. I shared that I too had been baptised as an infant, but in recent years, I learned that adult baptism is different. It was difficult to explain in Portuguese about the significance Jesus placed on baptism as a decision of obedience.

I asked her, "Was Jesus baptised as a baby or an adult?" Using my bilingual Bible, we found the passage where Jesus is baptised in the Jordan River as an adult by John the Baptist. Then we read in the Gospel of John where Jesus talks to Nicodemus about being 'born again'.

Anya questioned this. "But will this mean I won't belong to my church here anymore?"

"Not at all," I replied. *Help me, Holy Spirit!* In the next lesson, I found other scriptures about Jesus' instructions to us as believers and our obedience.

I visited Saul and Sarah after dinner and shared my questions. Sarah suggested, "Maybe it would help if Anya had some Bible studies with other interested women."

Plans and Ideas for the Year Ahead

I brought this up with Anya the next day, but the thought of study intimidated her after having bad experiences with headaches and learning. She believed she was stupid.

I reassured her. "No problem. We can continue as we are, just you and me, the Bible and our lessons." *Maybe she will be interested in doing a discipling study on our own?*

One morning, after an argument with Zé over smoking in the house, Anya remembered a method I used for memorising Bible verses. In large letters, she wrote out a verse in Portuguese from Deuteronomy that helped her with anxious situations. Taping the sign to the wall by the front door at eye level, she said, "My brother and my older nephews who can read Portuguese will see this too."

In English, it was one of my favourite verses too: "The Lord himself goes before you and will be with you; he will never leave you nor forsake you. Do not be afraid; do not be discouraged" (Deuteronomy 31:8, NIV).

She is getting bolder with her faith and isn't watching novellas or soap operas so much during the day. Hallelujah, baby steps!

A few weeks later, Anya came back from the family flour mill with great excitement. People were bringing in sacks of corn. Needing small change for their payments, but unable to leave the mill, she remembered a testimony from our friend Marion when in a similar situation. Marion prayed for people to bring small change when buying remedies at her health clinic. Anya prayed, and soon after, a woman passed by from the market, having sold her vegetables. She offered Anya some smaller change (*trocar*) in exchange for bigger bills. Anya said, "God heard my prayers!"

"*Fantástica!*" (Awesome!) I replied, sharing in her excitement but keeping my thoughts to myself. I wouldn't explain just yet that God doesn't always answer yes; sometimes he says wait or no. That could wait for another time.

The Good Samaritan Orphan Programmes

An opportunity to teach a seminar for an orphans' programme helped me better see the Father's heart of love. Marion asked if I felt ready to teach a one-day programme at a weekend seminar at her place. My role would be to assist healthcare workers (*socorristas*) from remote villages with activities, songs, and Bible teachings for their orphans.

I had visited Marion's Good Samaritan Clinics once in 2013 and again in 2014. Four main towns had a hub clinic, supporting more bush clinics in their areas. These bush clinics were in villages that did not have any preschool programmes available. The clinics used natural medicine to improve the lives of local people and ran a nutrition programme for orphaned and malnourished children. The *socorristas* had been trained in the Word of God as well as in growing plants and making and administering natural remedies from their own village clinics. They would come from the bush clinics to learn in one day what they could do for the orphans that they fed.

I prayed about the offer to teach another weekend seminar. I remembered how Marion was so enthusiastic and helpful last year when I taught. The healthcare workers were eager to learn how to benefit their orphans too. Though I felt insecure, I also knew I could depend on God's help.

I had peace about saying yes to Marion because my prayers and several specific Bible verses spoke to me.* *Wow, God is really talking to me, and it's amazing how fast and directly He silences my anxiety and doubts.* I was more aware, in this second year of service, that many people were praying for and supporting me. Though it

---

* *And God is able to make all grace abound to you, that you, always having all sufficiency in everything, may abound in every good work.* (2 Corinthians 9:8, WEB)

was only a three-day weekend seminar, I was humbled to share the Good News of Jesus Christ.

Even though I was a preschool teacher in New Zealand, this was different. I needed to make the programme culturally relevant, present it in Portuguese, and more importantly, bring a message from the Bible. After God's Word confirmed the way forward and I completed another week-long preschool training seminar at Whitewater Ministries with my colleagues, my confidence grew.

Marion was encouraging and had a great sense of humour. We both enjoyed a good laugh. She assured me that she would assist me with Portuguese, so I could teach in English or Portuguese. She worked with a local team member who could translate the notes into Makua, the main language for most of these healthcare workers coming from the bush. I wrote out notes in Portuguese on big A2 sheets and had my own notes in English, but I needed to shorten my sentences for translating.

The focus of the seminar was 'The Father Heart of God is Love'. Marion suggested using one story from the Old Testament and one from the New Testament. Reviewing my notes from previous preschool seminars, I wrote out a shortened version of what was important when teaching young children.

The *socorristas* represented thirty-five health clinics. Between thirty-five and forty men and women with babies and young children would attend. Marion organised the logistics of transporting them, the supplies needed to feed everyone, and places for them to sleep, as it was quite a journey. She also planned the overall programme, letting me know how much time I had and when my turn came in it.

An enclosed compound protected us from random acts of chaos outside. A large courtyard was to be the teaching area and cooking place. There were two big rooms in a separate building, one for teaching in, the other a dormitory for the visiting *socorristas* to sleep in. A small clinic next door sold herbal remedies, and people could request prayer for healing common ailments, too.

"You can stay with my German students inside my cottage," Marion offered. The cottage had a private toilet and shower area painted deep blue. By now, I was used to washing with cups of cold water from the buckets. *Very refreshing!* Two tiny rooms had skinny beds with, of course, mosquito nets drooping over them.

Marion hired some enormous cooking pots from Anya, used back in the family's restaurant days; Anya used every opportunity to generate cash for raising her nephews. A woman from the nearby village would come every day during the seminar and cook huge pots of food for everyone.

I was excited to be given this opportunity to share a biblical programme for children under the age of ten who were probably unschooled. After praying, I sensed the Holy Spirit lead me to present two stories: one about Daniel in the Lions' Den and the other a passage in Matthew where Jesus told his disciples to let the children come to him. The seminar would be in a couple of weeks, so I had time to prepare with Anya's language help.

Storytelling Props: Dolls and Lions

I talked over my plans with Lisa and Irene, explaining the need to make resources that would not only tell the stories but would teach the *socorristas* how to retell the stories and help children make the same props. The props needed to be created with free materials at hand.

The story of Jesus talking to the children inspired them. They explained how they made dolls or *bonecas* from a special weed (*capine*) and scraps of fabric. Growing up without toys or money had taught them to be inventive. They knew the exact type of weed that was needed and arrived the next day with a boxful. We all met on Anya's veranda one afternoon for the project-making. I visited local tailors asking for scraps of leftover fabric, explaining in simple terms what the fabric was to be used for. They sold me a bundle of scraps to clothe the grass-weed dolls cheaply.

We had great fun making these *bonecas* while Anya prepared afternoon juice and snacks for us and their young children. Cris really enjoyed having two other children to play with, something that didn't happen very often at Anya's. Meanwhile, I had asked Cedru to collect dried corn cobs from the market and from Anya's flour mill. With cardboard, a pen, and string, I made a lion to use in retelling the Daniel in the Lions' Den story. After making two examples to show the healthcare workers, we gathered boxes of all the resources they would need.

On my A2 sheets of paper, I used a black marker pen to write the topics and relevant Bible verses for the two stories in Portuguese. My bilingual Bible was very useful for this, as no internet was available for Google Translate. I used these A2 notes more as a teaching aid for myself, as almost none of the volunteers attending could read.

After all the preparations, I was ready in time for the seminar. Anya had helped me prepare a short devotion in Portuguese, then we all sang praise and worship songs in Portuguese and Makua. I began the programme with a short explanation about how young children learn. I spoke in simple English, which Marion translated into Portuguese and our bilingual young man translated into Makua. My pre-made teaching aids helped me stay on track with the programme, since other health training would also occur throughout the day.

As research has proven, learning is easier when doing rather than listening. With Marion's help, I involved everyone in doing everything themselves in this new-to-them children's programme. I taught them a couple of songs to welcome the orphans at their own clinic's programme, explaining that when all the children had arrived, the songs could help each one feel included.

The previous year, at Whitewater Farm's model *escolinha*, we developed the song *Fazer de rota* (Hold hands and make a circle). The next song of welcome introduced each child and created a sense of belonging to the group: *Estamos Feliz por estar aqui (child's name)*, which translated to mean 'We are happy you are here (child's name)'. However, we used an even simpler phrase in this rural area, *estamos feliz daqui*.

As it was useful to teach a bilingual programme, the *socorristas* could introduce the children to Portuguese words through song, which would assist them if they got the chance to attend school. There were usually one or two adults who were bilingual and could translate the Portuguese into Makua for understanding.

In another short teaching point, I introduced them to the idea that children learn through their five senses. Children would remember these stories better when the teaching included some of these learning paths. Throughout the day, we showed ways to achieve that. As was common in this area, most adults had very little formal education.

The first story was Daniel in the Lions' Den. I chose two Bible verses to support it, one of which was from the Old Testament: 'He will not fail you nor abandon you, so do not lose courage or be afraid' (Deuteronomy 31:8). We then went outside and sat on the ground, making lions using dried corn cobs, cardboard, and a number of black felt pens. I made one as a model while I told the story as I would tell it to young children. Everyone, men and women, enjoyed making their own lion out of local materials to retell this Bible story.

Songs about God caring for us were based around a verse in

Psalms that says, 'He listens to me every time I call Him'.* After sitting for a while, I introduced two more songs to teach the children about God loving us: *Cada dia* (Every day) and *Escuta minha coz* (Listen to my voice). I explained ways of making the songs fun and memorable using loud voices or whispers.

After a shared meal of *xima*, *feijao* (beans), and *cabrito* (goat) with *matapa* (greens), we had a short siesta, then came together for the second story, this one from the New Testament in the Gospel of Matthew. To support the story of Jesus welcoming the little children and not sending them away, as the disciples suggested, I shared with them that Jesus said he loves them just as the Father loves him.† I had written this in Portuguese on a large A2 sheet and the translator explained it in Makua, showing how to find it in the New Testament. *Hopefully, they will remember this part to share with the children when they retell the story.* Only one or two volunteers in their village might be literate in Portuguese.

We then made the *bonecas* or dolls from weeds and scraps of fabric, which gave the *socorristas* an idea to use back in their health posts for telling the story. Even the men seemed to enjoy this creative time. We also gave them time to practise retelling the story to each other, as their oral abilities would help them recall the stories.

Being involved in this seminar was truly fulfilling and enlightening. I was thankful for Marion and the others, who helped to make it an enjoyable learning experience for everyone. I took many photos during the seminar so I could show Lisa, Irene, and Cedru how their resources provided for the lesson and blessed the *socorristas*. Marion and I hoped that these stories, songs, and homemade

---

* Because he has turned his ear to me, therefore I will call on him as long as I live. (Psalm 116:2, WEB)
† Even as the Father has loved me, I also have loved you. Remain in my love. (John 15:9, WEB)

props were activities that could assist the volunteers in enriching and adding value to the orphans in their villages.

The orphans could learn to make their lions and dolls, then retell the stories to their adopted families. Both stories told them that God loved them, that they were all children of God, that they—especially the orphans—were special to God, and that He heard their voices when they prayed and sang songs to Him. We prayed the children would learn about God and remember Him when confronted with challenges in daily life. I reminded myself: *we are planting seeds*.

Marion was grateful I could assist in giving some practical help towards the orphans' programmes, as she had so many other responsibilities. I could not have done any of it without Anya's faithfulness and the dedicated time I spent with her learning the language, in particular the words I needed for specific experiences. My move into town and living with Anya and her family were just what I had needed to progress with this challenging language.

As time went on, practising in the market became more enjoyable and less threatening or embarrassing. I learned to laugh at my mistakes and not let them define my identity.

Rabies and Rosso

Dogs in this part of Mozambique were regarded differently to dogs in more affluent countries, like New Zealand. At Anya's house and courtyard enclosure, dogs had always been part of the family, but their roles were more watchdog than pet. Rosso had been in Anya's family for more than ten years. He walked with a permanently crooked leg due to an injury from a thief. He also had many scars and, like most dogs, was skinny. Anya could not afford medications like worming tablets or veterinary visits.

One day Rosso was acting strangely. His mouth was foaming,

and he was making unforgettable rushing-around types of movements. *Is this what rabies looks like?* To my relief, the power hadn't gone off in the past few days, so my phone was charged. I hoped and prayed for an internet connection to find a YouTube video on what a dog looks like when sick with rabies.

Many of the signs were there, but I was unsure how to show Anya and Cedru without offending them. I knew how important Rosso's guard dog duties were for the family. *However, Cris could wander into the courtyard to pat Rosso and get bitten!* I emailed my prayer team to pray for an immediate solution. When I figured out the Portuguese translation of what the video was saying, I showed it to Anya and Cedru. They agreed that poor Rosso likely had rabies. *Whew! That went well.* I prayed for God's protection for Cris and the family, thankful I'd had all the rabies shots, which would supposedly protect me for life. I didn't want to test it out, though.

Cedru managed to corral Rosso into a secure corner of the courtyard while the rest of us stayed locked inside the house. Anya said he would probably put Rosso out of his misery with a donk on the head with the shovel in the morning. She explained there wasn't a vet in the district anymore, adding the previous vet had been useless anyway.

"Why?" I asked.

Laughing, she replied, "Because he was afraid of dogs!"

The other option was to ask the local police to come and shoot him, but this involved more than they were prepared to bargain with. As nightfall came, I prayed for a rapid solution and a peaceful sleep.

Early in the morning, when Cedru was looking for the shovel, he discovered Rosso had escaped. According to Anya, he then took off, running around looking for a dog with a foaming mouth and erratic movements. Not far away, near the market, a woman saw Cedru looking frantic and waved him over to ask if this was the dog he was looking for. There was Rosso ... dead. The woman said he ran into her courtyard at dawn and began crazily digging in the sand. He had a couple of seizures, then just died. So he didn't get a donk on the head with the shovel, and he didn't bite anyone. That, I thought, was an answer to prayer.

Rosso had been a faithful guard dog, having sustained attacks by thieves with machetes or catanas and other abuse over the years. Cedru, who had a tender heart, was probably thankful he didn't have to kill him. He brought Rosso back to bury him in Anya's courtyard. We marked his grave with a little wooden cross.

Puppies Finally Appear, Only to Escape

Anya's female dog, Pelúcia, was pregnant to Rosso. A month after his death, when the time came for her to give birth, she hid under the building. After a week, we found out she had a litter of seven puppies. When they got older and needed to be fed solid food, Anya cooked ground maize swept off the floor of the flour mill by Cedru into a porridge with nothing else to supplement it.

Knowing she couldn't afford better food, I offered, "*Posso comprar boa comida para cães?*" (Can I buy good food for the dogs?)

She shook her head. "*Não obrigada, então eles não comem a farinha de milho*" (No thanks, then they won't eat the maize meal).

I'm amazed the puppies grow on that diet.

The puppies ventured out more and more from under the rubble into the courtyard of rusty and broken equipment and vehicles. Before long, they were covered in fleas and so full of worms that their tummies were huge. Anya, Cedru, and I dipped them in salt water and towelled them dry. They had no money for any stronger remedy, even if it was available. Anya and Cedru had raised puppies in this environment for many years. I was beginning to understand that this was a situation where it was better for them to manage with their limited resources. *Maybe I should just look, listen, and support their decisions on this matter.*

But the worst predicament was yet to be revealed. Anya and Zé had inherited their parents' flour mill, where people brought their dried corn to grind into flour to make their *xima*. Anya took me to see the mill, which was in an open shed near their house. I was shocked to see no one wearing masks. *Maybe masks are not available, and more importantly, not affordable. Solutions to poverty are complex.*

Frequently, Zé would find out when the mill managers were paid for grinding the grain and collect the money to spend on whiskey before Anya could get it. Anya explained that it was imperative he did not find the money from my lessons and lodging. I could do nothing but pray. I found God indeed intervened at dire times when the aggression was building at Anya's home.

One particular time, after many weeks of drinking, his behaviour was hard to live with. I finally felt enough was enough.* Filled with the power and language of the Holy Spirit, I did spiritual warfare in my bedroom next to Zé and Esa's room. In a very short time, Zé left the house and stood out in the courtyard, looking dazed and lost. Five minutes later, I heard him leave the premises on his motorbike. I was surprised at the short and immediate effect of praying fervently and made a note to myself to do this more often. *Sorry, God, for taking so long to ask for Your help in this matter!* I looked for Anya to share the news, but Cedru said she had gone to the market.

However, when Zé sped out of the courtyard, he left the big iron gate open, and the puppies wandered out into the main street. I wasn't aware of this until I heard Anya, returning from shopping,

---

* *For God didn't give us a spirit of fear, but of power, love, and self-control.* (2 Timothy 1:7, WEB)

yelling something about the puppies outside the courtyard. There she was with an armful of squiggling puppies. A kind man followed her with more puppies in his arms.

"What perfect timing to return, Anya!" I exclaimed. "I didn't realise Zé left the gate open."

After the gate was closed and the puppies reunited with their mother, I explained to Anya in my best Portuguese about Zé leaving suddenly after I was praying. He did not return to Anya's for many weeks after that episode.

Despite the lack of sterilisation available for animals, many puppies did not survive in this part of the country because of the hazards and tough lives. Anya guarded her puppies more closely after that. She was able to sell three of the seven before snakes or big lizards (*lagartos*) ate them or they were stolen.

I was thankful for my prayer partners back in New Zealand. The puppies were so cute despite having fleas, and there were definitely little Rossos in the litter! Anya hoped to raise one pup to replace Rosso as the guard dog.

Superstitions and Witchcraft Practices

After a few months of living with Anya's family and with more immersion in the language, I understood more about how superstitions affected their lives. Earlier in the year, I had not understood Anya's fear of young Cris playing out on the front veranda or outside of her courtyard. When I first moved in, I knew Anya and Cedru discussed big topics, but I couldn't understand them. Anya got local news through the grapevine, and Cedru heard about local events through mingling with people while fetching water or buying fresh produce at the market.

One morning, Cedru arrived at Anya's and shared some village news that I could see was very upsetting for her. I was able to catch

Plans and Ideas for the Year Ahead

what they were talking about, as they slowed the conversation, helping me to comprehend what they were saying. I retrieved my little pocket English/Portuguese dictionary to assist in my understanding, as it seemed quite traumatic news.

It was shocking, to say the least. A school-age child who Anya was acquainted with had gone missing. He had been walking home alone from school a few days earlier. Everyone's greatest fear was that he had been abducted for the witch doctor's purposes. There were reports periodically of dead children found in the bush with body parts missing. *So this is why Anya doesn't let Cris out of her sight!*

At first, I was incredulous of this news. I cross-checked it with the long-term resident missionaries and Peace Corps volunteers. It was indeed tragically true. Locals blamed the shameful practice on neighbouring countries who did this sort of thing. However, people here still believed that potions and incantations by the witch doctor helped with whatever problems they were experiencing. From what I understood, a witch doctor or *feiticeiro* was different to a herbal healer, a *curandeiro*. A *feiticeiro* dealt with the spirit side of life, manipulating or appeasing spirits. Christians perceived this as operating in the demonic realm. The *curandeiro* worked with herbal remedies for the good of people.

Often people professed belief in God and the Bible yet still went to the local witch doctor for help. Cedru had a close relative who attended the local church but also visited the witch doctor for a remedy for breastfeeding challenges. When God did not answer their prayers in the way they wanted or in the time that they wanted, they would go to witch doctors and try that type of healing. This is referred to as 'syncretism', when both beliefs merge. People believed in the spirit world and manipulating the spirits or ancestors, then when they heard of Jesus and the Holy Spirit, He became just another spirit that they brought into an existing belief system.

Many missionaries, I was told, considered animistic practices had a greater hold of fear over the local population than any other belief system. Marion learned from her healthcare workers that they believed a child's skin would get an 'itch' if they looked at a rainbow, and they would make an X from ashes on the child's forehead and warn them not to look. I remembered that when I first arrived, Anya's nephew Cris had a fetish tied to his wrist from his Makua mother or grandmother. Anya had big arguments about it but stood her ground about these not being allowed in her house. Otherwise, she told his mother, Cris could not stay with her. This was a courageous stand.

One week, while living in town, news spread that kidnappings of albino men, women, and children were taking place. *Why?* It was explained to me that potions made from their body parts were thought to possess special supernatural powers. I found it hard to believe such practices and beliefs were still around in this century. *It's definitely something tourists would not find out about!* The locals were generally ashamed of these customs. However, I learned that Mozambicans were not alone. Long-term missionaries confirmed that these evil practices were widespread across many African countries.

I was able to confirm this belief about gaining supernatural powers by reading an email from a trusted news source. The article described the practice of kidnapping albinos and how much money was paid for such persons—around $35,000 US dollars (in 2015) for an albino man. Our town had one or two albino families with children who I often noticed walking along the road. I prayed for their protection and safety after becoming aware of this danger.

Soon after that episode, I learned more about their traditional belief system. Anya explained that the people believed an evil spirit was plaguing this community. One night, drumming and chanting outside woke me, sounding like a parade. It was 4am, a frequent time to hear drums in the bush beating out messages to the spirit world, not a time for a parade!

At that time, Zé was sober and staying with Anya. I opened my bedroom door, and he came with me to the front veranda that overlooked the main street. I saw men, women, and school-age children marching, shouting, banging pots, and beating drums in a sombre sort of mood. He told me it was a march around town by people to scare off the *chupa sangue* (bloodsucker).

Zé explained this was thought to be an animal-type creature that went around sucking people's blood when they were asleep, leaving marks on their necks. The group would march around the whole town to scare away this entity, believed to be a local witch doctor who transformed into a spirit that looked like an animal. People who had been attacked recently and survived the *chupa sangue* attacks showed marks on their necks and arms. Later that day, Cedru confirmed the attacks to be true through the 'water-collecting' local news network. I understood what they were explaining. *My language is improving!*

I had learned in the cross-cultural course before my mission service that animism and witchcraft practices were a method of controlling the spiritual aspects of everyday life. However, they were fundamentally based in fear. I went to bed, remembering how the previous year, I had heard drums beating near Whitewater Farm as well as from Saul and Sarah's house on the outskirts of town. I felt sad that young children were taught these beliefs that would later become spiritual bondages for them. It reminded me why believers, including myself, sacrificed our lives to come and share the truth about the Gospel. We believed that, with a real relationship with Jesus Christ, people could be free from superstitions and fear.*

---

* *The light shines in the darkness, and the darkness hasn't overcome it.* (John

Before being saved by the grace of Jesus Christ, I practised what the western world calls 'New Age' beliefs. In reality, they were occult and thus also witchcraft. I messaged my prayer partners with the spirit world practices I had become aware of, asking for intercessory prayers. *In my heart, I want to see them free from these bondages too, Lord.*

On a positive note, we watched colourful parades, dance performances, and competitions amongst school children from Anya's veranda. Mozambique seemed to have numerous days and weekends off for celebrations. Some of the bigger holidays that honoured and celebrated women, children, and workers were *Dia da Mulher* (Day for Women), International Day of the Child, and Workers' Day.

1:5, WEB)

WO's Global Conference in Thailand

This year was a significant anniversary for global mission service around Asia and Africa. World Outreach proposed that instead of holding local conferences, everyone based in Africa and Asia would meet in one place. Amazingly, this was more cost effective than hosting one for African-based missionaries.

Saul and Sarah shared the news with me. "Guess what? You are coming with us to the World Outreach global conference in Thailand! All the WO missionaries will be there."

Because I had been accepted as a full mission partner last year with intentions of long-term service, I was able to join my colleagues in attending this momentous event. I had never been to any Asian country before, so I was looking forward to the experience. Tina offered to arrange accommodation and activities after the conference for a group of us wanting to see more while we were there.

Arriving in Thailand from a rural Mozambique location felt like entering a first world country. Flowers, especially huge stands of orchids, greeted us at the airport. The markets sold a large variety of tropical fruits, with frequent stalls offering freshly juiced fruits of any combination. People were polite, engaging, smiling, and helpful, and they were often able to speak English. The roads were paved, and there were regular rubbish collections. Though Thailand was more crowded, it was clean and beautiful, without much litter. We all enjoyed the clean bath and toilet facilities everywhere we stayed.

But I was shocked to see the abundance of huge Buddhas and shrines both in public temples and private shrines outside houses. I don't know why I was surprised, as Thailand is primarily a Buddhist country. I was very sad as I observed these people lost in their traditions, and I wanted to share the truth of the Gospel.* Though my heart was troubled, and my intentions were to share the goodness of God's grace, my evangelising voice had not yet been realised.

The conference brought in over 350 missionaries and WO personnel from a variety of locations. For many, it was an opportunity to finally meet volunteers in person. We heard amazing stories of God's miracles and testimonies in extreme situations. World Outreach focused on unreached people groups, often in remote or extreme places. I was inspired to hear collective evidence of God's protection, provision, and healing. Many were long-time missionaries, so there was a real wealth of stories. *Why didn't I become a Christian earlier in my life!?*

We had personal ministry too, assisting us in seeking God's plans and directions. I needed clarification about whether to return full time to Mozambique the next year. Approaching sixty-five, I

---

* *For God so loved the world, that he gave his only born Son, that whoever believes in him should not perish, but have eternal life. For God didn't send his Son into the world to judge the world, but that the world should be saved through him.*(John 3:16–17, WEB)

was wondering about continuing with preschool teaching. *Should I renew my three-year teacher registration for employment whenever I return to New Zealand? Could I work for half the year and volunteer in Mozambique for the other half?*

We also discussed ideas related to the Christian drop-in centre at Anya's, such as offering training seminars for preschools, discipling women, and encouraging mothers with young children in their faith. I was unsure of my next step, so WO mentors helped me with prayer and a time of reflection. Ultimately, the peace of God restored my soul. I trusted Him to show me in His timing.

After hearing all those amazing testimonies and stories of miracles, I struggled with comparing myself to others. However, I was learning to believe that God's Word was greater than my feelings of inadequacy and doubts. I focused on being inspired and encouraged, privileged to be a member of this Holy Spirit-led movement that was serving globally.

My roommate at the conference was an amazing single woman who had followed the call of God on her life to teach and serve in southern Mozambique. I was in awe of her steadfastness and inner peace as a single woman of God in a foreign nation. She was a Kiwi (New Zealander) too, so we enjoyed many things in common.

Tina had organised for us to stay at a Christian accommodation compound near the conference centre. Mealtimes felt like a gathering of one big family, with adults and children giving thanks to the Lord. I had never experienced this before, being a relatively new Christian on the mission field.

Families from all over the world had come here to rest and recharge after serving in countries like India, China, Laos, and Vietnam. I thought they were brave to work in challenging conditions with their children. *They must have super strong faith in God's protection!*

Tina also introduced me to an amazing orphanage near

Bangkok called the Rainbow House. They cared for, trained, and educated handicapped Thai children who would otherwise have been abandoned or left to die under tragic circumstances due to lack of care. A new preschool part of the orphanage was just opening. There were currently opportunities to come and volunteer for three months or more, which I added to my list of future possibilities. *Thailand?* A new thought for me.

Again, I consulted the Word of God. A Bible passage encouraged me to 'keep on keeping on' where I was already volunteering and wait for God's timing.

I learned so much from the eye-opening experiences in Thailand. Reinvigorated, refreshed, and encouraged from the conference, I returned to Mozambique with the other African-based missionaries. I was confident God had called me back to this place and that He would provide all I needed for whatever was next. My time here was not yet finished. I wondered what He had in store for me next!

WO Leadership Seminar at Whitewater Farm

A few weeks after returning from Thailand, we all reunited at Whitewater Farm for a World Outreach Leadership Training course for the local Mozambicans. After listening to Brian at the Global Conference, I was intrigued that he would share his wisdom and knowledge in this remote Bible School.

This was an important meeting, joining forty-seven pastors and leaders from various areas. Many local believers who were trained pastors in their villages were encouraged to upskill in leadership qualities from a biblical background. Brian spoke in English, with Saul or Kevin translating into Portuguese. I stayed for some of the seminar, but mostly I prepared and served food to the team. Others were involved with the pastors' meals. *Okay, so I'm serving leaders.*

That's important, but what gem can I personally take from this seminar? My answer came soon after the training sessions.

Sarah asked Brian about the process of writing a book, as she knew he was a published author. My ears pricked up. I had also been thinking about writing about my experiences someday. He gave us some good tips: "Find one defining sentence that tells what your entire book is trying to say and write this at the head of each chapter. It's important to set aside a regular time to write, maybe thirty minutes or an hour, and to focus on writing during this time. Don't be surprised if only one sentence results during a writing session. It could develop into a bigger idea later." *Wow, I had never considered that could happen, so if it does, I won't despair of being unproductive!* He mentioned that a session might also produce hundreds of words.

The significant timing of this encouraging advice startled me. I had never spoken about writing a book or known anyone who had published one, yet these suggestions could lead into more of what God had in store for me.

I had begun gathering notes, diaries, records, and photos after a long-term missionary in Kenya prophesied about seeing me writing a book on missions. I still didn't know what my defining sentence would be, though. Hopefully that would become clear when I began writing.

I was touched by this seemingly small part of the WO visit that demonstrated God knew and directed my steps before I was aware.* *Trust in the Lord ... and He shall direct my path.*

---

* *Therefore, don't throw away your boldness, which has a great reward. For you need endurance so that, having done the will of God, you may receive the promise.* (Hebrews 10:35–36, WEB)

Practical Missions

Refreshed after the conference, Sarah and I discussed holding a one-week training workshop for preschool volunteers from areas outside of town who needed fresh insight into simple Bible themes.

"The front part of Anya's building would be a perfect place to hold it, since it's a central location," Sarah suggested.

"Perfect! I can ask her this afternoon during our lessons."

When we prayed about holding this seminar, we had a sense of God's peace in it all. Later, I spent extra time in prayer, seeking God's strength, the Holy Spirit's direction, and courage, as anxiety could come in at any moment and paralyse the flow of ideas.

Sarah handled publicity and registered the people interested in attending. I was thankful she was bilingual.

We also involved Juli and Bev, two healthcare workers from the Peace Corps, USA. Sarah and I had previously assisted them as judges for an English language competition with high school students from three schools.

Practical Missions

"Are we teaching in Portuguese? And do we need a person to translate it into Makua?" I asked Sarah.

"Thankfully, all the volunteers coming have had some schooling, so they speak Portuguese. If you want, we can use large A2 notes written up for them to focus on."

"You mean they can write down the notes from those sheets?"

"Yes," she said, then clarified, "Only if we supply the pens and small notebooks for them, of course. They are unable to buy them."

I realised that since these preschool volunteers were not from the bush-bush, they would require new methods of learning and teaching! My brain was busy, imagining new ideas for them.

Lisa and Irene, who had attended Whitewater Farm's *escolinha* training seminar earlier in the year with their two toddlers, wanted to show the other volunteers what they had learned, so we included them in our planning sessions. We were so proud that these young mothers were willing to learn and put into practice new methods of teaching at the *Igreja Actos* preschool.

Sarah pointed out the importance of their involvement. "It's super that they feel confident in teaching their peers, as it will be more sustainable in the long term when we are no longer here to support them."

We listened to Lisa and Irene's ideas and what they were comfortable to demonstrate. They were happy to teach two songs: 'The welcome song' (*Bem vindo*) and 'I am special' (*Eu sou especial*). They were especially excited to teach the 'Head, shoulders, knees, and toes' action song (*Cabeça, ombros, joelhos, pés*), demonstrating a bit of fun with a fast and slow (*rápido e lento*) tempo. This method of learning was a new concept for many of these rural people. *This should be interesting and fun!*

Anya's role was vital. She would cater for a week's worth of meals, Cedru helping with food preparation. Anya had saved all her family's restaurant pots, so she could cook large amounts of beans, goat, potatoes, rice, and *xima*. Her eyes lit up when we assured her it would be an opportunity to earn extra money, but I knew she was just happy to be involved in what was a passion of hers, cooking and feeding people.

Juli and Bev offered to teach a session on accidents and emergencies involving young children at preschool. They were excited to be included and, thankfully, aware of the challenges in rural Mozambique.

"I could show them some simple hygiene, like hand washing," Bev said.

Juli suggested, "How about we bring samples of natural medicines that would be good for the young children at preschool?"

It really took a team to pull the seminar together. Cedru got involved too; we needed a second toilet, and our activities required resources he could help find around the market.

My daily lessons with Anya had noticeably improved my speaking and comprehension. Reading my bilingual Bible aloud assisted with these skills, plus gave me a background to write daily devotions for our week-long seminar. By now, I had a larger vocabulary for preschool activities and had planned, in Portuguese, the orphans' programme for Marion with her health clinic workers.

Sarah and I agreed that the best way to demonstrate developmental stages and how young children learn through their five senses was through practical activities, songs, and games. It was great to have some toddlers and preschool children attending with our volunteers to practise what we were teaching.

We learned about the background or location of each preschool and created a programme suitable for teaching around twenty-five children. One teacher shared that she had twenty-nine but two had died in the last month. It was a reminder of how fragile life was in these communities.

Practical Missions

* * *

Cedru found fabric scraps, magazine pictures, cardboard, and string so we could demonstrate how to make a calendar of the days of the week. We glued the magazine pictures onto cardboard to create puzzles. Using the town's only working photocopier, we made copies of the seven days of creation for each preschool. We supplied crayons for the attendees to colour the days and laminated the sheets for them. We also showed the teachers how to make simple matching resources using cardboard and scraps of fabric.

We explained how recognising patterns and sequencing was important for later language and reading skills. Each preschool received a bag of coloured plastic pegs, which had a variety of uses in teaching mathematical skills, such as patterns, counting, colours, grouping, and fine motor skills. We collected empty milk cartons to teach how to measure using 'found' materials, as we couldn't supply measuring tapes. We asked a local friend who owned a shop to save all her bottle tops from soft drinks for counting and creating simple games. Sound-shakers were made by filling empty containers with different contents like pebbles or sand for a variety of noises.

Juli brought a couple of simple new games: Statues (*Pedras*) and a version of Simon Says (*Faz Isto/Faz Faz*). Bev's health workshop was great. Sarah taught the topics that required better language skills than I had, such as administration ideas and developmental stages, while I taught circle-time songs and how children learn through the five senses. We also taught the teachers how to watch for boredom or restlessness during circle time and how to manage it so that the children had an enjoyable time.

We encouraged the teachers to consider themselves as learners too, which was a bit challenging because of their perceptions of what a teacher is and does. It was hard to condense our years of training into something that made sense to them and was simple enough to add value to their preschool programmes. But overall, everyone learned something new to enrich their programme.

I learned how the Holy Spirit could equip me spontaneously with courage and ideas in addition to what I planned.* Anya was pleased with her earnings. Cris joined in with the other children while we were demonstrating. It was a successful, rewarding experience and one we thought we would repeat the next year. *Thank you, God, for bringing all these activities together.*

Motorbikes to a Bush-Bush Village!

The previous month, Saul had preached from the Gospel of Luke at *Igreja Actos*. This was our home church, and we attended fairly regularly. Sarah and I had prepared a short play on the story of Martha and Mary (from the passage in Luke 10) about two women with different priorities when Jesus visits their household. We had great fun dressing up and finding props to support our storytelling, then presented it in Portuguese that was translated into Makua.

Saul thought we did such a fine job of telling the story that he came up with an idea. "Why don't you two ride out with me on motorbikes to the little church in Nadila? They would love to see your retelling of Martha and Mary—especially the children."

This little village was twenty kilometres out of town down a sandy, dusty road. I had been gaining confidence in riding my electric start motorbike with twice-weekly visits to the *Igreja Actos* preschool. I'd also been riding on the highway regularly out to Whitewater Farm for a bit of doggie time and practising on the dirt tracks around the cashew, mango, and lychee orchards. Overall, I felt confident and excited about travelling to this rural village in

---

* *My grace is sufficient for you, for my power is made perfect in weakness.* (2 Corinthians 12:9a, WEB)

Practical Missions

tandem, although doubts crept in. *Am I capable of doing this?* Another thought occurred to me. *Would this remote village benefit from the solar panel I brought over at the beginning of this year?*

I was thankful for the small backpack to put my 'Martha' church clothes and props in, since I dressed for safety when riding the bike. We set off on two motorbikes, one black and one red. Sarah, though an experienced bike rider, was Saul's passenger this time. I followed close behind. It was a challenge to get out of the loose sand of the driveway, although it had been good training as the paved road shortly turned into a sandy road. I rode looking out for patches of soft sand, heart racing and senses amplified.

As a novice rider, these road conditions challenged me mentally and physically. Saul was conscious of my limited experience. He slowed down and showed me where to avoid the deep sandy parts, finding the best path through them. *I'm in my sixties. If someone had prophesied to me a few years ago that I would be doing this, I would have fainted!*

I prayed for God's protection all the way there, fuelled onward by a sense of adventure coupled with my desire to take a Bible story to this little village of people who were basically unschooled.

Despite some tense moments and white-knuckle riding, we arrived safely and parked behind the church. Dusting off the red dirt, I quickly wrapped my *capulana* around my legs and donned a headscarf to respect their culture. I felt honoured to be in such an isolated part of Mozambique.

We had a warm reception at the little mud-brick, thatched-roof church. When I entered, my eyes took time to adjust. It didn't have the typical little wooden benches like other bush churches, just some tattered mats for the women and children to sit on. We sat on a couple of well-worn plastic chairs situated up the front.

I was amazed at the number of children attending. Before long, we were singing and praising God in Makua—simple, repetitive songs, thankfully—and Portuguese. After Saul's short message, Sarah and I dramatised the Martha and Mary story, much as we had at *Igreja Actos* weeks earlier. Surprisingly, I even remembered the story in Portuguese. *I must finally be improving,* I thought with relief.

We realised our props, one-word signs in Makua or Portuguese, would be useless here. The people were oral-based, so we had to be creative in our storytelling. Since our Portuguese was translated into Makua, the story needed to be simplified and the pace slowed. Everyone looked and listened with interest. It seemed such a simple lesson from the Bible. I was astounded by the level of excitement and gratitude everyone showed us.

Sarah and I were inspired by the possibility of mentoring and teaching these believers to run a simple *escolinha* programme. While it was something to think and pray about for the future, we needed to pray for the right direction and God's timing. *The opportunities are vast here. Will I be coming to this place next year with Sarah?*

Africa is so filled with enormous opportunities for enriching people's lives that it can get overwhelming. I needed to pray and ask for wisdom and for God to open doors where I was to walk through and close doors when it wasn't in that direction. I was learning how to be more reliant on the guidance of the Holy Spirit.

As we prepared to leave, I quietly asked Saul, "Would this be a good place to gift the solar panel?"

"No, not here. But I will give the matter some thought and pray about where it could best be used," he replied, putting on his bike helmet. "Showing favour to one place more than another can create jealousies or false expectations." Supporting newly trained pastors took Saul to many isolated rural churches. He assured me we would find a home for the solar panel in one of the bush-bush villages sometime.

When arranging our visit, Saul had declined their offer of food, knowing how poor they were. As soon as we had packed our Martha and Mary clothes, the three of us headed back to town on our bikes. I wore my yellow tinted goggles, a recent purchase, thankful the red dust couldn't fly in my eyes. I was so excited about this adventure that I found myself disappointed when the town appeared sooner than I really wanted!

Practical Help and Prayers for Healing

Lisa lived a long way away, and today wasn't a preschool day. There must be a very important reason for her to have walked into town with her son Issac strapped on her back to see us.

I asked Sarah for insight, as she knew Lisa's situation better. "She looks really distressed. Why didn't she phone us?"

"Even though we gave her and Irene phone credit so we could keep in contact, it probably ran out. They often use it to talk with their neighbours."

After the usual greetings and pleasantries, Lisa explained that her baby sister, Marta, was very sick with diarrhoea and vomiting. *Oh dear, not again.* It seemed to be a common health issue here. They had even taken the baby to hospital and received a drip to take home, but she was still sick.

"Follow us on your bike," Sarah told me. "And remember the route through the trees and huts, as you will be returning without me." Sarah jumped in the car, taking Lisa and Issac back to Lisa's parents' hut to see the baby. We arrived together, and Sarah and I quickly determined that Marta was still dehydrated. As Lisa's mother was Pastor Tino's wife, we all agreed in prayer for Marta's recovery.

Sarah had to go elsewhere while I did the rescue mission. I hopped back on my motorbike to return to Anya's. Praying I wouldn't get lost, I remembered some of the trees and shrubs pointing me through the maze out to the main road. *I think I remember where I have stored my sachets of electrolytes. And I will fill a large bottle with filtered water.*

How I returned to the hut with the electrolyte solution and explained how often and how much to give the baby was a miracle. And I missed the tricky sandy patches too! I was very thankful to have been able to bless them with prayers and practical help. Thankfully, Marta got much better over the following days.

This was another faith-building experience for me, praying for sick people and seeing a good outcome. Navigating my way there and back from the main road and following winding tracks built my faith in my riding abilities too. *My red Honda Hero bike! A fitting name.*

A few weekends later, Lisa came to visit us, looking distressed. Issac, after being sick with malaria, was very slow to improve. Lisa had previously lost a baby from malaria, so she was concerned. We all prayed, encouraging her that God heard her prayers. Issac recovered fully soon after. *Why am I always surprised?!* Until I lived In Mozambique, I never knew so many people became extremely ill with malaria. It claimed many lives as there was still no vaccine. The only protection locals had were the free mosquito nets supplied by the government.

We witnessed amazing answers to prayer, but they were not always what we had prayed for. Eva, a Christian woman from our church community, had HIV/AIDS and became very ill. My local friend and teaching volunteer, Hope from Whitewater Farm, travelled to Eva's house daily to feed and bathe her, explaining that Eva's family deserted her when she became ill. I admired Hope's faithfulness in caring for our sister in Christ. I visited a few times to help where possible and prayed with Hope. *I don't think nursing is my calling!*

One day, I heard that Eva had passed away. *Did God not hear our prayers? What happened?* However, Hope shared some positive outcomes with me. Eva had passed away in peace with the Lord and had no more pain. Plus, Hope had assisted her with some reconciliation between the family members. Sometimes God's best answer is not physical restoration but healing the wounds of our spiritual hearts.

God's ways are higher than our ways, I reminded myself. Even Jesus prayed, "Let your will, Father, be done, not mine." The Bible teaches us that God's answers are always for the good of someone, but often we can't see or understand them. I was learning more and more about the sovereignty of God in answering our prayers. I also had to remind myself I'd only been living my new life in Christ for ten years. *I still have much to learn!*

An Old Wheelbarrow and a Freshly Painted Wall

It was Cedru's job to locate a source of water for our daily needs when the big water tank ran dry. He had to push an ancient heavy iron wheelbarrow loaded with well-worn yellow twenty-litre containers. One day, in a shop window, I noticed a new red wheelbarrow with rubber air-filled tyres. This could be an opportunity to help him! *That would be a lot easier for Cedru to push through the sandy paths, especially with a load of full water containers.*

Excited, I hurried around to Anya's and asked Cedru to come and look at something down the main street. When he saw it, he said firmly, *"Não, obrigado."* I was shocked, unable to understand why he would refuse something that would obviously make his work easier.

Disappointed, I walked back to Anya's. She patiently explained that if Cedru was seen with such a fancy new wheelbarrow, robbers (*ladrões*) would follow him back to the house and make a plan to steal it. It would bring attention to her residence and courtyard. The fact that a foreigner lived here too would bring a dangerous element of robbery into our lives.

I was impressed by Cedru's personal sacrifice, not accepting an easy-to-push wheelbarrow because it could adversely affect Anya and her household, including me. Cedru worked so hard for our safety and comfort, and I really wanted to bless him.

Every morning when Anya, Cris, and I met for breakfast or *mata-bicho*, our view across the dusty, sandy side road was of a big wall, two stories high with very faded paint, in keeping with the piles of rubbish outside the screened porch. As we drank hot tea and fried bananas in freshly baked buns, I silently asked God to somehow bring a cleaner view through the screen. *Please paint the wall, Lord!* I didn't share my thoughts with Anya, though.

Watching two women in colourful *capulanas* walk by with well-worn buckets filled with small stones on their heads, carrying babies on their backs, I wondered whether my prayer request was trivial. However, only days later I couldn't believe my eyes. Some workers came and painted the wall, as well as the little apartment and front porch beside it. The white paint with green trim certainly brought a touch of freshness to look at while we ate our breakfast. Anya was amazed, as paint was expensive, and no other area had been repainted. *Wow!* We were in awe of God answering our smallest prayers.

Eye Clinics and Drilling for Water

For four years, two retired ophthalmologists from South Carolina, Jorge and Andrea, had been supplying eyeglasses and mobility aids from the United States to help local pastors in bush areas of Mozambique. A two-day road trip was made to meet up with missionaries at a southern port and help transport a mobile eye clinic back to our area. Arriving at a small apartment, we were welcomed by Gene and Tania, long-term World Outreach missionaries. They had plenty of floor space for us all, including Jorge and Andrea.

A container had arrived at the port with equipment to set up a simple eye clinic under trees, as well as wheelchairs and mobility aids. I wondered how the wheelchairs and crutches would work in sandy places. Noticing long lengths of white PVA piping being loaded on top of the ute, I asked Jorge, "What are these pipes for?"

"I have developed a system to hand drill for water in villages where people have to walk many hours to fetch their water. It's a cheaper option than hiring a truck with big drilling equipment, which costs thousands of dollars."

Andrea added, "Our simple hand drilling system doesn't always find water, but it's worth a try. Sometimes we have been successful."

We stayed a day or two and observed how Jorge and Andrea trained a few local volunteers to check people's eyes using the optical tools. The volunteers then practised their new skills at a one-day eye clinic in the city. After that, we loaded up two twin cab utes to transport people and equipment to the far north. Jorge and Andrea would train us and some locals to supply reading glasses for people living in poor, remote villages. Jorge would also try to hand drill for water and train locals how to operate this simple equipment.

Loading up the boxes and boxes of spectacles, I asked, "Where did you get all these glasses, Andrea?"

"In the United States, the eyeglass shops can have many glasses every year that are not fashionable anymore. They donate them to us for Africa."

Antonio joined us, as Jorge and Andrea had trained him a few years ago. He spoke Makua as well as Portuguese, a valuable skill.

As soon as we arrived back at Whitewater Farm after another two days of travel, we enjoyed a dinner prepared by those who had stayed behind.

Those of us going to conduct the eye clinic had a 4.15am start the next morning. Locally baked bread, bananas, and strong coffee with condensed milk filled us for breakfast.

"Take plenty of water bottles and some snacks," Andrea advised. "It's going to be a nonstop day of seeing everyone. No stopping for lunch."

That's going to be a long day, alright. And Andrea and Jorge are older than me. Impressive!

By now I was used to dressing for the bush villages: a long skirt down to my ankles and a headscarf to cover my hair. As the temperature was often in the high 30s, I wore light fabric. I packed a notebook and my little blue camera to record the occasion.

All the necessary equipment to set up an eye clinic for the day had been packed. Our destination was a bush village where one of Marion's Good Samaritan natural medicine clinics was established. When we arrived after a few hours of off-road driving through dirt tracks, the clinic had some chairs for us and benches for people to rest on while waiting their turn. The women and babies sat on the ground on mats, as they found this more comfortable. Around fifty men arrived on foot, with a few on bicycles. Most women in these subsistence farming communities would be working in their fields (*mashambas*).

We set up tables under the mango trees. I sat at one table recording people's names. *Thankfully, Antonio helps me spell their names properly.* Saul had trained pastors in the area years ago, but now they could not see well to read their Bibles. As well as being blessed with free glasses, they received a little Gideon New Testament in Portuguese. *Those mini Gideon Bibles are everywhere!*

It was a joy to see the smiles on these humble, hardworking

Practical Missions

people when they could see well enough to read their Bibles. A few people needed long-distance glasses. Andrea and Antonio used the optical tool to determine what type of lens they needed. I noticed some men kept the stickers or tags on the donated glasses, thinking this added value to their appearance! We prayed with people not only for their physical eyesight but for their spiritual eyesight to be renewed.*

By the time we returned home after our full day's activity, it was dark. After a hot meal and a cold shower, most of us headed off to bed for a sound sleep.

Now that we had experienced a couple of eye clinics in bush villages, Jorge and Andrea asked Pastor Tino of Acts Church (*Igreja Actos*) whether his community could benefit from free reading glasses. Word spread quickly, and local friends and neighbours came to Saul and Sarah's house for a fitting. Anya, who needed reading glasses, went there too, as she only lived a couple of houses away.

"*Talvez este ajuda-me com a cabeça doente,*" Anya said hopefully. "Maybe this will help me with my bad headaches." I hoped so. Anya had experienced frequent recurring headaches since she was young. As far as I knew, no cause had been diagnosed. I had prayed for God's healing, but it had not happened. *Why not? I have much more to learn about God answering prayers for healing.*

Jorge's schedule included hand drilling for water at the church. I mentioned to Sarah, "Wouldn't it be wonderful if they found

---

* *Jesus answered them, "Go and tell John the things which you hear and see: the blind receive their sight ... and the poor have good news preached to them."* (Matthew 11:4–5, WEB)

water? The children could wash their hands, and there would be drinking water for the *escolinha*."

Lisa and Irene organised a cooked lunch of beans, *xima,* and greens outside on a fire for the volunteers. People appeared from nearby, most requiring reading glasses. Just before starting for the day, Jorge and Andrea realised they had left a $10,000 optical tool (a refractor of some sort) back at Saul and Sarah's.

I offered to help. "Tell me where it is, and I can hop on my motorbike and go get it."

After lunch, I rode my Honda Hero a few more times, as they needed more reading glasses. *Where did all these people come from?*

The children from the *escolinha* were given a lesson in well-drilling for water. Unfortunately, they did not find water in this dry season, but many parents became more familiar with Acts Church and the preschool programme. Most left with reading glasses and little Gideon Bibles. It was so satisfying to see their hesitation on arrival turn into visible joy when the correct glasses were found to help them.

End of Year Activities

Sarah suggested a *festa* (feast) for the school year, which ended in November.

I agreed. "Lisa and Irene's first year for the new *escolinha* programme definitely needs to be celebrated."

We consulted with our two volunteers, who had sacrificed a lot for this five-day-a-week preschool, wanting their ideas on how to include the ten to twelve children and their family members. "What will persuade the children's parents to come for our mini graduation *festa*?"

They did not want a cake or popcorn, explaining instead, "A *festa* is not a *festa* without beans and rice!" Providing a midday meal after the ceremony would encourage parents to attend, especially as rice was a luxury.

Lisa and Irene offered to cook the meal if we provided the food. They had recently cooked a successful hot meal over a fire in the back of the church when the eye clinic visited. They arrived at 6.30am to start the cooking process. The *festa* would be held from 10am to 12 noon.

"Let's provide fizzy drinks and popcorn as well," suggested Sarah.

"Good idea!" I agreed.

We decided to demonstrate some learning activities with a brief explanation of why they assist very young children in learning. Lisa and Irene would show some activities too. A booklet had been prepared with the children over the past few weeks, focusing on how God created each child special. We measured their heights and weights and included handprints, footprints, and self-portraits, showing how unique they were. The children also coloured in a booklet of the seven days of creation to take home after the ceremony.

"I can make little graduation certificates for the children too," Sarah offered.

"Let's use the end-of-year photo of the teachers with the children wearing their preschool tunics," I suggested. "I know where to get it printed, and I'll make a thank-you card for Lisa and Irene. We could add an encouraging Bible verse to it."

Sarah agreed. "Include the money for the beans and rice inside."

We hoped that someone who came to the *festa* would be interested in assisting Lisa the following year. Irene would be unavailable, as she was returning to night classes at the high school for young mothers who had dropped out. Perhaps our encouragement in teaching and learning had influenced her to continue and finish her high school levels.

Lisa's father, Pastor Tino, came as a guest, as did two other pastors from churches further north. Parents with babies and toddlers arrived at the simple church building, some sitting on mats and others on chairs. It was a fun and successful end to a very challenging year for us all. Through ups and downs, sickness, and personal obstacles, we had prayerfully persevered, receiving God's strength and love. *Gracias de Deus!*

Earlier that week, during a time of fasting and prayer for the preschool, I had received a prophetic Bible verse about the future of the *escolinha* here. I shared it with Pastor Tino after discussing it with Saul and Sarah. I had never had much experience in prophetic words for people here or in New Zealand, but I felt this one was important to pass on. I asked Sarah to translate it into Portuguese. "There will be many children wanting to come and learn about God, Jesus, and the Bible," I shared with the pastor. "However, spiritual blockages are stopping them, and more spiritual warfare is needed."

I wondered what the outcome of that insight would be in the months and years ahead. *The needs here are overwhelming.* Although I didn't feel called to intercede in spiritual warfare at the time, I prayed for someone to rise to the challenge. *I probably need to know more about spiritual warfare or be called by God to do it so He can guide me.* I was thankful He hadn't called me to embark on that calling yet!

A Small Island

As Mozambique World Outreach field directors, Saul and Sarah visited and encouraged other WO volunteers, especially those in remote and isolated areas. One morning during breakfast, Saul asked me, "How would you like to travel with us to a small island up north, where a missionary family has been living for the past eight years?"

"Wow, yes, I'd love to come along and see what other missionaries are doing, especially on such a remote island. How long will it be for?"

"Pack for a week away."

"Seven days! Why?"

Sarah explained, "It will take two days to get there, with an overnight stop at a guest house on the coast that supports Christians travelling in this challenging area. Plus, there's a one-hour canoe trip to reach the island if the weather and currents are favourable."

Hostilities were a real threat towards Christians in this sensitive area, so this family's identity and precise location were kept confidential in the WO mission magazine. I learned that Hans and Ingrid had a heart to share the good news of Jesus Christ through building relationships. Ingrid made connections with other mothers through their children. Occasionally, tourists arrived on the island. Hans taught men to make handcrafted souvenirs to assist with their living expenses. The couple had opened a small shop to sell items made from coconut shells and local fabrics.

Because the roads and transport systems were even more rough and unreliable in the far north, we travelled in convoy with Tina and Andy in their off-road vehicle. Their three-year contract with Whitewater Ministries was coming to a close, and they were heading back to Europe soon. Sarah and Saul's car could only go part of the distance, so the twin cab ute would take us further.

After five hours of challenging roads, the guest house was a welcome retreat. Our time included taking showers and playing card games, as well as having devotional times in a beautiful, peaceful garden overlooking the sea.

The next day, we drove to an area where it was safe to leave Saul and Sarah's car. Andy and Tina met us with their off-road vehicle and drove to a beach area with parking. A good-sized skiff with a small outboard motor arrived to transport all of us and some much-needed supplies for Hans and Ingrid. The one-hour journey over the water to the outer island was refreshing and exhilarating. *They weren't exaggerating. This really is isolated!*

While Saul and Sarah mentored the couple on the island, I

End of Year Activities

spent time in prayer and reflection. I was nearing the end of my second year and looking forward to my third, although I was still unsure what it would look like. I immersed myself in God's word, focusing on how He 'talks' to me, encourages me, reassures me, and reminds me that He sees and loves me.*

That morning, I noticed a rare baobab flower, a glorious sunrise behind tall palm trees and sunlit clouds, and a little yellow bird in the garden amidst the morning birdsong. Then I spotted a heart-shaped leaf just outside my window on a vine. The plants around the house were sparse, so this little leaf stood out. These timely images of God's creation touched my heart, telling of His love for me. *He sees me!*

The little island had no motorised vehicles, so it was very quiet. I found beautiful tropical private places to seek God's guidance. Reflecting on the past year of personal and combined achievements, I was so thankful. I bought a few items, some clever fabric bookmarks and a keyring made from polished coconut shells, from the craft shop that Hans had opened, thinking they might give Anya or Lisa ideas for generating income in their town.

Every day, we came together for a swim somewhere safe and for fellowship, prayer, and the evening meal. These were deeply enjoyable. We were a multicultural group representing five countries, yet we belonged to a common family who followed Jesus Christ, obedient to God's guidance as we followed His unique plan for each of us. It was so refreshing to be here with friends and amazing to share this special time together on a remote island off the coast of Mozambique. *God bringing His children together.*

I was learning more and more how to 'trust and go' without

---

* *It is because of the Lord's loving kindnesses that we are not consumed, because his mercies don't fail. They are new every morning. Great is your faithfulness.* (Lamentations 3:22–23, WEB) knowing the details. None of us knew what the future held, but I was growing more in my faith and trusting God to show me the way step by step.

On the way home, my ear became sore and blocked, with pressure building. *Oh, no! It's probably just seawater stuck after a few swims. I hope it will leak out soon.* There weren't any medical facilities in our area, so as soon as I arrived back at Anya's, I looked in my extensive first aid kit.

Thankfully, I found some antibiotics and took them straight away, praying for rapid healing. In less than a week, I would fly from Mozambique to Johannesburg, South Africa. Anyone who has flown knows that an ear infection is not at all comfortable with the changing air pressures while landing and taking off.

Looking Back and Looking Forward

Before we all returned to our home countries to rest and reconnect with supporters, family, and friends, Sarah and I sat down to discuss possible scenarios for the first few months of 2016. We both knew the Bible encourages planning and having a vision. She and Saul would be on a short sabbatical for a few months, preparing to teach the World Outreach online missions course, among other activities. As far as I knew, I would return early in February after the worst of the wet season while they were still away.

We hoped that Anya's family was more peaceful, and I could resume living there and continue with Portuguese lessons. Sarah recommended that when I returned, I connect as soon as possible with Lisa, Mama Cinda, and other women I had developed friendships with. She strongly encouraged me to continue fellowshiping at one of the evangelical churches I had known before, possibly going with Rénia to her church. The pastor's wife there had expressed an interest in starting a small preschool in their

End of Year Activities

church area. And of course, I would support Lisa as she got her preschool in town up and running, hopefully with another volunteer.

Sarah asked, "Remember those two Makua women who wanted a discipling course, but illness overcame them?"

"Yes. Didn't they want to lead deeper Bible studies with the women in their village?"

"Maybe when I get back, we could go ahead with that discipling course."

It was still on our hearts to do, despite the setbacks. However, we agreed that God's timing was best.

"I also believe Anya needs discipling for a firmer foundation in her faith. Let's pray she will be more open to that next year," I commented.

"I think we have some discipling study guides stored somewhere that might work for Anya and you. I will ask Saul where they are and show you."

I was excited. "That would be great because I've run out of ideas. The Bible verses I showed her haven't made any changes in her understanding, as far as I can see."

"Developing literacy among the Makua and Nahara people could be another possibility," Sarah said as we brainstormed ideas. She thought I could visit Anna, who I had spent some time with when in South Africa. Anna had much experience with teaching a simple method of creating a written language to oral-based communities in their mother tongue. Perhaps we could use some of that knowledge up north where literacy was very low.

Another long-term missionary couple, Gus and Rona, were living among a remote people group in the northern coastal area. Years of learning their tribal language and developing friendships enabled them to teach and train the locals to write Bible stories in their mother tongue. There were no believers or churches nearby or

Bibles in their own language. I spotted a half-finished outrigger canoe lying in the bushes.

Gus explained, "Some remote coastal areas are only accessible by sea or bush paths."

Maybe I could visit them and learn more about their methods of teaching literacy to help when Saul and Sarah return to our area.

Having lived here for over twenty-five years, Sarah understood the obstacles to young girls and women of getting any education to develop their God-given talents and gifts. Basic education in hygiene could avert many health issues, which would also build self-esteem. Sarah's idea was to hold an after-school programme for young women to assist with literacy, numeracy, hygiene, basic health issues, confidence building, and other needs they might like to explore.

Anya's empty restaurant could be a venue to hold these 'deportment' classes, with Anya supplying the food. The recent *escolinha* seminar we had held there was successful, and everyone seemed satisfied that the premises could continue to be used in this way. The classes would supply Anya with extra income from renting out the space and supplying the meals, and Cedru would earn extra, as his jobs would increase to service the proposed training courses.

We also had a vision for developing a supportive reading programme for parents who had to leave school at an early age. We could supply Bibles for the adults and paper, pencils, and art supplies for the children. Sarah and I also wanted to visit more remote areas out of town on our motorbikes.

We were certainly not short on ideas. But, aware of the slow speed and obstacles involved in developing these plans, it was looking like a five-year vision! After our brainstorming session (*chuva de ideias*), Sarah suggested, "Before we go our separate ways, we should pray and seek God's direction. His timing and provision are essential."

End of Year Activities

These future possibilities created excitement and awe in me. I looked forward to the following year.* They also helped me continue to inform and involve my supporters, both churches and individuals.

I was developing a fondness for these friends and people, despite the challenges presented in this land. *To be part of a mission team is such a blessing.* However, I still had to remember not to compare myself with what others were doing in their areas of activity. I felt very privileged to be able to return with a bigger vision. *Help me, Lord!*

Packing and Preparing for a Return to New Zealand

November was the end of the mission year for most of us, who were residents of other countries. We planned our departures for early December when the rains started in earnest. The locals seemed to hibernate and rest, hoping they received enough rain to water their first crops of the season, but not so much that it would cause flooding and cyclonic destruction to crops and houses.

When we returned from visiting the missionary family on the island, we got busy packing and organising personal items to store until our return in late January. My motorbike and some belongings were to stay at Anya's. While I was there packing up, Anya shared with me that her brother Zé had asked her to pray with him every night for a week as he stayed off alcohol.

"Maybe he will even get a job," she added as I locked away my motorbike, which she and Cedru had promised to keep safe.

---

* *The Lord answered me, "Write the vision, and make it plain on tablets, that he who runs may read it. For the vision is yet for the appointed time, and it hurries toward the end, and won't prove false. Though it takes time, wait for it, because it will surely come. It won't delay."* (Habukkuk 2:2–3, WEB)

Anya was excited to see some answers to her prayers. I was surprised too! *I should also pray for him to stay sober and get a job.*

Some of my other belongings went to Saul and Sarah's to store while they would be away on a much-needed retreat. I would be house and dog sitting until their return in February. Arnaldo would still be employed, so he could support his family. Rénia, who lived in the little cottage behind their house, would keep the house clean of dust and feed Scrubbles, the wee dog. We would be happy to have the company of each other and the dog, especially at night.

Before we all went separate ways, Sarah came to me. "We found the Portuguese discipling study guides! Try them with Anya. She might be interested in starting them while you are away."

That afternoon, I presented one of the studies to Anya during our language study time. We looked at it together and began one lesson. She seemed keen to continue while I was away.

Friends in New Zealand had stored a small amount of my household goods at their farm for my permanent return, whenever that would be. Another friend from work and church, Kelly, had reserved a bedroom, attic storage, and a postal address for me to call home when I was in New Zealand. She also kindly shared her car with me for those weeks around December and January.

During my years of serving in Mozambique, I had to call 'home' wherever I laid my head at night. *Now, where is that thing I'm needing? Is it here or there? Sigh.* I sensed God developing these types of situations to grow a greater trust in His provision for all my needs and to practise not worrying.* I had to learn not to get frustrated with my stuff being spread out all over the world and instead focus on some sense of order in my immediate time and place.

---

* *A man's heart plans his course, but the Lord directs his steps.* (Proverbs 16:9, WEB)

End of Year Activities

YWAM Base on My Way Home, and Delayed!

With preparations for our temporary absence completed, suitcases packed, and the Toyota ute filled with people, including locals who had relatives in the city, we set off to stay at the YWAM base. Vic and Louise, with their five children, were its live-in overseers. Families from different nationalities lived at the base, a place of study and training that sent leaders to share the Gospel of Jesus Christ in remote areas.

It was a welcome retreat, with bunk rooms, running water, flush toilets, showers, and little kitchens with refrigerators! These were luxuries we did not have in town. I hugged and farewelled friends returning home before me. After shopping locally, I had enough supplies to keep me fed until I flew out, due to be only days after the others left for their home countries.

However, my blocked ear was causing more and more pain. Louise asked her husband to take me to a clinic where most visitors went so that we could avoid the local hospital clinic with its long waits and language barrier. Vic, being multilingual, helped me explain my symptoms at the medical clinic. They strongly advised that I postpone my flights until the inner ear blockage healed. I agreed! After two years in Mozambique, I was getting used to my plans changing, but having to trust God and be patient while an ear infection disrupted my flight home to New Zealand was still a challenge.

I was thankful the YWAM base was quiet at this time so I could have a bunk room to myself. Vic's practical medical help, interpreting, and prayers for healing were a huge blessing. I emailed my independent travel agent back in New Zealand, who was incredibly helpful with changing my travel plans, complicated by international times and connections. He always sorted me out with revised flights.

After a week of more antibiotics and prayer, my ear had not improved. During the past ten days, I had spent time walking within the fenced compound, with beautiful trees in bloom. Despite not knowing what was going to happen, a sense of peace through reading God's Word sustained me and drove away my fears. I clung to verses that spoke of God caring for me and exhorting me not to worry. *He will make me strong, firm, and steadfast. Amen.*

Memorised songs bubbled up from my heart to lift my spirits. When I had no internet, these comforted me and strengthened my faith, helping me to release my fears to God.

A pastor friend in New Zealand, unaware of my immediate problems, emailed me a timely message called 'Your trial is producing maturity'. *Really?* The devotional taught me that, at times, God delivers us in our bleakest moment into the miracle that we need. Other times, He uses trials to produce the miracle within us, as a refining fire brings out the best in us and burns up the dross. I felt as though I was in this trial of fire. *A timely message indeed!*

I was well enough to join a lovely women's Bible study group on the base. Their faith and prayers gave me hope that this earache would heal, and I could go home to New Zealand.

I made some special friendships at the YWAM base, including a teacher at the primary school who shared the same birthday as me. A few families invited me to their cottages for dinner, prayed with me, and gave me their friendship, which meant a lot to me during this time of waiting. My faith was being tested, as my healing was taking a while to arrive! My hope was in God's words, and I was thankful to be surrounded by fellow believers.

Somehow Vic heard of Dr Nina, a Russian doctor who was dedicated to helping low-income locals and who specialised in ear conditions and allergies. *How convenient—or rather, what a bless-*

End of Year Activities

ing! After examining me in her apartment, Dr Nina concluded I had an allergy to mangoes. *What?*

Through Vic's translation, Dr Nina said, "Stop all antibiotics now. You need antihistamines." I was shocked, yet convinced that our 'coincidental' meeting was another example of God providing just who and what I needed in His timing.

While in Mozambique during my first year, I had a passion for mangoes, eating them at Whitewater Farm whenever I walked the dogs, even peeling them with my teeth. I now remembered seeing a white sap when I peeled them. Researching on the internet, I discovered that this sap was related to poison oak, which I had suffered a severe rash from as a child. Dr Nina's prognosis that the allergy to mangoes could cause a swelling or blocking of the ears was correct. After a few days on antihistamines, my ear cleared just in time for me to make my rescheduled flights back to New Zealand. *Praise God!*

I spent my last day scrubbing both pairs of my footwear. I did not want to bring any unwanted African pests into New Zealand soil, and clean shoes were a strict requirement at the airport.

Despite not being able to stay in Johannesburg with friends as initially planned because of tight international connections, I was thankful for that delayed departure. I had learned more about trusting God's timing and experienced how He can bring good from a bad situation.

My times spent at the English church at the base were timely, too. I attended a Bible teaching that addressed three misconceptions about God's nature: when God is inattentive, when God is uncooperative, and when God is late. *That's helpful to know.*

I was further reminded through reading particular Bible passages that when I think God should do something, He can answer instantly. But sometimes He waits, and in the meantime, I can trust Him.* *Thank you, God, for your timely words that reassure me.*

I was relieved to have my ear passage not swollen anymore but sad to find out I now had an allergy to mangoes, possibly from overindulgence. Oh well, there were many more fresh fruits to eat there. Papayas and lychees!

Goodbyes are never easy, whether short or long. I had made some special friendships at YWAM, and I left with a tinge of sadness. I looked forward to returning in better health next time. I was to discover that this base would be a part of my heart and prayers for Mozambique.

Home for a New Zealand Christmas

After the long flight that I was used to by now, I arrived in Auckland with a sense of joy. Clean, green New Zealand, my home. It was a sight for sore eyes! Plus, my son was there with his family. It was great to catch up with family, friends, and supporters over the Christmas holidays. Since it was summertime, some were away on boats or at beaches. Such a contrast from conditions in rural Mozambique to the 'land of milk and honey', as it seemed in comparison.

Soon after my return, I was asked to help with relief teaching at the daycare. Not only was it enjoyable but it helped with finances. The children had grown since I'd been away! It was great to see the new outdoor spaces, and of course I loved working with the team of old and new teachers and meeting up with families again. More puzzles and books were donated too.

---

* *But may the God of all grace, who called you to his eternal glory by Christ Jesus, after you have suffered a little while, perfect, establish, strengthen, and settle you.* (1 Peter 5:10, WEB)

End of Year Activities

I spent Christmas with my son and his family, making Christmas cookies and sharing them with other friends. Then in the New Year, it was my birthday. Surprise! Old and new friends came, making the day special. My support network came together with cake and tea to offer encouragement and prayers for the year ahead in Africa. Friends, food, and fun! Beach and coastal walks were so refreshing for my soul.

Shortly after my birthday, I found out that my plans to return to Mozambique were to change dramatically.

Part 5: The Return 2016

Change of Plans!

My brother in Oregon sent me an urgent request to help with our mother, a widow of six years and very independent but with failing health. My brother was self-employed, married, and had two teenagers. They lived only a few houses away and had been trying to assist with her health challenges. She was going between home and hospital frequently. At the time, I was unaware of the full extent of the difficulties and challenges our mother was presenting, but I got the sense they needed more help.

My sister and her husband had recently moved permanently to South America and were employed at a university teaching English as a second language. My other brother and his wife, a university professor and self-employed cello maker, lived over one thousand miles away from my mother and were also busy with work. I was in New Zealand but on my way back to Mozambique with ongoing projects. We were all in the middle of commitments. *Should I go? How will this fit in with the plans we made in Mozambique?*

Though I had lived in New Zealand nearly all my adult life, as the oldest child in my family, I felt some responsibility.* My mother was my mother, and my youngest brother sounded in desperate need of help. I gave it some thought, though I could not see a way for me to go. A song came to my mind about God making a way where there seems to be no way.

I was weeks away from returning to Mozambique when I suddenly felt to pray specifically about whether I was to go. *Why does it take me so long to commit these questions to the Holy Spirit for help?* But I didn't feel comfortable using any of the donations given for Mozambique missions. If I was to go to Oregon, how would I pay for it, and more importantly, what would become of my commitments in Mozambique?

I felt God quickly indicate my direction when I read a passage in 1 Timothy that I had never noticed before.† It spoke to me about going home to care for our relatives. I felt some conviction. *Really, God?! How can I pay for this?*

I put the word out to my prayer partners about this urgent developing situation, and a surprising answer came that same week. A couple in the little Far North church believed it was imperative that I go home to see my mother before she passed away and gave me an anonymous donation. *Wow, what a quick confirmation!* I bought the airline ticket thanks to people I didn't really know. I was humbled by their obedience to the Holy Spirit's prompting to give without any desire for repayment when prompted.

I was blessed to be able to go, but with this sudden change of plans, I needed to email friends in Africa and America. My travel agent quickly got me connections that worked around existing

---

* *But if any widow has children or grandchildren, let them learn first to show piety toward their own family and to repay their parents, for this is acceptable in the sight of God.* (1 Timothy 5:4, WEB)

† *But if anyone doesn't provide for his own, and especially his own household, he has denied the faith and is worse than an unbeliever.* (1 Timothy 5:8, WEB)

Change of Plans!

bookings. I was to fly from New Zealand to South Africa, then to Dubai, a major airline hub in the Middle East. After a few hours in Dubai, I had a sixteen-hour flight to Los Angeles with another short flight to Oregon. It was a long series of flights and transit stops, but it gave me plenty of time to check out inflight movies as well as read God's Word, which calmed my anxious thoughts.

As I boarded the last short flight, I looked forward to meeting family. However, I was faced with another delay. It was so foggy that we got turned back to LA. After a night spent sleeping in the airport, I prayed for clear skies. *This body isn't as comfortable as in my younger years, straddling airport seats and trying to sleep.* On our second attempt to fly the last three-hour leg, I was pleased to see the Cascade peaks through the fog as we approached Oregon. Suddenly, the fog cleared, the runway came into view, and we landed. We all clapped, happy to reach our destination. *After two days of travel, boy, do I need a shower!*

Quickly after my arrival, my brother and family filled me in on my mother's health. I was shocked to see her in such a state, as I hadn't visited for years. Our weekly phone conversations had not revealed the full story. She always sounded so much better on the phone. I could now see she was very unhappy, battling everything and everyone. I was pleased my family had informed me of the urgency of her situation despite it being difficult.

My brother had tried to look after her deteriorating health for a long time. It was my turn now. My Mozambique plans were on hold; for how long, I didn't know. I focused my days and weeks on my mother's changing healthcare, developing relationships with local health professionals, and most of all, trying to be a listening ear for her and my family. *How can I help more?* My prayer life was a source of comfort, guidance, and direction during the turbulent days ahead, as failing health issues forced changes upon Mum that she found difficult to accept.

I was so thankful for the social workers, counsellors, and eventually the hospice professionals. They also helped family members cope with the evolving crisis. I stayed in the house, observing Mum's failing abilities to care for herself yet aware of her need for independence. She did not want me to tell anyone about any inabilities that became evident. *What do I do, Lord? I worry about her safety but need to respect her wishes to be private.* Losing control of her daily life was Mum's biggest fear. Developing relationships and connections with her health advocate and hospice was essential for her, and for me too!

With my prayer life and listening to the Holy Spirit's 'voice' through reading my Bible, I retained a sense of peace, calm, and forgiveness with love. At first, Mum did not want anyone to visit her at home, including nurses, doctors, and especially hospice workers.

We had some good talks, and she shared how she and my dad met. She clearly missed him. He had passed away a few years before, and they had been married over sixty years. She was determined to stay in her house, but it was built on a steep slope with stairs to climb up from the driveway, not ideal for someone losing their balance. The inside of the house was not able to be easily adapted, either.

I had worked with elderly people in retirement homes for a few years and was aware of what they needed during this stage of life. One of my brothers was searching for retirement places she could afford that were close enough for family to visit. However, she was adamant she was not going into an 'old people's home', as she put it.

After a particularly bad night, I phoned my brother in Colorado. "Have you found any assisted living place nearby? Things are changing rapidly here, and I don't think it will be safe for Mum to stay here much longer."

"Nope, absolutely nothing is available that is affordable or suitable."

At this low point, I turned to more fervent prayer and even wrote my requests down, as it helped me focus on God's hand in it all. I, as well as other family members, could see that she needed to move to assisted living, but it seemed impossible. We needed more help from the hospice in this unhappy atmosphere.

On Sunday night, I cried out to God. *Lord, I pray for your help in this transition time. By your grace and mercy, may my mother understand more fully her need for other people's assistance more than what the family can provide. I pray she will gain more trust in hospice professionals to care for her at home. I also pray for your guidance on how long I am needed here, as there are projects in Mozambique about to start. Father God, thank you that you hear my prayers and are already answering them in ways much greater and better than I can imagine. I pray for more willingness in my mother's heart to accept outside help and even to realise she could have better care in another place than her home. I ask you for an opening in a nearby assisted care facility that she can afford, where family can visit and she will be happy to move to. I pray that her heart will soften toward some family members, and that there will be a time of forgiveness and reconciliation. Thank you for all that you have done in helping me cope and for answering prayers for help every day. Amen.*

On Monday evening, there was a positive change in my mother's outlook. This was such a testimony and witness to God answering my desperate prayer! Another visit came that day from the hospice people, who were able to help us now that she had a more open attitude.

Then I got a phone call from my brother in Colorado. "I found a place for her!" Within one week of that fervent prayer, my brother had located the ideal place just up the road from where she lived.

"Wow, really? Where?"

"It's the one up the road with all the trees. They have a sudden vacancy in a little studio apartment and will give her a discounted price, too."

We both agreed that might clinch the deal.

One lunchtime, we heard a knock at the door. My godparents, dear friends of my mother's, arrived for a surprise visit, bringing homemade soup and Mum's favourite cookies. Sitting with her and chatting brought her a lot of comfort. They quietly confided in me that in these past few years, she hadn't let them visit her. I could only marvel at the hand of God, bringing people together to help her. *It's true; God can do super abundantly more than we can ever ask for or imagine!*

The assisted care facility was situated very close to her house. *She will feel at home under the trees.* The caregivers were friendly, and the place was well kept. One nurse, after I shared my faith, assured me she would care for my mother in her last days and quietly pray for her as well. This was a great comfort for me. With my other brother's arrival from out of state and local family helping to organise the physical move, I felt free to return to Mozambique.

I was so grateful to have been here during this time. After spending a few more days with my two brothers and our mother, we tearfully hugged goodbye. The long flights gave me forty-eight hours to rest, process, and reflect on all that had transpired. I knew life would be demanding once I arrived in Mozambique again.

Return to Mozambique

Sadly, two weeks after my return, I learned that my dear mother had passed away. I was deeply grateful to have spent time with her beforehand.

Due to the stress and long flights of these past three weeks, I arrived in Mozambique's warm, rainy climate sick with bronchitis and flu symptoms. Thankfully, Rénia cooked simple and nutritious soups while I house-sat at Saul and Sarah's as planned late last year. *Now I can rest and recover.* Saul and Sarah would soon return from their holiday and time spent planning a seminar for World Outreach members.

In January, while I was in New Zealand, the huge rubbish pile —by now, the size of two commercial buildings—that took up the entire side street outside Anya's courtyard was completely cleared. Not only that, but a rough fence was erected with signs stating, "*Não deixe lixo aqui!*" (Do not dump rubbish here!). This was an answer to prayer and a reminder to Anya and me that God cares about every problem, big or small.*

As usual in the rainy season, roads were being washed out, and houses were falling down. I was not as shocked this year by the road washing out in front of Saul and Sarah's *casa* (house) while I house-sat, just thankful there was another entrance. I found it interesting that, even though the repair took a long time and required patience, it was a solution to unemployment. Dozens of men with shovels were put to work, shovelling sand dumped on the good part of the road.

Another discovery I made, once I recovered enough to walk over to Anya's for my afternoon language lessons, was a neatly chewed hole in the plastic screen over my desk. An intruder had been in my bedroom while I was away!

I showed Cedru, and he said, "*Rato!*"

Oh no, I hope it didn't chew my clothes stored here!

"*Mais pequeno*" (But small).

Whew.

He set about finding a small piece of similar screening and sewed a patch over it, then lightly touched a match to it to melt the ends. Cedru was so gifted at fixing anything with very little money, a skill developed during decades of civil war and a scarcity of supplies and paid employment.

During the month before Saul and Sarah's return, I continued to sleep at their place, eating dinner with Rénia and Scrubbles, the wee dog. Walking to Anya's for my language lesson only took five minutes. *Will I be returning to live with Anya and her family for the whole of this year?*

I was thrilled to hear that Anya's brother got a job before

---

* *Be strong and courageous. Don't be afraid. Don't be dismayed, for the Lord your God is with you wherever you go.* (Joshua 1:9, WEB)

Christmas and was still employed. An answer to prayer! I found out that Anya had many setbacks with working through the discipling study guide I left with her while I was away. Sarah had left another discipling manual behind, this one with the English translation beside the Portuguese, in case I wanted to work through it with Anya. I showed her this option, and she was interested in trying these lessons together when we were both ready.

As soon as my donations arrived, I paid Anya for language lessons and meals. Food was in short supply at the markets during the 'hunger season', as the main crops hadn't yet been produced. I returned to eating with Anya and family once Saul and Sarah came home. Anya prepared typical Mozambican meals for this time of year, using maize, squash, fresh boiled peanuts, and cooked bananas—ingredients only available if the crops were successful. Anya sent Cedru to see if he could find any other food. *Hopefully, no cyclones or droughts will happen this season, so the people can eat!*

One of my favourite meals that Anya cooked, with much preparation work from Cedru and little Cris, was simple yet delicious and filling. Small dried brown beans were ground, soaked, and cooked with plenty of garlic, onions, curry, and salt. We ate it with rice. Anya and the boys had a small amount of dried salted fish, but its smell was disagreeable to me. Thankfully, the crusty fresh bread buns were still available.

When chicken was available, Anya marinated it in lots of garlic dried from last year's crop, then barbecued it over hot coals, Portuguese-style. The garlic, crushed in her mortar and pestle with oil and salt, was super pungent. Eaten with rice and cooked greens, this was another of my favourite meals.

It was a bonus for me to share meals with Anya's family and experience her Portuguese and Mozambican cooking. She helped me translate a song from my New Zealand daycare that gave thanks for our food. Cris, and eventually his little brother Gabby, enjoyed singing it before we ate. *Obrigado Deus para dar nos comida* (Thank you, God, for giving us food).

Sadly, Zé and his job didn't last for long. He returned to heavy drinking, with unpleasant results, mostly in the evenings when he came home. I continued with my daily language lessons, discipling Anya through the Bible study, and sharing meals with her and the children. However, I was advised not to return to sleeping there. *Oh, it is such a sad outcome, Lord. I pray that an AA programme will come to this area soon.*

Motorbike Licence Renewed by Myself!

Saul and Sarah were still away when I realised my licence needed renewal. Normally, Saul would accompany me to the licensing place, as my language for officialdom was insufficient. I was feeling anxious about this visit, to say the least.

The application also often involved a little 'gift' in the processing, and I was not sure how NOT to do this and yet still get it renewed. I emailed my prayer team to pray for favour and guidance in this and prayed as well. When I had peace about the timing of going to the office, I kept God's word close in mind, battling the rising thoughts of defeat and fear trying to deter me. Maintaining a firm grip on memorised words from the Bible and even singing some songs, I rode my bike to the office in peace, taking my little pocket bilingual dictionary along with me. I confidently entered the compound (in God's strength and power) and asked in Portuguese for a renewal of my licence.

Realising they were trying to tell me the bike was too big for this type of licence, I pleaded ignorance when they suggested I give them a gift. *Not again!* Last year, Saul had explained that the bike was less than 100 cc. I didn't want to have to go to the city and sit the test. *I should have brought some small Gideon Bibles to give them. Lord, please give me patience.*

The phrase "*Não entendo*" (I don't understand) came in very handy. I asked them to speak slowly, and using my little pocket dictionary, sign language, and pictures, we managed to understand each other—or possibly, I wore them out by 'not understanding'! By God's grace and mercy (along with my smiling face), they finally reissued the licence as it was their lunchtime. God's timing was perfect. The bonus was that I did not have to give them a small gift of money. I may have also said that when Pastor Saul returned, he could talk with them about anything I had missed, or something to that effect.

I felt so relieved and grateful for this small but significant victory. The bike gave me an element of freedom and a connection to Whitewater Farm and the dogs. Most importantly, it meant I could support Lisa and Rénia's church with the Christian preschool programme.

Having readjusted back into this lifestyle, I looked forward to the twenty-minute ride along the highway to Whitewater Farm to visit people I hadn't seen since late last year. I prepared for the possibility of traffic police setting up a hidden checkpoint and jumping out of the scrub. Random checkpoints along the road often expected a 'gift' of some kind from westerners. This time, if they asked me for my licence, I'd surprise them.

Sure enough, there they were again, hiding in the same spot as last year. I understood they were claiming I had the wrong licence, hoping for a 'gift'.

"*Não entendo.*"

Since Saul was not in the area, I rang Kevin on my basic phone as I was halfway along the highway. He came in his truck and spoke with the police. I was free to carry on to Whitewater Farm. *Whew!* I was grateful for Kevin's help, knowing how valuable it was to be part of a team in these parts with limited language.

I continued riding my red Honda Hero bike to the Farm. It was such a joy to see everyone—and the dogs, too.

Discipleship Programme

Anya had malaria again. This disease was a majorly disruptive illness in people's lives. Even long-term missionaries would succumb to a few weeks of sickness and inactivity. We had to halt the language lessons, and I ate meals with Rénia for a while. *Life is so hard here.* I felt sorry for Anya and her responsibilities. *Please, God, bring healing!*

The bilingual discipling study that Sarah had left out for me to try with Anya seemed the best one yet. I had time to examine its approach during our delay. Reading the introduction, I learned about the importance of a progressive study through the Bible, starting with Genesis, the first book in the Old Testament. I discovered it was imperative for students to have their own revelation from God—that they were sinners in need of a Saviour.* *I never knew that!*

This new study provided other enlightening and interesting lessons for me. I learned from the English notes how important it was for the 'disciple' to realise that it's not humanly possible to follow God's laws, and that they needed to repent and seek help. Their heart needed to be prepared as well as their mind. The study stressed how vital it was to follow the lesson plan and wait. *Why?*

---

* *Go and **make disciples** of all nations, baptising them in the name of the Father and of the Son and of the Holy Spirit, and teaching them to observe all things that I commanded you.* (Matthew 28:19–20, WEB)

So the person would reach the understanding that they needed help with bridging the gap between God and themselves. *Aha!*

The study had been developed for illiterate people groups who lived in an animistic believing culture, but I thought Anya would still benefit from it. I had been discipled ten years ago, but I had never led someone through a discipleship study. *I am learning too!*

Anya was enthusiastic. She wanted her preschool nephews, Cris and Gabby, to get some instruction once a week about the God of the Bible and God's love for them. When her health improved, I provided her with some resources, such as the seven days of creation, which we coloured in together.

After learning songs from our preschool programmes in the villages, Anya decided to teach a shorter version at her home. Her house was a point of contact for many of her family and friends in the area. I prayed there would be more children joining in with her nephews when I wasn't there. *Bring them in, Lord!*

Last year, I needed to focus on preschool language and market situations in our language lessons. When we finally got started this year, we both enjoyed the additions to our studies.

A Surprising Development

Our studies began with the character and nature of God, the origin of Lucifer, and other aspects of the spirit realm. I was unaware that Cedru, who was bilingual in Makua and Portuguese, was listening to our studies. Though he was not able to read or write, his eldest son went to school and could read both languages. One day, Anya shared that he had asked if she could copy out the Bible studies and verses for his family too. *Wow, I did not see that coming!*

This was an unexpected turn of events. Anya and Cedru worked with my limited language and simplified our conversations regarding spiritual matters. The Holy Spirit also helped bridge the gap in my understanding. I photocopied Anya's handwritten notes so other people in Cedru's family could follow along with the Bible study. They knew about the spirit realm, and some were involved in going to their local witch doctor for remedies, which Cedru believed was wrong. However, they had also been attending a nearby church. He wanted to help his family understand and learn more about the God of the Bible and about Jesus.

Cedru's extended family included a number of scattered households about fifteen to twenty kilometres away from town. A big mango tree dominated the area and was a focal meeting place for people to gather. His son agreed to read out the lessons and Bible verses on Sunday afternoons beneath the tree. After a short while, Cedru sadly related that his son had gone off with his friends and had become difficult to locate. *Now who will be able to read the notes Anya has written?*

By now, Saul and Sarah had returned, refreshed and happy to be back in Mozambique. I asked them for advice about this new discipling situation.

Sarah suggested a teaching resource called a MegaVoice. "Why not try that?"

I asked her for more details. "I've heard of those, but I've forgotten what they are."

"They are solar-charged devices about the size of a phone that transmit an audio version of the Bible in the local dialect, Makua. A German missionary up north has imported some and sells them for about $30 US. We're going to visit him soon and will bring some back."

Sounds perfect!

Thankfully, I had enough donations to buy one. A week later, I gave a MegaVoice to Cedru to share the audio Bible-reading in Makua with his family. He rode his bicycle home on Friday, and on Sunday he hung the MegaVoice from a branch of the mango tree and counted twenty-eight people gathered under the tree listening to the Bible! On Monday, he was so excited to share the experience with Anya and me.

His son was nowhere to be seen, although Cedru still prayed and hoped he would return one day. He saved the Bible notes that Anya had copied out for him, hoping his son would read them and make a change in his life.

When I shared this news with Sarah, she mentioned there was a church on the way to the city with a Bible bookstore. "They even have some Makua/Portuguese translations. I'm going there next week. Why don't we stop and buy one of those Bibles for Cedru to pass on to his son?"

I had doubts. "Cedru lives thirty kilometres away. He's illiterate, and his son is becoming more unreliable." *I don't know how this will work.*

Sarah suggested we pray about it and ask God. By the time we drove to the Bible store, I felt at peace about buying it. We both committed it to prayer, asking God to make a way when there seemed to be no way.* *My faith is growing.*

---

* Now to him who is able to do exceedingly abundantly above all that we ask or think, according to the power that works in us... (Ephesians 3:20, WEB)

Exciting Occasions

The weather during this season was predictably hot and sunny. Women bought colourful new *capulanas* and matching headscarves. Parades and performances filled the day, with groups performing their special dances or skits celebrating women's role in society. Hundreds gathered at the public square under the flag and listened to speeches by the region's dignitaries. Last year, we wandered over to the all-day government-organised celebrations held in a covered concrete stadium. School groups of children and youth, as well as men and women, performed vigorous dances and humorous skits to celebrate the work done by women.

This was my third year of participating in the town's festivities, and I wanted to experience something different. While Saul and Sarah were away, I had attended Rénia's *igreja* (church), which was down a sandy, dusty road further out of town. I came to know the pastor and his wife, Rosita, along with Bella and Mario, volunteers from an evangelical church in South America. They decided to hold a day-long *Dia da Mulher* celebration with their church community, sharing a big meal and spending time in prayer, worship, and craft-making. In contrast to the government's celebrations, the church would focus on honouring women through a biblical perspective.

Rénia, Mario, and Bella invited me to come along to their church after the official celebration by the town's flagpole.

"Can you please transport a case of cold soft drinks from a shop's refrigerator in town? It will be paid for," Rénia asked.

I knew cold fizzy drinks were something locals only enjoyed at special events, especially on hot days. I also wanted to help Rénia, as otherwise she would have to walk from town to her church with the drinks on her head.

"Certainly," I agreed. "I would be happy to do that."

After the formal celebrations by the flagpole, I walked back to Saul and Sarah's. I rearranged my *capulana* and tucked my scarf under my helmet, then jumped on my bike to pick up drinks from the shop in town. I picked up Rénia, who came with me as far as the paved road. *I'm loading my bike almost like a Mozambican!*

On the outskirts of town, I looked at the sandy road ahead nervously. Memories of sliding off my bike into sand still haunted me. *Should I go or not?* I rode a short distance before wisdom told me to turn back. *The reality is I'm not as agile now.* Rénia offered to walk the rest of the way with the drinks on her head, as the church was now less than a kilometer away.

"*Obrigada, Rénia!*"

This was not the first time I was impressed by the strength and balance of women carrying heavy loads on their heads. I followed her carefully on my bike, arriving safely after a few stalls and stops in navigating the loose sand. I loved helping others, but God was teaching me to accept others' help. The pastor and his wife were thrilled we had delivered the cold beverages.

This vibrant church had recently been built from concrete

blocks but still needed a roof. Although the sunshine shining through the bright blue plastic tarpaulin covering us was lovely, a metal roof would be needed before the seasonal heavy rains.

The church service was uplifting and different, as Mario and Bella organised Portuguese worship songs with a Brazilian flair. A couple of people recommitted their lives, and we believed for miracles of changed lives to come. Brazilian-Portuguese praise songs continued to play while we shared barbecued food, enjoying the fellowship of believers and our cold purple fizzy drinks.

Later in the week, Rosita organised a time for me to help set up a preschool programme at the church. She had ninety children on the roll, with the potential of forty taking part in the preschool. Their timeframe would be between 7.30am to 10am. She wanted to include *pap* (porridge) for the children.

I was surprised. "A hot meal?"

"Yes, but don't worry," she assured me. "It is not your concern. You just bring some ideas for a preschool programme."

By now, I could see progress in my own experiences, and I had a few practical ideas that could work for the many children in this church community. I felt pleased to be able to help. *Thankfully, I can leave the rest up to God!*

Another Orphans' Programme

A year had passed since my last seminar with Marion's healthcare workers (*socorristas*), and it was time to hold another one. Last year's training had taught the *socorristas* how to treat ailments using natural remedies, to pray for the sick, and to care for their village orphans.

Since my knowledge and use of Portuguese had improved, I was determined to use only Portuguese with no English at all, which would help the translator. I still had to write out and plan

Exciting Occasions

what I was going to teach, but I had more confidence. I felt I could bring in a little humour too!

Many of the health workers and teachers had attended the previous seminar. However, some were new, so we would need to include review points from last year. Fresh Bible stories and crafts were introduced for this year's theme, 'God Gives Us Courage'. I knew immediately which Old Testament story to use: 'David and Goliath'. They would love this story. The New Testament story took longer to decide on, but I chose 'Jesus Feeds the Five Thousand' from the Gospel of John. Anya again assisted me, but this time she just proofread what I had written. *Thank goodness I kept my notes from last year. They're a great template and help me remember!*

The seminar schedule was divided into several sessions—some with indoor teaching, others held outdoors under the big courtyard tree. Lunch and dinner were provided, with time set aside for reflection and sharing what was learned. The day would begin promptly at 7am and finish at 8.30pm.

Marion asked me to lead the half-hour devotion from 7 to 7.30am.

"In Portuguese, I presume?"

"Yes. Sufu can translate it into Makua, like last year."

I nodded. "After the devotional, you could outline the day's schedule of events."

Marion had a new idea too. "They love using drama or learning a new song about one of the stories. They are really good at orally presenting what they learn in Makua."

"Sounds good. They will love performing David and Goliath."

"Maybe we could make it a competition!"

I found some large sheets of newsprint paper to write out the Bible verses in both Portuguese and Makua. Some attendees could copy these notes to take back to their health post. We also collected materials and resources for the craft-making session that they would be able to use with orphans in their own villages.

I needed to pack for the full weekend, as Marion's centre was some distance from town. I relied on fellow missionaries for transport, and trips to the coastal areas were infrequent. *Don't forget to take mozzie repellent!* I also remembered my anti-malarial medicine. The coast with its mangroves seemed to have more mosquitos.

I dressed in my *capulana* and headscarf, and Marion picked me up in her small pickup the day before, along with other seminar attendees. These *socorristas* were from very rural areas and wore traditional clothing.

Marion was there to assist with the programme, but this year she left it to me, with Sufu to translate. Although honoured by her confidence in my abilities, I was a bit anxious. However, as always, once I prayed and got started, my feelings of inadequacy faded, and the Holy Spirit assisted me. Being well-prepared gave me confidence, and last year's experience also guided me, allowing me to relax more and enjoy the whole day and evening.

Before we started, I asked the *socorristas* what they remembered from last year's seminar. I was surprised how much they liked and used the preschool songs that reinforced Bible verses. After briefly reviewing some ideas, I introduced our new theme. I asked them, "When we don't have courage, what do we feel like?" Naming **fear** as the enemy that robs us of courage, I shared that I had been fearful about teaching entirely Portuguese—until I prayed.

The morning devotional focused on how God knows each of us (including the orphans in the village) by name, loves us, and hears our prayers.* We prayed to truly know those truths, thanked God

---

* *See how great a love the Father has given to us, that we should be called children of God!* (1 John 3:1, WEB)

for hearing our prayers and promising to always be with us, and prayed for the seminar day.

In the first morning session, we taught the story of David and Goliath. For our creative activity, we dramatised and retold the story. The Mozambicans brought it alive with their talent for storytelling. It was hilarious! After the morning break, we taught the story of Jesus feeding the five thousand with only five loaves and two fish. We made props of fish and bread out of local resources to teach the children. Some of them created their own songs about the story. After dinner, Marion provided prizes and time to share and reflect on what they had learned.

Most of these healthcare workers had sacrificed time from their family duties to study healthcare aspects, such as making herbal remedies, and to learn the Word of God and how to apply it to their lives. This seminar provided a basic model for an orphan children's programme of Bible stories using different methods to bring the stories alive and make them memorable.

Marion and I hoped the *socorristas* were now confident to take a practical programme, demonstrating God's love and hope for their lives, back to their villages.

My Honda Hero Takes Me to Cedru's Family

On the last Sunday of May, I received a surprising invitation. Cedru's wife and sister invited me to lunch to show their gratitude for giving them the MegaVoice and the photocopies of Anya's Bible study notes. Their only day off from working in their *mashambas*, or gardens, was on a Sunday. However, they had to postpone my visit to mid-June due to sickness in the family.

Cedru and I drew a map for the location showing the nearby town and where I needed to turn off the highway onto a track. I sensed he didn't really understand map drawings for directions. By now, I'd been in this culture long enough to know that people often said yes even when they didn't understand, wanting to be agreeable and avoid causing offence. Hoping I had the right day and time to ride eighteen kilometres out of town to an area I'd never been to before, I checked with Anya.

Wearing my helmet, sunglasses, short leather boots, and gloves, I set off on my bike alone to find their thatched huts on the pre-arranged Sunday. Riding out of town further than I had before, I passed a small town with a large twin-towered church, a Portuguese remnant from many years ago. Fighting off 'what if' thoughts, I asked God to give me a generous dose of courage.

Meeting locals at arranged times could result in a delay or even a 'no show' due to cultural differences or circumstances beyond their control. I waited by the taxis as agreed. An hour passed, but still no Cedru. He was supposed to guide me to the path off the highway that led to their cluster of huts, and I couldn't proceed without him. Eventually, I gave up waiting and enjoyed another ride back through the wide-open highway in the sunshine. *I wonder what happened? Did I misunderstand the arrangements?*

A few days later, Cedru explained why he hadn't been able to meet me. Someone important had died, requiring everyone to spend more time at their church that day. The following week, his wife and sister walked to Saul and Sarah's house just to apologise for his absence! I was blown away that anyone would walk eighteen kilometres to apologise for not keeping an appointment.

We organised another time a few weeks later, on a Sunday in July, to meet all their children and other family members. They wanted to thank me for the MegaVoice audio Bible with a meal. I was going to surprise them with the Makua/Portuguese Bible I had bought with Sarah.

This time, I had more precise directions to their place off the highway, though I didn't anticipate the steepness and sandiness of

Exciting Occasions

the track! I truly felt the presence of angels helping me manage it.*
A little further on, family members waved me along the correct path to their cluster of houses. It wasn't far off the road, but the experience was nerve-wracking. With relief, I parked my bike under the mango tree. Most dwellings in these parts were free of any bushes or plants to keep snakes or rodents from hiding nearby. I didn't have to dodge any shrubberies on my bike, thankfully.

Cedru and his wife and family were beaming, so happy I had finally arrived. Having me as a guest was obviously a special occasion, and I felt honoured to be there. Cedru was wearing the bright yellow high-vis vest I had given him for cycling along the busy highway twice a day to and from Anya's house for work.

Cedru and his wife looked after their own children, plus some orphans of family members who had died. He organised eight out of the twelve children to line up for photos. His older son, the one who could read the Bible, was nowhere to be found. Taking the photos, I wondered, *Who is going to read this Bible to them?*

Meanwhile, the wood fire, made from three long pieces of wood and three concrete blocks, was blazing. Cedru's sister was cooking a big pot of *xima*, stirring it with a handmade wooden spoon. Many children of all ages gathered shyly around, looking at the bike, then me. Thankfully, someone found a chair for me to sit on. *I don't get up and down from the ground so easily anymore!*

A small child brought me some bananas while the *xima* cooked. I felt humbled by their invitation to eat the main meal of the day with them. None of them carried extra weight. Harsh living conditions created slim yet strong bodies. After the bananas, I was given some boiled white manioc root with a toasted sesame and salt mixture to dip it in. I felt shy eating in front of them. *Why isn't anyone else eating?* I found out they were waiting for me to finish,

---

* *I will go before you and make the rough places smooth.* (Isaiah 45:2a, WEB)

then they would eat what I didn't. *Yikes!* I needed to eat enough to show my appreciation but leave some for them. I was relieved when that part of my visit was over.

Cedru's older brother, in his seventies, had recently returned to the family land and was in the process of building his own house alongside his family members. I was curious to see how far along he was, so after lunch, Cedru took me to see. On the ground were hundreds of clay bricks formed from mud and straw they had mixed with water in a nearby pit. The bricks dried quickly in the current climate. They had also gathered the tall grass that they used specifically for thatching the roof. Cedru's brother hoped to earn enough money to reroof it with tin and cover the walls with a thin layer of concrete before the onset of torrential seasonal rains and cyclones.

A Surprise Visitor Who Helps!

Once the *xima* finished cooking on the wood fire, a small plate with some cooked greens, ground nuts, and tomatoes was presented to me with a large spoon in case I didn't want to eat with my fingers. *Good idea! My hands aren't the cleanest after the bike ride.* Trying to eat just enough, but not too much, I passed the plate to the rest of them to finish.

I wondered whether I should give the Bible to them today or wait until Cedru's son reappeared. At that moment, a tall, young Mozambican man with a red cap walked out of the nearby path and headed towards us. The family seemed to be familiar with him. Imagine my surprise when he said he had walked around fifteen kilometres from the edge of town. Agostinho was a Christian too! He was going to visit some family members out this way but gladly stopped with us to chat. Thankfully, he spoke Portuguese, so I could converse with him a little.

"Você pode ajudar aqui?" (Can you help here?), I asked.

"Sim!" (Yes!)

I was excited to find out he could read. I told him about the disappearance of Cedru's son, the only literate member of this family, and showed him the Bible I had bought. "Could you return to the people here on Sunday afternoons and read passages from the Bible?" I explained that Cedru would also be supplying notes from Anya's Bible study.

I was in awe at how God had worked out the details of this situation. I remembered how Sarah and I had prayed when I bought the Bible, wondering who would read it if Cedru's son didn't return.

It was such a surprising answer to prayer to have someone 'randomly' walk into our midst who could read, was a Christian, and was willing to regularly visit these spiritually hungry people. God's ways are much higher than our ways!* It was a simple encounter yet, despite delays and obstacles, God still came through to bring His Word. *How will this multiply?* I wondered.

My Solar Panel Finds a Home!

Pastors Saul and Tino had been riding their motorbikes to two remote churches outside of town. They had trained a pastor for one of them and regularly rode out to encourage him and the group of believers. It was quite a long ride on rugged sandy tracks and beyond my capabilities. But one day Saul asked me if I wanted to visit these bush-bush communities in the 4x4 truck.

"Yes, of course!"

"They need the roofing iron and water containers delivered.

---

* *"For my thoughts are not your thoughts, and your ways are not my ways,"* says the Lord. (Isaiah 55:8, WEB)

Also, more Bibles." Saul explained some characteristics of these settlements. Both churches lacked water nearby, and it took the community from 4am until 12 noon to walk to collect it, making many trips since they only had a few water containers. The roofs of their huts were grass thatch. With tin roofs, it would be harder for thieves to break in, but roofing iron required money. After selling charcoal made from felled trees, they had earned enough money for Saul to buy the roofing iron in town.

My heart went out to these people who struggled so much in their everyday lives.

"Do you still have that solar panel from New Zealand?" he asked.

"Yes. Why?"

"I was asking Pastor Florindo what else is difficult for them with living so far from electricity and roads."

Being too far out for electricity to be installed, they could only recharge their cell phones by walking into town. They used the phones to talk with their neighbours, especially with the other small church nearby with whom they combined services and Bible studies.

"Your solar panel would bless them in more ways than one," Saul said. "But we also need to buy a battery for them."

"Fantastic! I'm so glad you found some people to benefit from it. I have enough donations to buy the battery and a light, too."

The next Sunday we drove the truck loaded with iron, water barrels, Bibles, and the solar panel with a battery, cord, and lightbulb. I was so excited to be blessing it to this community. We brought some more plastic jerry cans to collect and carry water back for their daily needs, although this was a short-term solution to their water problems.

"Wouldn't it be great to get a well dug closer for them?" I asked Saul. He explained that Pastor Florindo believed the area to be too

Exciting Occasions

dry for drilling to be an option. At least, I would see a solution for one of their needs. *Let there be light!*

Pastor Florindo asked for the solar panel setup to be installed in his hut for two reasons. He would charge phones for a small price, generating an income to buy food or charcoal for his church community, and he could teach Bible studies at night in his house.

However, the battery, solar panel, and lightbulb setup was a valuable asset, tempting for *ladrões* (robbers). A bamboo panel loosely securing his entrance was his only door. The following month, after generating some income by charging cell phones, he bought a wooden door to make his house more secure.

Our arrival was very exciting for everyone in the area, and an interested crowd watched. Other men of the village were involved, as well as the pastor, so they would know what to do when repairs were needed.

Saul knew exactly how to connect everything. The battery sat inside Florindo's hut on a chair and the lightbulb dangled from the roof beam. The solar panel was outside, of course. Even during the day, it was dark inside the house as there were no windows. Yet this kept it cool from the sun and heat. When the lightbulb lit up brightly, big grins were seen all around!

The pastor's next purchase was roofing iron, which would keep everything safe inside the house, as the natural thatch needed replacing yearly. Saul promised to make another trip out to this area in the truck. It was such a rewarding feeling to see in practical ways how all of us, including generous donors from New Zealand, were able to improve their challenging lifestyle. They seemed so grateful for anything. Even just visiting them touched their hearts. I was inspired by these people's tenacity despite the hard conditions.

When I returned to town, I read a Bible passage to encourage Pastor Florindo. I wrote it in Portuguese for Saul to deliver with the roofing iron on the next trip. "You are the light of the world. A city located on a hill cannot be hidden ... Even so, let your light shine before men, that they may see your good works and glorify your Father who is in heaven" (Matthew 5:14,16, WEB).

We heard that the nearby village church also wanted encouragement and a fresh Word from God. The following Sunday, we returned by truck with more supplies. Their water source was a four-hour walk each way. To see them in their cleanest clothes was therefore surprising. *How do they do it?!* I learned they worked together as a community, some doing the water transport and others cooking to feed them. These were desperate-looking villages, according to my eyes, but they showed a generous spirit, sharing what they had with us.

We didn't know how bad the physical state of their church building was until we saw they didn't even have enough water to make mud to patch up the cracks and holes. *Dry, sun-scorched places.* I recalled this description in a Bible passage when I was wondering where in Africa to go. *Looks like this is one of those places!*

I prayed, hoping to bring an encouraging word of God or maybe even a song for the children. Pastors Saul and Tino were team-preaching this day, with Tino translating from Portuguese into Makua. As usual, three plastic chairs were placed up front for us. The men, women, and children sat either on a few thin benches or on woven mats. Despite their outward appearances, booming voices filled the little church, singing to *Deus* (God). Bare feet shuffled on hardened mud floors. Faces beamed. Their passion for worship was evident. *Our belief in Christ knits us together like nothing else does.*

At the front, a battered, empty tin holding a small bunch of green leaves and one flower sat on a rickety wooden table. Underneath was a small pile of pumpkins, beans, and onions. A couple of large bags of peanuts were stacked in the corner. I hoped they weren't for us, as this would be a source of substantial income for

Exciting Occasions

them. But they were. We were presented with the vegetables after the service, along with two live chickens, one for Pastor Tino's family and one for Pastor Saul's.

I whispered to Saul, "How can we deprive them of their precious produce, especially the live hens?"

He assured me it would be worse to insult them by refusing. But we gave Pastor Tino most of the vegetables for his large family. He promised to kill our chicken back in town, thankfully. Meanwhile the hens' feet were tied up, and they sat on the floor behind our seats, staring at me with beady eyes. Another unforgettable Sunday!

I felt very privileged to have joined them out in this tiny bush church with a bigger faith than I thought possible in their circumstances. Once again, God was showing me how His powerful Presence fills us all with overflowing hope and gratitude in our hearts and is not dependent on outward circumstances.

I thought about these children's potential, living out in the bush-bush, not going to school or having any other learning experience, just working for their family's existence. I followed up my 'wonderings' with prayer, asking God if I was to be a part in His good plan for their lives.

I would need to trust Him and be patient as I waited to find out what the second half of the year would bring. I had a hunch, though, that like the weather, major changes were developing, forming up like distant thunder clouds on the horizon of my destiny.

Anya's Baptism

It was a joyful day seeing Anya take the step of baptism in her faith journey. After many months of discipling, Anya finally reached a point in her understanding; she needed to be obedient to Jesus' requirement to be baptised. *Hallelujah!* Her baptism as a baby did not count, as she had been unaware of what the decision to follow Jesus meant.

I confirmed with her that this was an outward declaration of her faith in Jesus Christ, following Him into death, resurrection, and new life. I had never baptised anyone, nor discipled anyone else, for that matter. This was indeed a momentous occasion!

Marion was a long-time friend of Anya's, and when she heard the news, she offered to be in the pool with me on the other side of Anya.

"I think this celebration needs cake, Anya! What do you think?" I asked.

Laughing, she agreed to make one of her delicious cakes.

Sarah and Saul thought the pool at our favourite courtyard restaurant and retreat would be a perfect location for Anya.

"I will ask her tomorrow," I offered.

"She can bring her two young nephews for a swim afterwards too," Sarah said.

After discussing the choices, Anya was comfortable with being baptised in a swimming pool at the local restaurant courtyard rather than at the beach. As we went there every two months for refreshments, they graciously permitted us to bring Anya's homemade cake to celebrate with. Including Anya and her two nephews, Pastor Saul and Sarah in a pastoral and friendship role, and Marion and I baptising her, there would be five adults and two children ordering lunch.

Having come from a formal religious background, Anya wanted a certificate. Pastor Saul and I designed and printed one, and Saul signed it. I added some special Bible verses that came from the Holy Spirit at the time to encourage her journey and deepening relationship with the Lord.* We emphasised to Anya that this was only in remembrance of the event. Her heart's decision was what 'sealed the deal' between her and God. I was confident she understood this.

As Marion and I got into the pool with Anya, Pastor Saul stood at the side and read some commitment words for her to agree to. He knew that as he was a male pastor, who had lived in Mozambique for over twenty years, she would believe this was an official baptism.

It was a truly memorable experience for us all. Marion had been Anya's friend for ten years, and Saul and Sarah's sons had been taught Portuguese by her. Encouraging, prophetic words were spoken, and we enjoyed Anya's cake after our meal. The boys, Cris and Gabby, enjoyed their swim too.

This amazing experience came as a surprise to me. After two years of living and studying with Anya and discipling her, her decision to be baptised was an answer to prayer. Her life had been hard, and her acceptance of raising her brother's and sister's children and being unable to marry was such a sacrifice.

I prayed her faith would grow and deepen and that every day she would believe more of who she is in Christ, knowing God does hear her prayers. *Perhaps she will inspire others in her large extended family, especially those of another faith, to seek Jesus.*

---

* **Go** *and make disciples of all nations,* **baptising** *them in the name of the Father and of the Son and of the Holy Spirit, and teaching them to observe all things I have commanded you.* (Matthew 28:19–20, WEB)

Meeting Needs

Two people from a village without a nearby school had a passion to offer unschooled children an opportunity to learn. The question was whether a preschool or kids' club would best serve this community, which had over eighty interested children and teenagers.

Estima, a wife and mother, and a young man named Stácio both attended the evangelical church in the area. They sent word to Sarah through the church network that they needed help to create a workable programme. Estima had seen how Whitewater Farm's *escolinha* worked. However, she and Stácio hadn't expected so much interest and were struggling to implement a meaningful programme. The space inside the church was crowded, and there was a large age gap between the young children and teenagers.

"Let's ask Lisa to share what she has learned from the past eighteen months of her *escolinha* experiences," I suggested. I was excited to be experiencing the next level of training, making it sustainable for when we were not here.

Meeting Needs

Sarah said, "Saul thinks it would be a good idea for Lisa's father, Pastor Tino, to take part in the initial stages of setting up the preschool in this *Igreja Actos*. It's within his area of pastoring, and it will be good to establish links between the two church communities."

Lisa was excited to join us, ready to step into a shared leadership role.

Arriving at the church, we could see why Estima and Stácio were overwhelmed. The eighty-plus children were keen to learn anything! Estima had asked a nearby neighbour to cook a big pot of *pap*, maize porridge, on her outdoor charcoal fire for them all. We called everyone outside, singing *Fazer de círculo* (Make a circle), and started with some simple games—a challenge with so many children of all ages.

When the porridge was ready, the children sat on the dusty red earth and waited patiently for bowls to be shared out. Some picked leaves off the few bushes nearby, and I watched as four children shared one small bowl, dipping into it with their leaves and sucking the porridge off. Sarah said the meal was probably the major reason they attended. For some, it could have been their only food of the day. A sobering thought.

In our discussion after that overwhelming session, we found out that Estima and Stácio only wanted children aged three to six to attend, not the whole town's children. We agreed that the curriculum should include biblical content and provide a bilingual approach to help Makua-speaking children enter school more successfully. Before our second visit, Sarah, Lisa, and I met to choose resources to pack into a box to demonstrate their use in teaching. Pastor Tino was keen to come along to build links between his church and this out-of-town church. Rénia was also interested in coming along and volunteered to help.

I asked Lisa, "What would you like to teach Estima and Stácio?"

She enthusiastically replied, "*O que está a faltar?*" (What's missing?) and added, "*calendário também*" (the calendar too). We used a simple sign of the days of the week in Portuguese to teach young students.

The first game involved a tray of assorted objects. Each item was named in Portuguese to prepare the children for school. Then, the tray was covered with a cloth and one object was secretly removed. When the cloth was removed, the teacher asked the children, "What's missing?" This simple game, easily created with local resources, trained young children to remember objects and helped with their reading skills.

We had to condense the learning for teachers to create a curriculum they felt was important for the children, and we only had a limited time to do this. Sarah hinted that some major changes were coming for us. *I wonder what those changes will bring.*

Our priority was to limit the number and ages of the children. We drew a line on the wall of the church entrance. If the child was under that line they could enter, but if they were taller, they had to stay outside and peer in through the windows. The result was thirty-nine preschool children under the age of seven. It was heartbreaking to see so many children hungering for any opportunity to learn something. At least, the taller ones could lean in and observe through the church windows.

It was so rewarding to see Lisa step up and teach the volunteers what she had learned through workshops at Whitewater Farm and in town at our own training sessions. Running her own preschool with Irene for eighteen months had also given her confidence in passing on knowledge gained through experience. I still felt frustrated in my use of Portuguese at times, but my basic command of the language curbed any desire to make programmes too complicated for these adults who had no education due to the war.

I created some simple resources from materials, often discarded rubbish, to show them what they could use from their own environment. It was amazing what games and teaching aids could be created using bottle caps, cardboard, seeds, pegs, and stones. By now, I understood how essential it was to train the locals to become independent by encouraging them to use their ideas. The history in this country was often one of dependency on outside organisations to give a handout instead of a hand up. We and our supporters did not have ongoing resources to pay the volunteers, plus we did not know how long we would be able to be here. When I first arrived on my mission, I found this a new and challenging concept. However, I now better understood the need for wisdom for a long-term outcome.

Sharing about the Bible, who God is, the days of creation, and how special each child is in God's eyes was just the beginning of an introduction to the God of the Bible. We used songs and actions in most of our teaching, supplementing these with a few books and a maths game using dice, stones, and cards with numbers. Our simple materials offered flexible, open-ended learning experiences.

On our third and fourth visits, a small group of volunteers came to help make a pool of resources. We supplied glue and clear plastic Duraseal to make simple puzzles from discarded magazines and cardboard cartons. During our training sessions, we helped the volunteers to colour in their own resources of the seven days of creation numerals. Soon we had three boxes of supplies with lids, which Estima would store in her house. The church had no space to secure them safely yet. We spent a short yet intense time supporting these enthusiastic adults, who wanted to enrich their village children's lives in the best way they could.

Since we were all believers, we prayed at the beginning and end of each training session. Simple prayers were spoken with children, who were from various faith backgrounds, to introduce them to the loving God of the Bible. After we passed the Bible around, one song they loved was *Escuta minha voz* (Listen to my voice), which we sang in whispers and loud voices. Estima remembered the creation song from previous training sessions, so we could leave that to her to pass on. Lisa, who planned to visit occasionally to support the programme, remembered it as well.

Reflecting on the 'Great Commission' in Matthew 28, I often wondered what difference I was making. *Am I doing enough for God?* I had experienced greater satisfaction in my contributions during my third year. More and more, however, I realised I was learning as much, or more, than the people I worked with. I needed to be content with not knowing the full picture of what God was doing here. I had a new thought: *His call to me was to 'Go' to Mozambique, and that is enough. Really, God?! Wow.* I was further encouraged by this verse: "We know that all things work together for good for those who love God, for those are called according to his purpose" (Romans 8:28, WEB). *Amen!*

A Surprising and Timely Seminar

After our busy time helping Estima and Stácio set up their preschool, Saul collected a ministry team from South Africa off the plane. A seminar had been planned for the pastors in churches north of us, with a women's seminar, prison ministry, discipling, and an issue I was excited to see happening in this part of Mozambique: ideas about running alcohol (AA) and drug addiction programmes. *Hallelujah!*

I shared the news with Anya at my language lesson. "Maybe

Meeting Needs

this addictions programme will come to your town, and Zé can be helped!"

Anya exclaimed, "God heard my prayers!"

Before we all travelled up north in two vehicles, we spent a day fasting, praying, and singing worship songs. These problems were widespread, and the positive impact would be far-reaching. We knew this training would need God's help and protection.

"How long is the seminar?" I asked Sarah, who had clarified details with Saul as she needed to prepare Rénia to look after the dog.

"It will be one week, with each day full of training and information. We will be staying at various missionaries' houses. I think you will be with the Efe family."

I had some packing to do. *I wonder if we will get to swim?*

The seminar reached a number of leaders in the area. It reached my heart too. I was especially impacted by the prison ministry seminar, which was new information for me as I had mainly been involved with the education of young children.

I don't know who said it, but I wrote in my notes: 'We go into prisons to create destiny by changing their lives and healing their hearts with the love of God.' Only Jesus can set people free from visible and invisible prisons.* We, as followers, are His hands and feet.

We even visited the town's prison, which was a sobering sight, especially seeing the number of young men. *Gosh, this is grim.* Thinking of the prisons two thousand years ago in the Bible, I wondered how different they were to this.

The pastor of the South African team planned to return with

---

* *The Spirit of the Lord is on me, because he has anointed me to preach good news to the poor. He has sent me to heal the broken hearted, to proclaim release to the captives, recovering of sight to the blind, to deliver those who are crushed and to proclaim the acceptable year of the Lord.* (Luke 4:18, WEB) training manuals translated into Portuguese. *Great!* But it wouldn't be for another year. Things moved slowly here. He would also bring a team to help train local pastors and leaders. This sounded so positive. I hoped and prayed it would extend to Anya's town where Zé lived, so it could benefit them too.

This seminar was a start to the overwhelming problems of alcohol and drug addictions here, where there were no programmes yet to help them get free. Without our belief in Christ within us and helping us, the problems would seem insurmountable. The ministry team encouraged everyone not to give up hope.

We were all thankful for and encouraged by the people who travelled from South Africa. And we did manage a swim before we travelled home!

Unforeseen Changes

Soon after the seminar, I began to sense in my spirit that my days here in Mozambique were coming to an end. I did not know what was coming. I could listen to my old self-talk that suggested anxious times ahead, or I could recall the promises of a faithful, loving God who was going ahead of me to prepare the path. *Help me, Lord, to hear and trust you!*

It was a time of retirements and relocations within the World Outreach mission organisation itself. My core support team, Saul and Sarah in town and Kevin and Ginnie on the farm were considering relocating. World Outreach had asked Saul and Sarah to transfer and be the WO representatives in South Africa. They would continue to visit Mozambique as WO field directors.

After many years, the time had come for Kevin and Ginnie to transfer the leadership to the next generation of local Makua men to train and disciple men to pastor village churches. Before returning to their home country, Kevin and Ginnie planned the continuation of the four preschools, the infant feeding programme, and the training of Makua women to disciple other women through audio Bibles. Whitewater Farm would be sold by World Outreach; however, Whitewater Ministries would remain functioning with local leadership. With occasional mentorship from Kevin and Ginnie once a year, local leaders would become more capable and the programmes self-sustaining.

Yikes! Both of them relocating from this area! Questions flooded in. Where would I live? Saul and Sarah would probably sell their house. *What about our plans and ideas for the ministries in town for women and children?* Without better language skills, I couldn't do those on my own.

Changes had come for Anya's household too. Zé was out of work again, and his wife was expecting a third baby. With Anya's extended family relying on her to supply food and lodgings (if their mud-brick house fell down from weather), her house was no longer suitable for me to stay in.

As a single woman in the district, it wasn't safe for me to live on my own. This was not New Zealand. There were bars on every window, padlocks and chains on doors, and courtyard walls with glass on top—visual reminders of the dangers here. Without better language skills, especially when dealing with officials and immigration needs, I could get into difficulties. It didn't bear thinking about!

Then there was my soon-to-expire New Zealand teacher registration, which required me to resume teaching in New Zealand, since my experience here did not count towards registration requirements. Plus, I would reach retirement age in less than two years.

My feelings tried to dominate my thinking. Initially, I felt sad and disappointed. *My language is flourishing, and with it, there could be more outreach possibilities. Am I letting my supporters down?* Then I remembered something: when there is **dis**appointment, God comes with **re**appointment. This simple phrase stilled my soul for a moment or two, but it wasn't enough to stop the

Unforeseen Changes

tsunami of panic threatening my peace. Fortunately, I still had my ukulele with me for my worship times. "I need you more, Lord!" I sang.

In the sunshine, under the coconut trees of Saul and Sarah's courtyard, I sensed God 'talking' to me. *Peace I give you, my peace I leave with you ... Do not let your heart be troubled, neither let it be afraid.** *Nothing can separate you from MY love.*

My peace was restored. *So, am I to stay or go?* I needed more time to hear from God! I decided to try other 'doors' and see if they opened. I visited friends in the area to investigate what others were doing and whether I could be of assistance. After a few weeks, the direction I was to take became clear. Even though I visited some incredible mission families in the area, I didn't sense a green light from God to join them. I had no peace about any of those possibilities. In my heart, I knew my time in Mozambique had come to a close. *But what is ahead?*

Before I became swamped with the unknowns, I sought advice from those closest to me at the time, Saul and Sarah.

Pastor Saul shared news from a recent email. "Because some key leaders are transitioning into new roles and places, a World Outreach retreat for Mozambique missionaries will take place soon."

Sarah reassured me we would be receiving expert support. "Trained mentors will come from South Africa and New Zealand to help guide, advise, pray for, and counsel us as we go through transitions. You already know some of the people."

I felt better already about the new season ahead. *I am not alone!* I recalled God's promise that the Lord himself goes before me and

---

* "Peace I leave with you. My peace I give to you. Don't let your heart be troubled, neither let it be afraid." (John 14:27, WEB)

he will never leave me nor forsake me, and it encouraged me not to be afraid or discouraged.

I didn't know it then, but I would require mentoring through this season of transition. The biggest challenge long-term missionaries face can be transitional times, which involve external global factors like cultures, climates, seasons, and internal pressures that cause confidence to crack or doubts to appear. However, while changes can be spontaneous, transitions can be planned and prepared for.

The three-day seminar focused on transition using reflection, prayer, and mentoring to navigate through these turbulent waters. I learned some important aspects of managing transitions successfully: You must end before you can begin; between the end and the beginning is a gap, which can be a creative time; and transitions can be a source of renewal.

I needed to guard my heart and mind from the lies of the enemy, who wanted to tell me I was a failure. I knew in my heart that God had called me here. But what was next? *One day, I'm looking forward to months, possibly years, of living here in Mozambique, and the next day, the door is shutting. What am I going to do?*

The teaching sessions were focused and useful, with time spent in worship, prayer, and reading specific Scriptures for transitions. One verse was particularly relevant: "Always rejoice. Pray without ceasing. In everything give thanks, for this is the will of God in Christ Jesus toward you" (1 Thessalonians 5:16–18, WEB). *And remember, the gap between the ending and the next beginning can be creative and refreshing.*

After some powerful prayers and prophecies, and with a fresh perspective, my decision to return to New Zealand came with peace. Well, not totally. I had been away for three years, so my permanent teaching position was gone. I had no car, no house, etc.

I realised I had changed. Things would be different for me. But knowing God was on my side, I mostly felt encouraged and enthusiastic about the possibilities ahead. However, as I learned in the seminar, transitioning from one phase into another can be slow. My faith in God working things out for me was stronger, though. *In His timing!*

One possibility was that I could return to Mozambique for a few months the next year as a short-term missionary. Or I could resume full-time teaching for a year or two and then return for longer. I had so many unanswered questions and needed to rein in those wild horse thoughts. *Wait! I say it again: Wait on the Lord.*

A Door, Donations, and a New Owner for the Hero!

Meanwhile, more immediate issues needed my attention. I woke up one morning to a new thought: *Before I leave, I must look at my finances and the donations that people have pledged for this year. Who can we bless before I go?*

I asked Sarah, "What do you think about buying Anya a smartphone so we can keep in touch with her and her family? I have enough donations to be able to bless her. She could keep me informed of Cedru's family too."

"That's a great idea! I can show Anya how to use it and get you two connected."

When I met with Anya to discuss the changes ahead, she confided that she had been secretly saving the money from my lessons and lodgings to buy herself a scooter. She needed help purchasing and transporting it from the Big City. Saul and Sarah were happy to assist, using the twin cab ute they had recently purchased from departing missionaries, Tina and Andy.

Anya chose a bright yellow *motinha* (scooter) and told me in

Portuguese, "Now I can take my two nephews to preschool and deliver my special celebration cakes to customers."

I wondered how the three of them would fit on it.

She laughed. "*Não problema!*"

Over the past three years, I had brought medical supplies with me each year. My plastic boxes held basic first aid items, including a digital thermometer that could be helpful for Anya and her extended family. I wanted Lisa and Irene with their young children to be able to benefit too, so I asked Anya if she could share the medical supplies with them.

"*Claro! Não problema*" (Sure! No problem).

I added, "*Eles podem andar aqui*" (They can walk here). Anya was always so gracious with my basic Portuguese, though she still corrected me sometimes.

Cedru's bicycle was in desperate need of replacement. He was thrilled to be blessed with a new one to help with his lengthy daily travels. Both the scooter and the bike would need to be securely locked away from *ladrões*, probably in the spare kitchen where my Honda Hero bike was now.

Usually, I rode my motorbike to Acts Church, but one day I decided to walk, hoping to find Lisa. While visiting the new *escolinha* that her father and others had built adjoining his church, Lisa asked, "Do you want to see my house?"

She led the way through the *bairro* (neighbourhood) of many huts and paths to her little hut, carrying Issac on her back with a wrap of cloth. I could never have found this place on my own! A cyclone had demolished her previous house, so she had been living with her parents and their other children. Last year, during the dry season, her father and brother made the mudbricks to build this three-room house.

The kitchen was just big enough for three concrete bricks to hold a pot while cooking with wood she had collected. The bedroom was the size of a woven sleeping mat for her and three-year-old Issac. The front room contained a sack of dried beans or corn. In this dry climate, the mud floor was cool and smooth, and the bricks looked solid. But without a thin covering of concrete, it would quickly disintegrate.

"You must be relieved to have a tin roof for your new house," I commented.

"Yes, but I don't have a door. We ran out of money for that. I am borrowing one from my brother," Lisa replied, adding, "It's not safe for me and my baby to live without a secure door."

"Of course," I agreed. After a brief discussion with Sarah, who had come with us, I shared my thoughts about the situation.

Lisa was overjoyed when I suggested she find a local timber merchant to make her a door. "*Muito obrigada!*" (Thank you so much!).

I also let her know that she and Irene could use the medical supplies at Anya's.

I had noticed the newly built *escolinha* at Acts Church had a grass-thatched roof. Saul and Sarah didn't have enough funds for metal roofing this year, nor did my donors. *How can we help with a short-term solution?* We bought several plastic tarpaulins, which were installed between the thatch and the rafter poles. *Lord, there never seems to be enough provision, but I believe you can multiply our efforts. I pray that roofing iron will arrive before the next big cyclone. Amen.*

The floods last year had destroyed one wall of Arnaldo's house, where he lived with his wife and twin girls. Though Saul and Sarah had employed him as a caretaker and gardener, the country was experiencing inflation, and his savings weren't enough to buy the cement he needed to plaster the outside walls.

One evening, Sarah said, "Well, this is the last meal we will eat together from this table and chairs!"

I looked up, surprised. "Why?"

"We are gifting them to Arnaldo's family tomorrow, with four bags of cement. He has admired them for some time. Do you want to come with us?"

"Sure!" I was always pleased to visit local families.

I feel sad to be leaving, and I've only been here a short time compared to the decades Saul and Sarah have invested into this community. They must be feeling super sad.

For the remainder of our time there, we ate our meals without the table and chairs, but in our hearts, we were satisfied to know they had gone to a good home.

With only six weeks to go, it was time to face my departure. The countdown had begun. I asked Sarah, "How do I sell or pass on my Honda Hero? Who should get it?" I needed to make a decision and put a plan in place before we all left.

"Arnaldo can't ride, obviously, due to his childhood accident that left one arm and leg crippled. Why don't you ask Marion? She has many healthcare workers in need, and enough wisdom to know how best to bless someone."

When I caught up with Marion at Whitewater Farm a few days later, she excitedly exclaimed, "What great timing! Mama Grace's little motorbike fell apart months ago. She struggles to get to the Good Samaritan clinic out of town."

I had been friends with Mama Grace for the past two years, often stopping at the clinic where she made herbal tinctures and dried herbs.

Marion's ministry from Europe enabled her to pay the staff at the health clinics. "Did you know she earns money at her job there?" she asked. "I can work out a small payment plan for her to pay you for your Honda bike. It's better if she pays something for it rather than it being a total gift."

I was thrilled. My bike would be going to someone involved in

Kingdom work who truly needed a bigger bike! Mama Grace, a large woman with an equally big heart, often transported passengers alongside produce from the town markets. Her small bike had looked so tiny under the load, and I marvelled at how long it had lasted. *Thank you, God, for your solution. Nothing is wasted.*

When her final payment came, it was time to hand it over. I will always remember her wide smile as she waved goodbye. With a roar and a cloud of dust, I watched the motorbike drive off. Just like that. Gone.

Plans to Leave, but for How Long?

Suddenly, I was no longer focused on building better language skills, planning training for the *escolinha* volunteers, or discipling new believers. My world here had come to a screeching halt. I was informed of major changes of leadership positions within the mission organisation. However, the seminar we had recently attended to help us navigate these transitional times had been hugely helpful in preparing me to plan my exit.

Practical issues, like delegating donations to those I worked closely with and passing on possessions, were easy. Emotional and mental transitions were more difficult. I worried at first that I would be disappointing my supporters back home. Throughout my time as a supported missionary, I had needed to remember that my sponsors were giving to the Lord as He prompted them. In return, they were blessed within themselves for their generosity and obedience. But maybe things were changing for my supporters too. *Might it be a relief for them to reconsider their donations?*

During my first year, I was plagued by comparing my 'performance' to others. The Bible warned against this. I learned that when God said *Go*, I went. Looking back, I was thankful for what I had achieved for myself and others here. I had to entrust God with any desired outcomes I hadn't yet seen.

Doubts of God's provision tried to derail me. *I don't have a house, a car, or employment back home.* However, in Mozambique, God had demonstrated many times that He goes before me, preparing the way.*

My 'suddenlys' over the past few years had taught me that God is faithful, that He hears my prayers, and that His answers are far beyond what I could ever ask for or imagine. There is power in speaking the Word. The truth in God's scriptures set me free from clouds of doubt, fear, disappointment, and self-condemnation. I learned more than before how to trust God for everything. *Now is no different to any other time my plans changed. Will He surprise me with a car, a rental unit, and a job all at the right time? In Your time, right, God?*

Whether I returned next year for short-term ministry was completely up to Him. I was rich in profound experiences in Mozambique and multi-national friendships for life. My health was strong, though some issues were developing.

For now, I faced another decision.

Surprising Detour to Zimbabwe

Checking my emails one morning, I saw a message from my friends Ray and Lois, who managed an apartment complex in Harare, Zimbabwe. They had heard things were changing for us in Mozambique and offered me an invitation to visit with free accommodation on my way home. *That's tempting! I hope my travel agent can organise this slight change in plans.*

---

* *The Lord will keep your going out and your coming in, from this time forward, and forever more.* (Psalm 121:8, WEB)

Unforeseen Changes

One observation by my WO mentors at the 'Transition' seminar was that I did not have a holiday plan in place. *This could be my time to rest, refocus, and recharge!* Decision made. I had peace about it after seeking wisdom and guidance from God; that was the main thing.

Africa called us at the same time in 2013. Ray and Lois had lived in Kerikeri for seven years after emigrating from Zimbabwe. But now they had grandchildren in the capital, Harare. Three years ago, they held a garage sale prior to leaving Kerikeri, running a sausage sizzle to raise a donation for my trip to Mozambique.

Even though they had found a place to live, with employment and a good church to fellowship in, times were tough, and life was precarious. I felt they needed some encouragement, and we'd had a good friendship back in New Zealand. *Maybe there will be another mission opportunity there for me, Lord?*

With our bags packed and belongings shared out, the 'Fab Five' headed to the Big City to fly to our various destinations. While waiting for our flights, we spotted a local outdoor café. We ordered our favourite meal, ice-cold drinks with Portuguese BBQ chicken and chips, and someone pulled out cards for a quick game of Up and Down the Creek. All too soon, our plane to South Africa arrived. I blinked back tears, wondering when I would next see these very special friends who helped me laugh.

Before heading our separate ways in Johannesburg, we hugged, prayed, and promised to keep in touch. Inside OR Tambo Airport, I paused to look up at an enormous mural with an African proverb: *If you want to go fast, go alone. If you want to go far, go together.* I had gone farther than I ever dreamed possible with all my supporters,

WO missions, and companion missionaries on the field. Now here I was, on my way to Zimbabwe for a new adventure.*

I headed for my departure gate, looking forward to meeting up with Ray and Lois. I felt certain I would return to South Africa—but then, it was also possible I might suddenly find myself on a different path!

* * *

My arrival in Zimbabwe was refreshing in more ways than one. It was a joyous occasion to be met at the airport by my friends Ray and Lois. Being in an English-speaking country was such a relief too. *I'm going to enjoy being on holiday here!*

The studio apartment that was to be my base for a few weeks was vacant, following some renovations. I was struck by how clean it was, with my own shower, sink, and toilet. *Water comes out of the taps, and there are no buckets of water in the bathtub!* The small kitchenette had a fridge to keep drinks cold. *Nice!* The bed had clean sheets, blankets, and pillows, with no mosquito net. The colder nights meant no mozzies. *What luxury!* But most outstanding was a large vase of fresh flowers, which weren't available in the arid areas of Mozambique.

After I rested, Ray and Lois took me to garden cafés with lovely fresh food. Sipping coffee one morning, Lois asked, "Would you like to visit the Nyanga National Park area? We can stay at our relatives' rustic cabin and visit Troutbeck Resort beside the beautiful lake."

"Sounds perfect to me!" I seemed to connect with God in nature. "I'm ready for some relaxing outdoor spaces."

---

* *We know that all things work together for good for those who love God, for those who are called according to his purpose.* (Romans 8:28, WEB)

Unforeseen Changes

We took off in Lois's packed little car for a sightseeing adventure of Zimbabwe's countryside. A week in a cabin was the best tonic for my weary soul after going through so many transitions. Walking between the pine trees and sitting quietly by myself, undisturbed in God's creation, was just what I needed. "He leads me beside still waters. He restores my soul" (Psalm 23:2b–3a, WEB). *So true.*

The dramatic beauty of my surroundings and the stillness of being away from civilisation noises refreshed me. The open blue skies of rural Zimbabwe during the dry season gave me space to talk and listen to God. The clear night skies hosted a delightful display of stars in the surrounding darkness. *It's true. The heavens do declare the glory of God.*

A week later found us in an amazing national park, Lake Chivero, with its flocks of interesting birds and ancient rock paintings. Chengeta Game Park was another memorable experience, with a giraffe casually strolling through the resort cottages with their thickly thatched roofs. With the assistance of the wildlife guides who cared for the elephants, we got up close to some, even a baby elephant. They needed protection from poachers and the ivory trade.

The most memorable experience was attending the local church a few times. What surprised me was how they prayed for the government in power! The political difficulties in Zimbabwe were not immediately obvious, though Ray and Lois had informed me about them as we spent time together. The church's hopeful messages, filled with uplifting verses, strengthened its congregation's faith in troubled times. I was impressed with the country's strong Christian background which, despite hardships, brought many people a source of hope for the future.

After three action-packed weeks, I felt refreshed as well as informed about another African country. However, I didn't feel led to stay, so I continued with my plan to return to New Zealand.

As the plane left African soil, a popular expression came to mind: 'You can take the person out of Africa, but you can't take Africa out of the person'.

Finally, Home in New Zealand!

Looking back as I left African soil, I realised God had guided me in many unexpected directions. In a small way, I obediently followed Jesus' Great Commission. I went where God called me, and I discipled Anya, baptising her when she became aware she needed to take that step. But that was only a part of what I did. With so many connections and opportunities to bless people, I will never know the full extent of this amazing mission experience.*

After the long flights and connections, I was relieved when all my luggage arrived safely at Auckland Airport. I emerged from customs after declaring everything and being cleared to go, looking forward to what lay ahead. What a joy to see my son waiting for me! It was already afternoon, and we had a four-hour drive north ahead of us. We departed promptly, chatting nonstop as we caught up with family news. Then, after ninety minutes of driving, my phone rang.

"Hello, who is this?" The reception wasn't great in the truck, especially with the sound of rain and wipers. "Auckland Airport? Yes, my suitcase is a burgundy-coloured tartan bag. What? I have the wrong bag?"

I turned to my son. "We need to stop and check whose bag I have! It seems like it belongs to someone in New Plymouth. She

---

* ... *giving thanks always concerning all things in the name of our Lord Jesus Christ to God, even the Father.* (Ephesians 5:20, WEB)

Unforeseen Changes

turned my bag into the baggage claim and alerted someone to ring me. She had to catch her flight to New Plymouth."

We stopped and looked in the back. The bag looked like mine but had a different name on the label. *Oh no! How did that happen?* "I'd better text my friend Kelly and tell her we won't arrive until at least 10pm."

We turned back, flicking on the truck's lights in the early dusk, and drove in silence. I began praying intently. *Help us find a car park close by!* Fortunately, we found someone at the airport to open the office where my suitcase was stored, and I returned the New Plymouth suitcase. It looked identical to mine!

By now, darkness had set in with steady rain. I made more prayers for protection and travelling favour.

"Are you hungry? How about we stop for a burger and coffee before we go again," I offered.

My son's good nature returned after a meal, and we were back on our way. After navigating our way out of the road construction around the airport, our conversation resumed.

He had looked for a car for me when he heard I was coming home for good.

"You will love it, Mum. It's a bright red Mazda station wagon. It's under $5,000 and not too high in mileage. Friends of mine are selling it locally."

"Sounds great. Tell me more tomorrow." *I need to look at the donations bank account as soon as possible. I hope I have enough money for it.*

Traffic was favourable, and the rain stopped. Without further mishap, we safely arrived at 10.30pm to a warm welcome by Kelly and her cat. *Thank you, God.* I hugged my son, thanking him for collecting me and my luggage—twice!

I turned to Kelly. "You won't believe what happened!"

Leaving all the luggage until morning, I finally crawled into my own bed. *God is good.* I woke to sunshine and a view of cows across the valley. The complexity of reconnecting into life here immediately overwhelmed me. I made my way to the kitchen, praying for God's peace and direction, and found a note on the bench that Kelly had left before heading to work. *A three-month relieving job is available at an early childhood centre in Kaikohe. Ring this number. And help yourself to coffee! P.S. I can take you there tomorrow on my way to work.*

Wow, that's one answer to prayer! It seemed like things were falling into place quickly. In Mozambique, the pace was a lot slower. I was used to delays and obstacles—expected them, in fact. Here, life moved quickly and efficiently.

I hadn't checked my bank account for weeks, so when I hooked into Kelly's Wi-Fi, I was shocked. I only had enough for a deposit on the car. Without any public transport in the Far North, owning a car was essential for resuming work as a reliever in the early childhood sector. *Now what, Lord?*

My son's comment about the car came to mind. I rang him, asking if his friends would sell me their car with only a deposit and a note to promise the balance in four weeks.

They replied, "Yes! But not for a couple of days until we get our new car."

The following morning, Kelly dropped me off to the childcare centre, and I secured the three-month relieving position. *Woohoo! I'm on a roll.*

Next, I contacted my previous landlord in the afternoon to see if, by some miracle, one of the cottages was available. Bryan confirmed one was vacant. "Your timing is perfect! You can move in after we clean it this weekend. You don't need to pay any deposit, as we know you from before you left for Africa."

It's so handy and right next to my church, too. Only God could have orchestrated the timely solutions to all these needs. I collected my new car, paid the deposit to my son's friends, and organised full car insurance. Friends helped me move my stored household items from their farm while other friends donated furniture and carpet. Kelly brought my clothing on hangers and bedding to my new place. In a short time, I was all set. A new job, my own place, and a reliable car!

Another surprise awaited me soon after moving in. A church that had supported me rang, "We were just given a $4,000 deposit from an anonymous donor for you! It will be in your bank account shortly."

"What? That's amazing! It's the exact amount I need to pay off my car!" *Why am I always surprised?!*

Photos

Cris pats Rosso in Anya's courtyard

Here I go!

Orphans programme training Makua health workers

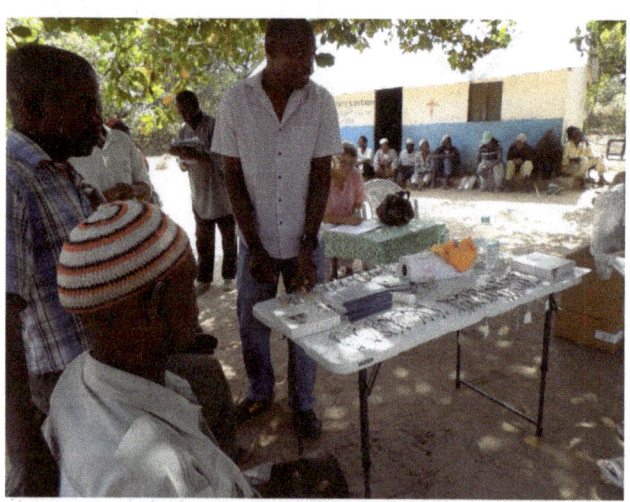
Helping with 'Sight for Mozambique' eye clinic

Photos

Cedru's family welcomes me. Visitor with red cap will read Bible to them

Solar panel gives light and charging of phones for pastor's village

Called to a Sun-Scorched Land

Lisa now training others for new preschool

Church in town makes mudbricks for preschool room

Photos

Arriving at another church to train preschool volunteers

Town preschool with Irene showing books from NZ daycare

Called to a Sun-Scorched Land

Bible story of Martha and Mary after our motorbike ride

Help arrives! Rénia transports the soft drinks up the sandy road

Epilogue

A few months had passed, and Kelly and I were having coffee together. She asked me some questions I had also been reflecting on. "Your newsletters were very informative. But looking back, what were some of the lessons you learned? What are you thankful for? What changed or impacted you?"

Where to begin? I paused, then said, "I thought I was going to assist mainly with training volunteers to help with preschools in remote villages. But there was so much more! I learned a lot about myself and God's nature, especially His faithfulness and response to my prayers."

Our informal conversation helped me put my thoughts into order to write in my journal notes. A summary of some of these insights follows:

- By joining an international mission organisation (World Outreach), I was very well prepared. I was thankful for those who joined my 'Sending Group' to assist me in all aspects of my life both there and here.

The various transitional times both on the field and when I returned were assisted by mentors.
- I learned to try new things and laugh at my 'failures', which were only learning experiences. Learning another language taught me to keep lighthearted and laugh at myself. It chipped away at my pride, teaching me to ask for help—but with wisdom.
- I became more dependent on God's direction, trusting Him more and praying more. He showed me through many examples that He heard my prayers, answering even the small ones!
- I learned not to compare myself with others. What I was or wasn't 'doing' became less dominant in my thinking.
- I had a revelation that people from various churches were giving to me as a missionary from their own obedience to God. The Bible says we will be blessed when we are a cheerful giver. I was only a part of the whole team, the one sent out to be the hands and feet of Christ. This released me from a burden of false responsibility.
- My physical health served me well. The developing 'niggles' related to mobility occurred on my return home to a nation that has a fairly good health system, thankfully!
- Mostly, I am eternally grateful for God's incredible love, faithfulness, and patience.* I'm grateful that so many people came with me on this journey—without them, I could not have achieved as much.

---

* *Always rejoice. Pray without ceasing. In everything give thanks, for this is the will of God in Christ Jesus toward you.* (1 Thessalonians 5:16–18, WEB)

Postscript, or Where to From Here, Lord?

It wasn't until six months had passed and I was back into a routine, renting and working part-time in the early childhood sector, that I asked myself, *What's next?* Resuming face-to-face connections with friends and family was a priority, as was fellowshipping in my church. Becoming more involved with grandparenting was also high on my priority list.

Coming back from three years on the mission field took a bit of adjustment. I had to deal with a sense of loss. But after some expert mentoring, I felt confident to explore new ministry opportunities and resume previous commitments. Once a week at a local primary school with a team of volunteers, I went back to teaching about the Bible and how it applies to children's everyday lives.

Realising that working with very young children might be more physically difficult as I get older, I trained online to teach English as a second language. Volunteering with new immigrants was rewarding, yet not an area I felt led to pursue for employment.

A retired teacher mentioned she needed an assistant with teaching English inside the regional prison. This progressed to going in with a local pastor to teach the Bible. Again, both were very rewarding. Then Covid hit, and the prison shut down.

Changes in income forced me to consider other options. Moving out of my rental cottage and into a local backpackers' lodge seemed a good solution. It satisfied my interest in sharing the Gospel with people from other countries as well as with locals who also found the campground an affordable place to live in.

When I slowed down with the 'doing' and came into a season of 'being', I heard God speak again. 'Write the book.'

What?! Write a book about my life? That's too big. Where would I begin?

I wrestled with these thoughts and tried to write but only got as far as multiple beginnings. Then I joined the New Zealand Christian Writers (NZCW) group. They helped inform and encourage me, supporting me in tackling this task.

After a timely NZCW Retreat, I saw a way forward—to only write about the mission experience. *Of course!* An obvious decision, but still an overwhelming project.

During my internship year with World Outreach, I remembered Kevin helping me with the enormity of being a missionary in Africa. He asked me, "How do you eat an elephant?" The answer was, "One bite at a time."

One bite at a time, I have followed God's prompting to 'Write the book'. I am convinced we don't have to be extraordinary people, just ordinary and willing to follow where God leads. All things are possible for those who love the Lord.*

---

* *Looking at them, Jesus said, "With man this is impossible, but with God all things are possible."* (Matthew 19:26, WEB)

Afterword

The mission projects in Mozambique, initiated by Kevin and Ginnie years ago, continue to expand and are in need of our prayers and donations. This area continues to suffer from cyclones and droughts.

The two organisations listed below, World Outreach NZ and Frontline Church, are trusted contacts, and their funds will go directly to support the various mission projects.

Hopeful for a brighter future — Are we willing to help them?

World Outreach NZ
nz@world-outreach.com: Training/Internships/Donations

Frontline Christian Church (AOG), Kerikeri, NZ
Donations: Frontline Missions Account, 03-0351-0026106-00
Reference: Mozambique

Acknowledgments

This book was made possible first and foremost through a personal God who created me, never gives up on me, and continually wraps me with His love. My grandparents and my parents cheered me on from the beginning to follow my dream to go to Africa. I hope to encourage the next generation as they did for me.

I am grateful to my son and his family who let me go there, celebrating Christmas and birthdays on my return visits to help us stay connected.

I would like to thank my extensive church family—the little church in the Far North, my home church Frontline (AoG) in Kerikeri, Northland churches, and Harvest Church with its Ground Crew mission group in Papakura, as well as the small home groups who supported me. I appreciated their encouraging emails when challenges seemed huge. Even just an uplifting word buoyed my spirits. Thank you!

A huge thank you to World Outreach International who offered me an internship with guidance, training, and mentoring both on the field and off. I am particularly grateful to Rod and Lynley Talbot, Paul and Sue Fosse, and Kevin and Ginnie, who introduced me to life on the mission field. Chris Low helped me bridge the gap with teaching preschool concepts in Mozambique culture. Andrew introduced me to a card game called Up and Down the Creek, which kept me laughing after a challenging week! Anya, her family, and Cedru all hold a special place in my heart—

your hospitality and patience with my language and cultural understanding were much appreciated.

I also have many to thank for their offers of practical assistance. My friend, Joanna Comely, offered her home as a base for my sending supporters who welcomed me home for 'R and R'. Teachers, family, and children at PECC Haruru Falls donated resources. Two women in the Bay of Islands, unknown to each other, donated funds to buy the motorbike, while an anonymous couple provided airfares for family reasons. There are countless people I would like to thank, for this has been a team effort.

I am eternally grateful to more recent friends and collaborators in getting this book out to the public. My editor, Sue, has been patient with me and super knowledgeable; my proofreader Althea, a published author herself, has been so helpful; and my long time friend Robyn, an avid reader, became my beta-reader. The NZ Christian Writers group have been very supportive and got me started on this journey, for which I thank them.

About the Author

Mary-Pat lives in the picturesque Bay of Islands, New Zealand, where she enjoys a fulfilling semi-retirement.

A former preschool teacher, she continues to nurture young minds through her volunteer work, playing ukulele for preschoolers. Outside of her community involvement, Mary-Pat cherishes time with her grandchildren, stays active with pickleball, e-bike rides, and regular gym sessions, and is deeply engaged in her church activities.

She is also a proud member of the New Zealand Christian Writers group. Another book of short stories from her adventurous life is still developing! She keeps in touch with mission activities from Africa, a region close to her heart.

www.ingramcontent.com/pod-product-compliance
Lightning Source LLC
Chambersburg PA
CBHW062045290426
44109CB00027B/2732